THE VINDICATORS

Books by Eugene B. Block

THE WIZARD OF BERKELEY
GREAT TRAIN ROBBERIES OF THE WEST
GREAT STAGECOACH ROBBERS OF THE WEST
AND MAY GOD HAVE MERCY

THE VINDICATORS

Eugene B. Block

Doubleday & Company, Inc.
Garden City, New York
1963

To Ruth, with love

The author, with a deep sense of gratitude, extends his thanks to the large number of men and women whose friendly help contributed to compiling of material for this book. They include:

Malden Grange Bishop, Three Rivers, California.

Sheldon S. Brown, Oak Park, Michigan.

Sherman Burns, New York, New York.

Chief of Police Thomas Cahill, San Francisco, California.

Chief of Police A. H. Fording, Berkeley, California.

Erle Stanley Gardner, Temecula, California.

Edgar T. Gleeson, Mill Valley, California.

Leonard Gordon, Detroit, Michigan.

Leonard Gribble, London, England.

Livingston Hall, Cambridge, Massachusetts.

Marshall Houts, Woodland Hills, California.

Arthur M. Johnson, San Francisco, California.

Captain of Police Daniel Klem, San Francisco, California.

Luis Kutner, Chicago, Illinois.

Harold K. Lipset, San Francisco, California.

Prof. Austin MacCormick, New York, New York.

Don Magnuson, Washington, D.C.

Luke S. May, Seattle, Washington.

Attorney General Stanley Mosk of California.

Inspector Edward J. Murphy, San Francisco, California.

Virgil W. Peterson, Chicago, Illinois.

B. J. Rhay, superintendent Washington State Prison, Walla Walla, Washington.

James B. Schick, Walla Walla, Washington.
E. Spencer Shew, M.P., London, England.
Dr. LeMoyne Snyder, Paradise, California.
Rabbi Joshua S. Sperka, Oak Park, Michigan.
Chief of Police Frank A. Sweeney, Jenkintown, Pennsylvania.
Shelby Williams, New York, New York.
Dr. David H. Wilson, San Francisco, California.

CONTENTS

INTRODUCTION

This book, as written by Eugene B. Block, fulfills a vital need in the field of law enforcement. I feel that the great majority of the American public casts the law-enforcement officer in the Javert image featuring the police officer as a relentless prosecutor, a public servant interested only in fixing guilt on the suspect and sending him to prison for the crime.

In modern law enforcement this theory is outdated, and I have seen in my own area officer after officer work as hard to prove the innocence of the suspect as much as his guilt. There are many reasons responsible for this ethical approach to crime solution, and chief among them have been the setting of high entrance standards, the establishment of competent training programs, and the adopting of a strong workable code of ethics.

If one were to pick an individual most responsible for this professionalization of police, one would have to turn to J. Edgar Hoover, Director of the FBI. For years he has been a standard bearer in the progress of law enforcement and has through insistence of strict rules of conduct for his own organization affected the over-all police picture. It was soon obvious to top police officials that the FBI through these qualities was able to win the respect, confidence, and support of the American public.

In this book Mr. Block describes a series of cases which

occurred both in this country and in England, and beginning with a Los Angeles case in which a police fingerprint expert was dubious of the rightful conviction of a man arrested for robbery, begins to tell in an interesting factual manner how officer after officer accepted his responsibility of effectively, efficiently, and fairly enforcing the law.

Throughout the book the facts as assembled by Mr. Block attempt to create a true and proper picture of the American policeman. I agree with him that the large majority are dedicated men who want to know the truth regardless of consequences and to overcome the too prevalent idea that police wish only convictions regardless of facts.

I am not going to say, and I am sure Mr. Block agrees with me, that despite these many instances of unselfish, unprejudiced investigation, the wrong man will not be convicted in subsequent cases, but I think that the reader of this book will form the same conclusion as did I, and that is that policemen are only human and are therefore prone to human error. I do not think that any officer will dispute that fact, but the succession of cases as set forth by Mr. Block will give the reader a deep confidence in his local police department and a realization that every effort will be made to avoid such mistakes.

This is a book that every police department should have as a matter of good public relations and also as a source of research for cases which can be used to refute the claim of "too eager an arrest."

Frank A. Sweeney
Chief of Police
Jenkintown, Pennsylvania

Immediate Past President
International Association of Chiefs of Police

THE VINDICATORS

FINGERPRINTS NEVER LIE

Throughout his long service in the Identification Bureau of the Los Angeles Police Department, Inspector Howard L. Barlow was a firm believer in the infallibility of fingerprints in crime detection. A recognized authority, he always insisted that fingerprints alone could speak the words "guilty" or "innocent"; that they were incontrovertible compared to even the strongest circumstantial evidence.

For years he had devoted himself to the relentless study of loops and whorls and the other intricate distinguishing marks in fingerprints until the subject had become almost an obsession far beyond the line of duty. Barlow often quoted Fred Cherrill, for years chief superintendent of The Fingerprint Bureau of Scotland Yard, who was recognized in many countries as an outstanding expert in his specialized field. Criminologists still refer to an often quoted reply by Cherrill when he was asked whether it was possible that the prints of any two men could be exactly similar.

"The chances," said the expert, "are more than the total population of the world against one that they could be alike."

Inspector Barlow's deep faith in the certainty of fingerprint tests accounted for his prolonged interest in the case of James W. Preston. It began on the dark night of October 18, 1924, when a desperate robber forced his way through a window into the home of Mrs. Richard R. Parsons, an attractive and well-to-do widow in her early fifties.

Lonely since the death of her husband, Mrs. Parsons was seated at the piano playing a sonata when she suddenly heard what seemed to be soft footsteps behind her in the living room.

Wheeling around on her stool, she was horrified to find herself face to face with an intruder holding a leveled revolver in his hand. His features were masked with a handkerchief in which large holes had been cut for his eyes. Despite her fright, Mrs. Parsons noted that he wore a gray felt hat and that his eyes were a deep blue.

"Stick 'em up," he commanded gruffly. "I want your diamonds." His victim at once became aware of a heavy nasal tone in his voice.

Fearing to make an outcry, she threw up her hands and the gunman, moving forward, slipped the rings from her fingers. "I want the rest of your stuff—all of it," he ordered, and again Mrs. Parsons took note of the voice that was to become an important factor in the identification of a suspect.

Terrified, the widow merely shook her head. "I'm—too—scared—to—think," she finally stammered. "I really can't tell you where I've put my things."

The robber took another step closer, still pointing his gun in a menacing manner. "Then go and look," he directed. "I'll follow you."

With the armed man at her heels, Mrs. Parsons moved from room to room, looking for rings, bracelets, and earrings which she seemed unable to locate. "Quit your stalling," the man finally snapped. "You're only playing for time."

"I'm really trying to find my things," she answered nervously, moving out of her bedroom into an adjoining study. It was there that the two, almost at the same moment, noticed an unshaded window through which neighbors might look into the lighted room. To Mrs. Parsons it offered hope; to the robber it meant only one thing—danger.

"You brought me here on purpose," he snarled. "Now give me the stuff and let me get out of here."

It was then that Mrs. Parsons made a foolhardy move. Ignoring the warning and the man with the revolver, she turned and dashed through the narrow hall. She had just reached the outside porch when a shot rang out and the fleeing woman felt a stinging pain in her back. In a moment she swayed and fell unconscious on the cement floor. Seconds later the gunman was gone.

Neighbors, attracted by the shooting, rushed to the woman's aid, summoned an ambulance and notified the police.

Mrs. Parsons' wound proved to be not so serious as was at first believed and in a few days she was able to give detectives a clear account of the robbery and an unusually good description of her assailant. "I can see him now," she related. "He was about five feet six inches tall, and I guess he weighed something like a hundred and thirty pounds. But those deep blue eyes and that voice. I could recognize them any time."

It was a good description and detectives were confident that should the man be apprehended, he could readily be identified by his victim. However, they had come upon still further help in their search. A close examination of the house had disclosed that the gunman, in forcing his way through a first-floor window, had left a clear fingerprint on the wire mesh window screen. The print, of course, was photographed and though the records of the Identification Bureau had been carefully studied, no matching print could be found. Obviously, it would be necessary to wait for an arrest.

Meanwhile, excitement was running high in the once-quiet neighborhood in which Mrs. Parsons lived and angry residents were pressing demands on the police for quick and effective action. An intensive search of the area had been started soon after the shooting and patrolmen throughout Los Angeles were under orders to keep a sharp lookout for suspicious characters. Descriptions of the fugitive were being broadcast over radio stations and had been sent to surrounding communities by teletype.

The break for which detectives had been hoping came unexpectedly on October 15, three days after the shooting, when a young man in the uniform of the United States Navy was found loitering in a manner that aroused the suspicions of a passing policeman. The sailor said that his name was James W. Preston, that he was twenty-eight years old, and had been honorably discharged from service a few weeks before.

"Then why are you still wearing that uniform?" the officer demanded.

Preston had a ready answer. "Another sailor stole my civies the day I got out. As soon as I can earn enough, I'm going to buy some new clothes."

Dissatisfied, the patrolman took him to headquarters where inquiry disclosed that the young man once had deserted from the Army a few years before enlisting in the Navy. He also had been arrested on a vagrancy charge.

While officers still were considering whether to hold Preston for illegally wearing his Navy uniform, one of them suggested that in some respects he resembled Mrs. Parsons' description of her assailant. Although Preston vigorously insisted that he knew nothing of the crime and had been miles away from Los Angeles at the time, he was taken to the Identification Bureau for fingerprinting.

Anxiously, inspectors checked his prints against those found on the window screen but they proved to be different in all essential respects. Still reluctant to drop the matter, police decided that even in spite of the fingerprint comparisons, they would ask Mrs. Parsons to view their suspect. They chose to wait until the following day before taking him to the hospital.

Meanwhile newsmen had learned of the arrest and, through an inexplicable error, two newspapers appeared the next morning with headlines intimating that Preston was the wanted man and that his fingerprints matched those found on Mrs. Parsons' screen.

The wounded woman already had read these accounts when Preston was brought to her bedside. No one ever has doubted her desire to be cautious as she looked into the prisoner's face, determined to judge for herself despite the newspapers. However, she definitely identified him as her assailant, explaining that she could "never forget those eyes." Preston was told to speak and she was certain that she recognized his voice.

Again Preston pleaded that a mistake had occurred but the police were willing to rely on so positive an identification despite the dissimilarity in fingerprints. He was charged with burglary, robbery, and assault with intent to commit murder, and his trial was set for March 11, 1925.

The prosecutor fully realized the weakness of his case with only one witness, Mrs. Parsons, and with the disparity in fingerprints a strong point for the defense. He therefore proposed a compromise, offering to ask dismissal of two charges if the accused would plead guilty to one. This Preston refused, reasserting his innocence. The assistant district attorney then offered to drop the three felony charges if the defendant would plead guilty to simple assault. Again Preston declined but his lawyer advised him otherwise, explaining that his maximum sentence could not exceed six months, while if he were tried and convicted on the more serious counts, he could receive a life term.

Preston remained obdurate. "Why should I plead guilty to something I didn't do?" he argued. "My conscience is clear and any jury will believe me."

He had calculated wrongly. A jury was impaneled and Mrs. Parsons took the stand, identifying Preston positively as her assailant. "I could recognize him anywhere by his eyes—those deep blue eyes—and, of course, by his voice with that nasal twang," she said. The prosecution closed. It had no other witness.

Preston now debated whether to testify. He realized that if he did not the jury would infer that he was guilty, yet if he did take the stand his previous record undoubtedly would be disclosed by the prosecution. He chose to risk his chances as a witness, and, after denying any knowledge of the robbery, he swore that at the time he was in Long Beach, twenty-two miles away. The jurors did not appear to be impressed.

Then, as Preston had feared, the prosecutor began his cross-examination by compelling the witness to admit his previous trouble with the law. The defense then called a new witness, a girl who said she had been with Preston in Long Beach at the exact time of the shooting. But she was a poor witness, speaking in a low and hesitating voice and, as the judge interrupted with questions of his own, it was clearly apparent that he doubted her story. Nothing was said by the defense of the dissimiliarity between Preston's fingerprints and those found on Mrs. Parsons' window screen. As it later developed, Preston's lawyer was unaware of this vital point in his behalf.

On March 14 the jury retired and soon returned with a verdict finding Preston guilty of two felony charges. Two days later the convicted man stood before the court for sentence. The judge obviously had read the false newspaper accounts of matching fingerprints, for he turned to the defendant with this question:

"Despite the fact that your fingerprints were there and despite the fact that fingerprints are the only infallible identification, do you still insist that you were not there?"

"Yes sir," the accused replied, in a loud, firm voice.

Again the judge referred to the fingerprints. "The jury did not have that evidence," he declared. "I suppose the jurors will be glad to know the court had evidence that you were identified by prints. You have a voice that not one in ten thousand has—possibly one in a hundred thousand. You committed one of the most serious crimes that can be committed. You had better take your medicine and try to learn your lesson. . . ."

Had Preston known of the fingerprint comparison he might at that moment have looked hopefully to his lawyer, expecting him to interrupt the court. However, he was as unaware of this vital point in his behalf as was his counsel. Not a word about fingerprints had been spoken at the trial. The judge continued:

"I sentence you to serve an indeterminate term of from eleven years to life in state's prison."

Preston gulped and sank into his chair. On March 21 he entered San Quentin Penitentiary and his name became a number.

Apparently his case was over—for everyone, that is, except Inspector Barlow in the Police Identification Bureau. It was he who had compared Preston's fingerprints with those left by Mrs. Parsons' assailant and had found them widely different. He was convinced that a miscarriage of justice had occurred and he determined to prove it however long that might take. With Barlow, the infallibility of fingerprints was something like a creed.

He took a card bearing the prints from the screen and placed it conspicuously on his desk. "I'm going to keep this here," he told a colleague, "and I'm going to check them against every print that comes in here. Some day—you'll see."

"That's a pretty big order," said the other, chuckling. "But I know you. Go ahead—stay with it till you're satisfied."

Inspector Barlow did just that. Day after day scores of fingerprints came across his desk—prints of murderers, burglars, forgers, arsonists, among others. Meticulously, the expert would pick up each new card of prints and compare it with the other he kept before him.

Weeks lengthened into months. A year passed. By now he had checked thousands of fingerprints but Barlow still was unwilling to give up. Occasionally, fellow workers stopped to watch as he went painstakingly through his daily routine. Sometimes they laughed or even grew sarcastic, but the inspector was indifferent to their taunts.

His long vigil came to an abrupt end on a busy morning in May 1928, more than three years after Preston had gone to San Quentin. The day had started with the usual routine, the fingerprinting of a long line of men rounded up during the night for a variety of offenses and Barlow moved from one to another, with no reason to suspect the drama destined for the next few hours.

As he finally finished his boring work with the last prisoner brought into his room, he turned to the stack of cards on his desk and began fingering them with no unusual interest. At last he came to one that bore the name of a burglar suspect—Earl M. Carroll, alias the Weasel. It was not a name unknown to the police.

Barlow was about to toss it carelessly into his wire tray when something about the ridges in the fingermarks moved him to look at it again, this time more closely. Suddenly he reached into his drawer for a magnifying glass, then stared long and hard at the intricate pattern of lines before him. What he saw set him quivering with excitement. It seemed far too good to be true.

"Could this really be it?" he asked himself, half-aloud. He had been fooled many times before.

Almost incredulously, he grabbed for the now well-soiled prints from the old robbery case and placed them close to the card he had been examining so minutely.

Now he peered even more sharply than before, his eyes moving anxiously from one card to the other. Then his lips pursed and he whistled softly, jumping excitedly from his chair.

"At last," he called excitedly to his assistant. "At last, I've found them—the matching prints in that old Preston case. This time I'm sure—come see for yourself."

The long, untiring watch was over!

Carroll was convicted of the robbery committed more than three years before. The wheels of justice then were thrown into reverse to undo a grave miscarriage of justice. Governor

Friend W. Richardson promptly granted Preston a full pardon
and he walked out of prison a free man.

Cases like this, though infrequent, continue to occur in
various parts of the United States. They occur because conscientious, skilled law-enforcement officers and private investigators are eager to use their talents to ferret the truth,
believing that it is just as much their duty to vindicate innocent people as it is to convict the guilty. They accept this
as a responsibility, recognizing it as basic in our system of
jurisprudence which follows the common law principle that
every man shall be presumed to be innocent until proven
guilty. Occasionally, however, the principle is reversed by
overzealous officials.

In some instances of error the victim does not suffer conviction and imprisonment as did Preston. In many, the mistake is discovered before the accused is brought to trial and
often continued investigation leads to the capture of the guilty
one.

But why do such mistakes occur? Who is responsible?

There are many reasons. Occasionally, such a case may be
attributed to human error with no one intentionally at fault.
But in most instances, the blunder is due either to careless,
inefficient methods and procedures, or to the deliberate action
of police officers and prosecutors eager to find a quick solution to a complex, baffling case and obtain a conviction to
satisfy an aroused public or to glorify their own records.

Fortunately, the vast majority of public officials concerned
with criminal procedures are dedicated, conscientious, painstaking people. For the most part, they are anxious to protect
the innocent and to proceed along careful, cautious lines,
utilizing the most modern scientific techniques and affording
the accused every legal right. But there are some exceptions
and in such cases the fault lies sometimes with the public
and occasionally with a biased press.

For example, a heinous crime is committed and a shocked
citizenry cries out for action by the police. There are angry

demands for capture of the criminal and his quick conviction. Often an element of vengeance overshadows a consideration for justice. It is a human frailty.

Intense police investigation starts. The press, responding
to public pressure, may goad the law with demands for quick
results. Officers hastily set about to reconstruct the crime,
interpreting whatever evidence may be at hand. If motive is
not immediately obvious, it becomes a subject of speculation.
A theory is developed and an arrest is made. The investigation may produce conflicting evidence but too often officers
are prone to disregard all that is incongruous with the theory
they are supporting and to magnify everything that fits it.

Consciously or unconsciously, they are sometimes moved
by a public attitude that judges the competence of police
and prosecutors by their records for convictions with no concern for the manner in which those convictions have been
obtained. This, obviously, is dangerous thinking.

Great importance is given to the testimony of eyewitnesses,
yet it has been established that rarely do two people see
the same thing in exactly the same way, nor are their observa-
tions always accurate. Too many, with honest purpose, relate
what they think they have seen—or should have seen.

Actually, the erroneous testimony of eyewitnesses, especially in identifications, is responsible for the vast majority of
cases in which justice miscarries, though often there are other
elements involved.

Startling conflicts in the testimony of eyewitnesses, whose
only purpose may be a desire for truthfulness, long has been
the subject of study by attorneys and criminologists. A
pioneer in that field, Professor Hugo Münsterberg, who occupied a distinguished place as professor of psychology at
Harvard University, often lectured on the widely different
accounts given by students and even professional men who,
in tests, had observed the same things at the same time and
under similar circumstances.

In his well-known book, *On the Witness Stand,* published

in 1908, Dr. Münsterberg frankly confessed how he, despite years of experience as a criminologist, had given police a grossly inaccurate report of what he had observed in his own home on a night when he returned to find that it had been looted.

He went on to relate a startling experiment carried on in Berlin in the University Seminary of Professor Franz von Liszt, a famous criminologist, who for a test had secretly arranged to have a group of students interrupt his lecture with an act of gunplay. When it was over the class was called on to write what had been seen and heard. After papers had been checked for errors, the ratio of mistakes ranged from 26 to 80 per cent. Similar experiments, carried on among groups of professional men, resulted in equally surprising conclusions.

Münsterberg occasionally cited the case of a family involved in a poison plot. One member stated that a beverage of which he had partaken was sour and disagreeable; another insisted that it was sweet, and a third said that it was tasteless.

Such discrepancies may be taken as evidence of the usual unreliability of testimony from people who have witnessed an accident, a murder or any other occurrence. Different people just do not see the same things in the same way. And, too often, a defendant is the unfortunate victim.

The fallibility of testimony from witnesses was often emphasized by the late Judge Jerome Frank of New York, a nationally known jurist, who was a close adviser to President Franklin D. Roosevelt. In his widely read book, *Not Guilty*, Judge Frank pointed out that many attorneys hold that of all sources of error in criminal trials, one of the most fatal is "an unreflecting faith in human testimony." He wrote that when a witness testified "I saw" or "I heard," what he really meant to say is "I believe I saw" or "It is my opinion that I heard."

Judge Frank further declared that "an eyewitness is not a

tape recorder or a photographic film. He does not necessarily reproduce sights and sounds accurately. A witness's observation of any event does not precisely mirror the event." Many people, he concluded, are too ready to assume that they have seen all that there was to be observed.

Circumstantial evidence often plays a major role but this, too, is fraught with dangers until it has been put to serious, honest and competent legal and scientific test.

Today, in most of our large cities, crime laboratories are maintained by the police. They are manned by trained technicians, well able to utilize the most modern techniques of scientific crime detection in their work. But many areas still are without such facilities. The accused frequently is the one who suffers.

Lack of competent defense counsel also is responsible in many cases for errors in our administration of justice. A defendant, through lack of funds, may be obliged to engage an unskilled, inexperienced lawyer or he may be represented by an indifferent, inefficient attorney appointed by the court to serve without a fee—a man incapable of matching wits with a clever, experienced prosecutor eager to build his reputation by convincing the jury that the man at the bar is guilty.

Some states do maintain public defenders but in many instances they are overworked and understaffed, so that adequate study and attention to every case is impossible. In only a few states can the penniless defendant call on publicly supported psychiatric and medical experts—another factor in which the prosecution has unfair advantage.

Then, too, there are inherent weaknesses in our jury system and the ever-present danger that jurors will be influenced by a prosecutor's prejudicial remark—words that the court immediately orders expunged from the record but which cannot be erased from the minds of those trying the accused.

The plight of the innocent who longs to continue his fight for vindication after he has been convicted must not be overlooked. Ordinarily public interest in his case has ceased after he has been found guilty and sent to prison. The victim and his family, drained of financial resources by the cost of trial, rarely are able to pay for continued legal skirmishing and investigation. When the prison gate closes behind the convicted man, his case usually is forgotten with him.

Only in recent years has there been an organized effort to remedy such mistakes of justice. This has been done largely through a dedicated and privately financed group now widely known as the Court of Last Resort, but more of this later. Succeeding chapters will relate cases in which officers of the law and private investigators, utilizing differing skills and procedures, have achieved notable results in finding the truth to vindicate innocent people. They are not all sensational cases but all of them involve human beings trapped in the meshes of cruel circumstance. Above all, they will demonstrate the eagerness of many peace officers and others to protect the innocent and to enforce the law with fairness and honesty.

Competent officials take pride in such a policy. The attitude of capable, dedicated officers everywhere is reflected by Chief of Police A. H. Fording of Berkeley, California, head of a department nationally recognized for its pioneer work in criminalistics.

"After observing literally hundreds of policemen over the past twenty-five years," he writes, "I am convinced that the vast majority derive infinitely more satisfaction from establishing the innocence of suspect individuals who are under the shadow of incriminating circumstantial (and at times eyewitness) evidence.

"Unfortunately, the prosecutions are highly publicized while the vindications go unnoticed."

California's Attorney General Stanley Mosk, head of his state's Department of Justice, also has strong views on the subject—views that doubtlessly are supported by his colleagues throughout the nation. "Justice carries a two-edged sword," he says. "One blade to defend the innocent; the other to cut down the guilty.

"In a well-ordered society it is equally as important to protect the guiltless as to punish the guilty, for in America, as distinguished from many unfortunate lands, the individual is all-important.

"Justice is not only punitive; it demands the moral obligation of impartiality from beginning to end. Justice does not seek a victim to expiate for a crime. Justice seeks out the facts, the truth, regardless of the consequences.

"From the scene of a crime, evidence that may point unerringly at the suspect or the accused must nevertheless be gathered together with careful consideration of the possible innocence of the person or persons apprehended. Our peace officers are morally bound to seek the truth, and to reject the false in assembling their evidence."

And from the opposite coast of the American continent comes this statement once made to a jury by Samuel Leibowitz, often acclaimed as the most celebrated criminal lawyer of his time, now a highly respected and nationally known judge in New York. He said:

"I hear many people calling out 'Punish the guilty' but very few are concerned to clear the innocent."

2

DETECTIVE AT WORK

A frail young woman, with a pretty face and soft auburn hair, sat across the desk from a famous detective, her cheeks pale and drawn, her eyes filled with tears. "I just know my husband is innocent—he's certainly not a murderer," she said firmly, struggling desperately for control. "You are probably the only man in the world who can save his life. Name your price and I'll pay it."

The man turned in his swivel chair and stared silently through the wide window of his well-furnished New York office. Then he swung around, looking his visitor squarely in the face. "I'll take the case on one condition," he finally replied, speaking slowly to emphasize his words. "If I should become convinced that your husband is guilty, I'll turn the evidence over to the government. Is that a deal?"

The woman nodded. She was Countess Nancy de Marigny, socialite daughter of the multimillionaire "Midas of the Bahamas," Sir Harry Oakes, murdered in one of the most bizarre and sensational mysteries ever to be front-page news on two continents. The husband for whom she was seeking help was Count Alfred de Marigny, thrice-married thirty-four-year-old playboy. He had been arrested the previous day —on July 9, 1943—for the murder of his father-in-law whose body had been found brutally bludgeoned and set afire in the bedroom of his luxurious home in Nassau.

The Count's attractive wife was torn between two loves.

She had adored her father, who had been outspoken in his hatred of de Marigny. She was equally devoted to her husband, whom she had married at the age of eighteen in defiance of her wealthy family's wishes. Added to her predicament were the assertions of her mother, Lady Eunice Oakes, that she strongly believed the Count to be guilty, a view which most of the island population shared.

To the American detective, Raymond Campbell Schindler, she looked now as her only hope.

Often referred to as the greatest investigator of his time, Schindler was a heavy, powerful man, then sixty-one, with a large, fleshy face, gray hair, shaggy brows and sharp penetrating eyes. He had earned his reputation through years of spectacular feats in crime detection that sometimes had freed the innocent and at others had sent the guilty to prison on the mute testimony of a hair or a single thread. Schindler was known for his uncanny ways of learning the truth, a talent which many said had come to him naturally. In his work he always disregarded public opinion and insisted on reaching his own conclusions in his own way. He was meticulous in everything he did; always alert to the most minute details.

He used the sciences and his own extraordinary intuition, usually bringing them into interplay. Though he was relentless on the trail of the guilty, he was equally dedicated to the cause of the innocent. He chose always to obtain every shred of evidence and to weigh it impartially, regardless of whether it supported a likely theory or pointed in an opposite direction. Many have said that he typified the highest ideals of American justice. He received large fees from the rich and often served the poor without charge.

In appearance Schindler looked like a successful business executive. Nothing about him resembled the popular stereotype of a detective. He never carried a gun or wore a disguise.

One of his highest tributes was paid by Homer S. Cummings, who, as United States Attorney General, once wrote: "In my judgment Raymond C. Schindler is a great detective. He never evolves theories of his cases until the last scrap of evidence has been developed and analyzed. I never knew a man to move more swiftly or with surer touch. He is loyal to the most exacting and ethical standards."

Schindler's career had an unusual beginning. Born in New York City, he supported himself in early boyhood first by delivering newspapers for thirty-five cents a day, and later by ushering in a theater.

In 1900, at the age of eighteen, he was persuaded by his father, John F. Schindler, to enter the insurance field which had provided the elder Schindler with a good living. Somewhat dubious, the boy obtained a job as salesman for an agency but his earnings at the end of the first year totaled only $18, his commission on a policy sold to the owner of a music store in Alliance, Ohio.

Grateful to his only client, he decided to show his appreciation by organizing bands in the community and urging the players to buy their instruments from the favored storekeeper. Only the music business prospered. Young Schindler's activities were without gain.

At his father's insistence, he left Ohio for Pittsburgh to sell typewriters. In two years he saved $2400—enough, he thought, to start a fortune by investing in mining stocks.

Lured by reports of quick profits in California, he moved there and exchanged his savings for shares in a gold mine, where he took a job working on the property. Financial troubles developed and the entire project finally was abandoned.

Now almost penniless, the disillusioned young man decided to try his luck in San Francisco but unexpected events delayed his arrival. He reached the smoldering city on April 19, 1906, a day after the great earthquake and fire, but, as circumstances later proved, the catastrophe gave him the opportunity that was to be the beginning of a new and famous career.

In a city of ruins he finally found a job as an investigator for a fire insurance company. It was at a time when these concerns, facing tremendous claims, were hard pressed to establish whether losses were due primarily to the earthquake or to fire alone.

In this work, Schindler's talents as an investigator soon attracted wide attention and as time passed he was entrusted with major assignments. Hiram W. Johnson, a leading attorney, who later became Governor of California and United States Senator, took notice of the young man's astuteness and hired him to research an important case. Schindler turned in a bill for $50. Johnson responded with a $500 check and a note on the error of underestimating the value of his services.

Months afterward, San Francisco's infamous graft prosecution began and a celebrated detective, William J. Burns, then in a high post with the United States Secret Service, was loaned to San Francisco. On Johnson's recommendation, Burns engaged Schindler as his chief assistant.

In 1909, their work done, Burns resigned his government position, launched his own agency, and took Schindler with him to New York as manager of the main office. Three years later Schindler opened his own agency in New York. It grew into a tremendous organization with operatives in many countries.

Directing activities from his New York offices, Schindler moved them about like men on a giant, world-wide checkerboard, and, sometimes when situations demanded, he would board a ship or, in later years, a plane at an hour's notice. He constantly studied the latest advances in scientific crime detection and was one of the first to demonstrate the practical value of the lie detector.

Schindler, with unusual ingenuity and resourcefulness, also had the talents of a playwright. These qualities were never better demonstrated than in the case of a penniless Negro who had been arrested in 1911 on flimsy circumstantial evidence for the brutal murder of a ten-year-old girl in Asbury Park. He was engaged to investigate the killing by a wealthy citizen who had been impressed by the Negro's persistent pleas of innocence.

After a thorough study of the crime, the detective singled out seven possible suspects, then eliminated them, one by one, until only an employee of a florist shop remained. Under the circumstances, it was obvious to Schindler that if this man were guilty it would be necessary to trap him into a confession.

A number of ruses were tried but when all of them failed, Schindler, in desperation, conceived a melodrama and set the stage for its production. First, one of his cleverest operatives was assigned to meet the man in the restaurant that he frequented, cultivate his friendship and win his confidence. When this finally was accomplished, the "roper" invited him on an auto ride into the country. By design, he stopped the car at an isolated spot, walked to the road, and by careful prearrangement, "chanced" to engage in a violent altercation with a "stranger," who, of course, was one of Schindler's men. When this person, feigning anger, drew a knife, the investigator took out his revolver and fired a blank shot. The "stranger" fell on his face, pretending to be dead, and the sleuth speeded away with his companion. The stage was set.

A few days later the detective told the suspect that he was going to Germany and the latter asked if he might go along—a request that had been expected. The investigator shook his head and long argument followed.

"On a long trip like that we might fall out," said the detective. "You've got too much on me—you saw me kill a man."

"If you had a hold on me like I have on you—then would you take me?" the other countered, falling headlong into the trap.

"Just what do you mean?"

"I mean that I'll give you a hold on me, too. I killed that little girl in Asbury Park. I killed her with a hammer. Now we're even."

Hours later the man was dictating a long confession to the authorities.

In another of his sensational cases, Schindler was summoned by a prominent family to investigate the deaths of a wealthy Grand Rapids manufacturer and his wife, supposedly from heart trouble, while they were house guests of their son-in-law. Before the funeral of the husband, who had survived his wife only by a few days, relatives were aroused by a mysterious anonymous telegram urging that an autopsy be demanded. They surmised that the son-in-law, a playboy dentist whom they disliked, might be involved, since he and his wife were to inherit a huge fortune. The burial was delayed pending an inquiry.

It took the detective only a short time to unmask the dentist, who constantly boasted of his rare surgical accomplishments. He was unknown at the hospital where he claimed to have performed miracle surgery; in fact, his practice had consisted mainly of street corner demonstrations in another country. Further inquiry revealed him as a pretender in every phase of his private life.

On a night when this man was out of the city, Schindler decided to search his apartment. Gaining access by a ruse, he quickly came upon a book on poisons. It was opened to a page on arsenic, carefully marked, and elsewhere in the suite were glass slides which had been used in cultivating bacteria.

When the dentist arrived at the railroad depot, he was promptly shadowed by operatives who trailed him to a garage. There, it was learned later, he had met an undertaker in a secret rendezvous, paying him $9000 to affirm that arsenic had been used in embalming the woman's body.

A chemist who examined the manufacturer's vital organs reported that they contained "enough arsenic to kill twenty men." This evidence, and much more that Schindler and his men had unearthed, was turned over to the authorities, who obtained a confession from the dentist that he had put the poison in the food of his house guests and previously had tried to kill a wealthy aunt with supposedly deadly germs which he had cultivated.

An attempt to escape the supreme penalty by an insanity plea failed, and the dentist was sent to the electric chair.

To this resourceful detective Countess Nancy de Marigny entrusted the life of her titled husband and the fortune she knew his defense would cost.

Raymond Schindler's first move was to board a plane for the Bahamas, arriving less than four days after the murder. He had not set foot long on Nassau before he realized that he faced a far more difficult assignment than he had anticipated. He soon learned that his presence was not wanted, for no one seemed concerned with any inquiry that might tend to vindicate de Marigny. The authorities, he was quickly convinced, were interested only in convicting the Count and were rejecting any evidence that might be regarded as favorable to his defense.

The island police who had arrested de Marigny a day after the murder already were at odds with the Duke of Windsor, then the British Royal Governor of the Bahamas, who had summarily summoned police officers from Florida to take over the entire case. He learned also, in those first hours, that fast-surging public opinion already had found de Marigny guilty. De Marigny was generally disliked while his murdered father-in-law was a favorite on the islands, Oakes' industrial empire having provided abundant jobs and contributed much to the economic wealth of the region.

In this atmosphere of hostility and confusion, Schindler set to work assembling as many facts as he could about the grotesque murder of Sir Harry Oakes and the events immediately following.

He learned that while Sir Harry's wife and children, including the Countess, were living at The Willows, their summer estate at Bar Harbor, Maine, Oakes had moved from his own palatial residence in Nassau to his fifteen-room beach villa Westbourne, once the home of the famous American actress, Maxine Elliott, and occupied later by the Windsors while their quarters in Government House were being renovated.

On the night of July 8, two days before he was to leave on a business trip to South America, Sir Harry had hosted a small farewell party. His guests were his close friend and business associate, Harold George Christie, a sixty-four-year-old bachelor; Charles Hubbard, and Mrs. Ducibel Effie Henneage. The evening was uneventful. Chinese checkers were played after dinner and at about eleven o'clock the party had broken up, all of the guests departing excepting Christie, who had been invited to spend the night with his host.

The two men talked alone for a short time, then went upstairs to the second floor to retire, Oakes in a large twin-bedded room, and Christie in a bedroom only a few yards away. A bath and dressing rooms connected the two sleeping chambers. Both bedrooms opened on a wide balcony where Sir Harry always breakfasted. The servants already had left, being in the habit of sleeping out, and though three outside stairways led to the balcony, neither man locked his doors or windows.

During the night there was a fierce rainstorm accompanied by thunder and high winds. It had awakened Christie twice, as he was to testify later.

Christie had arisen early the next morning, dressed leisurely, and stepped out to the porch, expecting to find his host waiting for him. It was seven o'clock, the hour they had agreed to meet, but Oakes was not there.

Thinking that Sir Harry had overslept, Christie walked into Oakes' bedroom and found it filled with smoke. He took one look, then stepped back, stunned by the ghastly sight before him. Sprawled diagonally across the smoking bed lay his titled friend, his face and head smeared with blood and his body badly burned. Red-stained carpets and bedclothes were still smoldering and an electric fan was stirring up a mass of pillow feathers covering the body.

Christie's first impulse, he said later, was to stuff a pillow under Oakes' head and to try to force water down his throat. Then he reached for the telephone, summoning Oakes' physician, Dr. Hugh A. Quackenbush, who arrived hurriedly and pronounced Oakes dead. Then he surveyed the grisly scene and notified the authorities.

Lieutenant Colonel R. A. Erskine-Lindog, the Commissioner of Police, rushed to the villa with Major Herbert Pemberton, head of the Criminal Investigation Department. Hasty examination soon convinced the doctor that Sir Harry had died of skull fractures resulting from four heavy blows which had left deep rectangular head wounds such as a steel bar might inflict. No weapon was in sight nor, indeed, was any ever found.

The officers, theorizing that the killer had first murdered the millionaire and then set his bed afire to conceal the crime, discovered gory handprints running along the north wall of Oakes' bedroom into the outside hall and on the railing of the staircase. They found red stains on the knobs of doors leading from Christie's room to the porch, but Christie insisted that he was too confused to even attempt an explanation. He declared that he had heard no noise at any time in the adjoining bedroom of Sir Harry, nor had he sensed anything unusual in the house when he was awakened by the storm. At no time had he smelled smoke. Dr. Quackenbush fixed the time of death at between 2:30 and 5 o'clock that morning.

In the confusion, fully three hours had elapsed before word of the murder had reached the Duke of Windsor and his unexpected action had thrown the entire situation into turmoil. The Duke, for reasons that were never explained, had chosen to ignore the island authorities. Having made this decision, apparently without consultation, he had phoned the Miami police and summoned Captain Edward Melchen, who once had served as bodyguard for Windsor during a visit to Florida and in whom the Duke evidently had great confidence.

Before Melchen's arrival with Captain James O. Barker, supervisor of the Miami Crime Laboratory, Nassau police had arrested de Marigny for the murder but they quickly withdrew from all participation in the case on learning that the Florida officers were on the scene. Not only did they abruptly end their work but they gave the Miami officers only a meager report of what they had learned and done.

Soon the men from Miami uncovered the first of a number of blunders in the early investigation and they found themselves handicapped because of erroneous information which they had received before leaving Miami. The Duke had mistakenly reported the case to them as a suicide and Barker, therefore, had failed to bring his camera and other necessary equipment which he would require. No one ever knew why he had not sent for it.

Although the Miami men were already aware of the dislike for de Marigny in the Bahamas, they were at a loss to understand why the Nassau authorities had arrested him so soon instead of first keeping him under surveillance pending a thorough investigation. They were equally puzzled by the failure of the Nassau officers to immediately press a thorough search for the lethal weapon and to take specimens of the bloodstains in Oakes' bedroom as would be customary under such circumstances. There were still other baffling questions involving the activity of the Nassau police.

Schindler's arrival in Nassau to work in behalf of Countess de Marigny and her husband had stirred immediate hostility and he found himself unable to obtain the slightest cooperation from either the Bahama authorities or the men from Miami. It was some time before he was even given permission to inspect the Oakes' home. However, working through his own resources, he sought to ascertain by himself why the Nassau police had been so quick in arresting the Count. The answer, he found, lay in the fact that bad blood had existed between the accused man and his father-in-law, a bitterness that began when Oakes had tried desperately to prevent his daughter's marriage. It was rumored that the Count had threatened his life and reports also were current that de Marigny was broke and was counting on his wife's large inheritance to pay his debts. Moreover, the Count, a soldier of fortune, living a Bohemian life, was regarded as a ne'er-do-well, an upstart, and thoroughly disliked. Now the tragedy had come at a propitious time to turn public opinion quickly —and bitterly—against him.

Inquiring into de Marigny's movements on the night before the tragedy, Schindler found that the Count, occupying a cottage five miles from Westbourne, had entertained guests and had driven two women home shortly after 1 A.M., his route taking him close to the Oakes home. This fact was seized upon by the prosecution to support a theory that he could have stopped at Westbourne on his way back to commit the murder, although de Marigny, in vigorously pleading his innocence, insisted that he had not been in his father-in-law's house for the past three years. Others, however, were inclined to suspect that he had returned home and left again later for the Oakes house.

There was other circumstantial evidence against the accused. Constable John Douglas of Nassau had reported that about the time the body was discovered, de Marigny had appeared at a police station to inquire about a truck license. "He appeared excited and his eyes were wild," the officer related. When told of the murder, the Count exclaimed: "The old ——— should have been killed anyway." This remark, the constable stated, was followed by inquiries as to whether a man could be convicted of murder if no lethal weapon were found. Later, when investigating officers discovered that de Marigny's beard and mustache showed what they regarded as signs of singeing, he had offered a variety of conflicting explanations, Constable Douglas stated.

Schindler turned next to the backgrounds of the two men, still groping for a lead. Sir Harry, a surveyor's son, had been born in Sangerville, Maine, in 1874. He had worked his way through Bowdoin College, and then taken an unimportant job in a New York pulp plant. Young Oakes showed little promise and his parents were frank in saying that in their judgment the future held little for their son. In fact, they occasionally pointed to the county poorhouse and told him that this was destined to be his home.

When gold was discovered in the Klondike in 1896, he joined the Alaskan trek. The venture ended in complete failure. Then for thirteen years he wandered almost penniless and ragged through many countries until fate took him to Ontario. He was, by now, thirty-seven years old.

There, by a strange quirk of circumstance, misfortune started him on the way to wealth. He had boarded a train without funds and a conductor had unceremoniously put him off at a small Canadian station. There Oakes encountered a friendly Chinese restaurant owner who listened to his story and loaned him sufficient money to invest in a mining claim. Before long he struck gold. Then Oakes staked another claim. It turned out to be the famous Lake Shore Mine, estimated to have yielded more than $200,000,000 in gold. The Chinese is said to have been generously rewarded.

From then on, Oakes had accumulated wealth at every turn. In 1923 he married and built palatial homes in one country after another. In the Bahamas, he drilled wells and formed a large and profitable water company. Though some pictured him as gruff, uncouth and of a pugnacious nature, never losing the roughness he had acquired in his lone wanderings, he was charitable and made huge gifts to worthy causes. One of them, $400,000 to a London hospital, brought the reward of a knighthood in 1939.

In all of his affairs, social as well as business, he was known for an unswerving determination to have his way. In this regard, the story still is told in Nassau of his visit to a plush hotel with a party of guests and his demand for a table in the best corner of the dining room. The headwaiter looked at Oakes' miner's boots and flannel shirt; then told him that all of his best tables already were reserved.

Oakes stormed out of the place white with rage. A few nights later he returned, announced that he had bought the hotel, and promptly fired the head waiter. The transaction, consummated by telephone, had cost him a fortune.

In high Bahama circles he was well respected but Schindler learned that shrewd business dealings had made some bitter enemies and the detective wondered whether one of these might have been the murderer. This suspicion was strengthened later when Schindler was informed that Sir Harry had confided to friends that he feared an attack. Of this the Miami authorities were aware, but they had made no effort to ascertain whom he feared or why. Oakes never carried firearms, as far as was known, but a revolver was found after his death in a bedroom drawer. His reason for having it there was never ascertained.

Schindler did succeed in locating several men who bitterly hated the murdered man because of business transactions. He interviewed them without success and when he demanded permission of the Florida police to subject these individuals to lie detector tests, he was curtly rebuffed.

What Schindler learned of Count de Marigny accounted well for the dislike that he and Oakes had for each other. Affectionately known as Freddy to his wife and close friends, the Count was a lean, dark-complexioned athletic type, wearing a Vandyke which gave him something of a distinguished appearance. He craved fun and had little concern for the cares or responsibilities of life. He had been born on Mauritius, a British island in the Indian Ocean, then inhabited largely by French-speaking people. From his mother he claimed to have inherited his title. He was fond of beautiful women and they seemed unable to resist his charm. He had been married twice before meeting Nancy Oakes, and divorced

each time. No wonder then that Oakes opposed the court-
ship of his young daughter to a man he often called a fortune
hunter and a sex maniac.

The romance was at its height when Nancy reached her
eighteenth birthday. She promptly took off for California
with a girl friend and her marriage to de Marigny followed,
but the enmity of the Oakes family for its new member remained unchanged.

Once when the young bride was ill of typhoid in a Palm
Beach hospital and her husband had gone there to stay with
her, Oakes had telephoned to him with the demand that "if
you don't leave her alone I'll come and throw you out."
The Count remained. There were many other such incidents
in the years that followed.

Having thus learned much of the two principals in the case,
Schindler continued his efforts to inspect the murder scene,
to interview the prisoner, and to inspect more of the specific
evidence claimed by the government. His persistence finally
won to a degree but he became convinced that too much
evidence had been destroyed by careless police methods to
enable him to reconstruct the crime.

He finally visited de Marigny in his cell and became impressed by the accused man's statements and by the way he
made them. Many interviews followed and before long
Schindler was satisfied that the accused man was innocent.
How to prove it, however, was another matter and the detective finally concluded that his strategy would lie in his ability
to disprove the prosecution's case in its entirety.

Schindler never commented on his evaluation of the prisoner as an individual, nor did he ever say whether he believed
there was justification for the dislike of de Marigny by the
islanders. Whatever conclusions he may have reached on
these points he kept to himself. Evidently he believed these
were matters on which he had no right to comment; that
they were irrelevant to his assignment.

The Count, during all of his intimate contacts with

Schindler, displayed no great bitterness toward his accusers. He remained optimistic in his belief that the New York detective, working with defense counsel, would succeed in proving his innocence. It was obvious that de Marigny was fully aware of the dislike with which he was held in the Bahamas and took it as a matter of course. He seemed content in knowing of his wife's unswerving loyalty and her confidence that he would be vindicated; nor was he troubled by the opposite attitude of his mother-in-law, which continued throughout his trying ordeal, an attitude obviously influenced by her personal aversion to the man and by her orginal opposition to the marriage.

Later Schindler spent days at Westbourne scrutinizing almost every inch of the enormous house. He examined the walls of Oakes' bedroom where bloody palm and fingerprints had been partly washed away by Nassau police who had chosen to use soap and water instead of cameras.

Schindler had been told that a telephone book in the bedroom had been handled by bloody hands. Several pages supposedly had shown fingermarks as if the killer had hunted for a number. These, however, had been discarded and there was no way to trace the authenticity of the clue.

A sheet, blanket and another bed cover, he discovered, had been burned far less than Oakes' body, indicating to Schindler that the millionaire had not been killed in his bed as the prosecution contended, but had been carried there after the actual murder. He took specimens of the burned bedding and carpet with him and experimented with them for weeks, saturating them with combustibles. He concluded that it would have taken fully forty-five minutes for these materials to reach their charred condition; that the killer, therefore, may have worked leisurely after the murder. Yet Christie claimed that he had heard no noises. The detective doubted that the feathers on the body had been blown by an electric fan from the burned pillows. He was inclined to suspect that they might have been sprinkled deliberately in some strange

voodoo rites by natives with whom Oakes had quarreled. And
he could not understand why Sir Harry's genitals had been
burned far more than the rest of his body, indicating perhaps
that a blowtorch had been used by a degenerate.

Then Schindler turned his attention to de Marigny's alibi.
The Count had driven one of his women guests to her home
and he insisted that he had returned directly to his cottage.
He was specific on the time consumed, a point corroborated
by servants who said he had not been gone for more than
three quarters of an hour. This the prosecution vigorously
challenged, contending that he could not have covered the
distance in that time. Yet Schindler made the run a number
of times, in differing weather, and proved that the Count's
time schedule could be correct.

The detective pressed still further. He established that one
of de Marigny's party guests, George de Vivolou, had lingered to chat with a woman friend until long after his host
had returned and gone to bed. When de Vivolou finally did
escort her home and returned to the cottage for the night, he
parked his car directly behind the Count's in a narrow driveway and took the keys. To have left the house later to do
murder, de Marigny would have been compelled to move his
friend's locked car. The machine obviously had not been
moved.

Schindler also learned that two watchmen were in the
habit of maintaining an all-night guard on a two-story addi-
tion that was being built to Oakes' Westbourne home to connect it with an adjacent golf clubhouse which he also owned.
These men were on the ground the night of the murder but
the New York investigator was kept from interviewing them
and they never were called as witnesses.

The authorities also had disregarded two servants living
in a house adjoining that of Oakes. They told Schindler that
they had seen a man running down the road at the approxi-
mate time of the murder.

Attacking the prosecution's theory of motive, the detective

disclosed that the accused was far from broke; that actually he owned a profitable poultry business and other moneymaking enterprises. Strangely, his dairy firm continued selling eggs to the government which was making every effort to convict him as a murderer. Schindler further ascertained that the Count recently had refused a business loan and had ample funds in banks.

There were other points, too, that further convinced Schindler beyond a doubt that de Marigny was not the killer. One of them involved a police examination of the shirt and other clothing worn by the accused on the night before the murder. The garments were all free of bloodstains. But the investigator was not prepared for a stunning surprise that lay ahead. This was to come at the preliminary hearing before Magistrate F. E. Fields, which began as a perfunctory formality and ended with a bombshell. The surprise came from Captain Barker, the imported Miami officer, who testified that he had removed a single gory fingerprint from a scorched wooden screen close to Sir Harry's bed—the print of Count de Marigny's right ring finger!

To the amazement of everyone in the tense courtroom, he proceeded to support his statement by exhibiting a photograph of the print which he claimed had been "lifted" from the screen with adhesive tape.

Routinely labeled people's exhibit J, this lone fingerprint was to become the pivotal issue in the Count's trial for his life. It engaged Schindler in weeks of intensive scientific study in which he was assisted by a corps of American experts. His work with this tiny bit of evidence finally was to be acclaimed an outstanding achievement, to be recorded by criminalists on two continents as a shining example of scientific crime detection at its highest level. One writer referred to it as "the most brilliant piece of detective work in American history."

At the moment, however, Barker's disclosure had caught Schindler totally unaware. He pondered the origin of this all-important evidence and the more he thought of it the more puzzled—and suspicious—he became. Barker had testified that on discovering the print, he had dusted it with powder and "lifted" it with rubber tape. What Schindler could not comprehend was why the Miami man had not followed the customary procedure of first photographing the mark on the screen itself. Nor could he understand Barker's admission that while he had found the print soon after his arrival, he had said nothing of it to anyone until ten days later.

Schindler became still more suspicious when at last he was permitted to examine the screen together with enlarged photographs of the fingermark on the tape. To his astonishment, there were little circles in the background of the print, though experience told him that, instead, there should be ridges from the wooden surface of the screen. It seemed incredible.

Comparisons had shown that this was in fact de Marigny's print yet the accused Count had insisted that he had not been in the bedroom until long after his arrest when he was taken there by officers.

Had Captain Barker actually taken it from the screen? Schindler wondered, yet the possibility of trickery at first seemed inconceivable. He realized all too well that his case now depended on this puzzling bit of evidence. A man's life was at stake and it was up to Schindler to learn the truth.

He flew back to the United States as he had several times before during his work on the case and in Washington he consulted his close friend, Homer S. Cummings, who had investigated certain aspects of the mystery and had become convinced of de Marigny's innocence. He also spent much time with such specialists as Maurice O'Neill, a noted fingerprint expert of New Orleans; Leonardo Keeler, a criminologist who had pioneered with the lie detector; and with Erle Stanley Gardner, the author of crime mysteries and a recognized authority on criminal investigations. With them he spent days and nights poring over technical books on fingerprints and reports of celebrated cases throughout this country and Europe in which such evidence was involved. When at last he returned to Nassau, O'Neill and Keeler accompanied him, determined to solve the mystery.

The trio went to work on the wooden screen. Laboriously, they fingered every inch of it and "lifted" every print. They had made hundreds and each one showed a background of ridges from the wood. They spent weeks trying to produce a print with a background of circles like the one that Barker had. It was impossible.

Then they turned to a minute examination of the spot marked by Barker as the exact location of the disputed print. And when their work was over they agreed that under no circumstances could a fingermark ever have been "lifted" there. To them there was only one conclusion—the print, however it was obtained, had never been on the screen! They speculated that de Marigny's fingermark had been obtained from him after his arrest, undoubtedly by a ruse, and they asked themselves whether other evidence might have been similarly treated.

The experts continued their efforts, conferring frequently with Sir Godfrey Higgs, who had been engaged to head the Count's defense counsel, but the lawyer, like the investigators, had found himself frustrated in many ways by the prosecution's refusal to give him access to evidence which the defense regarded as favorable to its side.

Meticulously, they prepared for courtroom strategy, hoping to blast the prosecution's major contentions with dramatic impact. At last October 18 was set for the opening of the trial before a jury and all Nassau counted off the days. Never had so sensational a case been brought before a court in the Bahamas. Speculation as to the outcome ran high— not as to guilt or innocence, for the defendant's conviction had long since been taken for granted. The only question seemed to be the severity of punishment.

The trial, held before Sir Oscar B. Daly, the chief justice, began calmly enough, as Attorney General Eric Hallinan, directing the prosecution, led Christie, police officers and others into a routine recital of the condition of the bedroom and of the body. It was not long, however, before Schindler's work began to reveal itself and dramatic clashes came in quick succession.

The first occurred after prosecution witnesses had told of de Marigny's ride from his home with a woman guest only hours before the murder was discovered. Carefully, with marked attention to time and distance, the government was laying a foundation for its contention that the accused had returned home as he claimed; then sneaked out to kill his father-in-law.

Schindler had anticipated this, of course, and had spent many nights with craftsmen to create an exhibit that could provide visual refutation before a jury. When the time came for cross-examination, defense counsel surprised a packed courtroom by placing before the jury a miniature reproduction of the Count's cottage, the narrow driveway, and the two parked cars. As jurors strained their eyes for a close look at what any child would have cherished as a rare toy, the defense lawyer dramatically pointed to a small-scaled model representing de Marigny's car, parked in front of a tiny replica of his guest's locked machine, arguing that it would have been impossible for the accused to have driven away without moving the car behind it, or at least awakening those asleep in the cottage. The prosecution suffered its first telling blow.

Witnesses told of the feud between the defendant and his father-in-law and the prosecution tried hard to establish motive for the crime. Officers described the condition of Sir Harry's bedroom and of his body. Against their testimony defense counsel hammered hard, bringing out the blunders of the police in trying to wash out the bloody handprints that might have proved valuable clues. At every opportunity, Sir Godfrey, fighting to save his client, injected stinging charges that the authorities, in their intense desire to build

a case, had shown no concern for the possibility that someone else might be guilty.

Anxiously the defense awaited the introduction of the lone
fingerprint, now admittedly the government's strongest evidence. When this point was finally reached, the prosecution
chose to show the jury not only the mark but the entire
screen itself. With an air of confidence, Captain Barker took
the stand and began his testimony. Relating how he had removed the print, he insisted that it had been made by one of
de Marigny's fingers, which had not been denied. It was
obvious that he was making a deep impression on the jury.

Barker's assurance faded fast, however, as Sir Godfrey began his cross-examination. First he called on the witness to
indicate the exact spot on the screen from which he had
taken the print. Barker fumbled, and when he finally did
place his finger on the screen, Higgs promptly demonstrated
to the jury that if this had been the spot, the fingermark
would have protruded from the outer edge of the screen.

The Miami expert tried to correct himself. He was asked
to explain two penciled circles, some distance apart, that had
been made earlier on the screen to indicate the exact location of the print. "Which of these circles is yours and which
is the correct one?" the defense lawyer demanded.

Barker stared back and finally answered that he had been
confused and may have drawn both circles.

Next Higgs explained that accepted procedure called for
"dusting" a print with powder, photographing it at once, and
later bringing the picture into court together with the "lifted"
print on tape. Why had not Barker followed conventional
methods, he demanded. The officer explained that in his
hurried departure from Miami he had failed to bring the
necessary camera with him. The court inquired why he had
not sent for it or borrowed one from a laboratory maintained
by the British military. Barker reluctantly admitted that he
could have done so.

The defense turned its guns on the "lifted" fingermark and

Barker was forced to admit that such a print taken from the screen should show a circled background. Then Higgs carefully exhibited to the jury the little ridges behind the print that Barker had introduced—ridges that did not appear on the screen.

"Will the foreman of the jury kindly place his right little finger on this screen?" he asked.

The juror pressed his ring finger on the wood and then withdrew it. Members of the jury gathered around to scan their foreman's print. Its background clearly showed the circles of the wood.

At this point Justice Daly interrupted. "Does the defense mean to infer," he inquired, addressing Sir Godfrey, "that the fingerprint may be a forgery?"

"I do, sir," he retorted. Then, turning to Barker, he snapped:

"I suggest that you and Captain Melchen deliberately planned to get the defendant alone to get his fingerprint. I suggest that you have evaded the truth and substituted fabricated evidence."

The officer shot back a heated denial.

Later he was forced to listen to O'Neill, the expert from New Orleans, who became one of the star witnesses for the defense. In his judgment, the expert swore, the print had been obtained by a ruse while de Marigny was being questioned after his arrest. He insisted that it could not have come from the screen.

Testimony and arguments finally came to an end after twenty-two days and Sir Oscar Daly began his instructions to the jury. His concern over the disputed little fingerprint was clearly evident when he told the jurors:

"The prosecution must prove beyond a doubt that the fingerprint of de Marigny was found where they say it was found. The jury must consider whether the police are trying to make the facts fit their theory."

At last the jury filed out with the Count's fate in its hands. Hours later it sent word that its work was done.

A hush fell over the crowded courtroom when the moment came for the verdict to be read.

"Not guilty" said the jury and a burst of handclapping started. A bailiff quickly rapped for order—there was still more to be read. The jury ironically recommended that the Count be deported immediately from the Bahamas. The crowd cheered anew, more loudly now, and Countess Nancy rushed forward to embrace her husband.

Although it was learned later that three of the jurors had voted for conviction, the verdict generally was regarded as a stinging repudiation of Barker and his methods. Why he had concentrated all of his energies to prove the defendant's guilt and had refused to consider contrary possibilities, even refusing to cooperate with Schindler, no one ever knew. There were many opinions.

That night a celebration took place in the home of the defense lawyer, Sir Godfrey Higgs, who shared congratulations with Raymond Schindler. At the height of the gaiety, Keeler, one of the defense criminologists, suggested that the vindicated Count de Marigny subject himself to a lie detector test. He readily consented and Keeler, experienced in handling the apparatus, announced later that the test had shown the Count to be innocent.

De Marigny and his wife promptly flew back to the United States. Schindler lingered long enough to write a letter to the Duke of Windsor in which he pleaded for a reopening of the case, insisting that with some official help he could identify the murderer and prove his guilt. But in reply Schindler received only a curt note from Windsor's secretary advising him that the Nassau police were capable of handling any further inquiry.

Disappointed, in spite of his victory, Schindler returned to New York to take up a number of cases that had been neglected during his long absence.

Time, however, has failed to let the Oakes mystery rest or to take it from its place in Bahama politics. In the spring of 1959, nearly sixteen years after the murder, a demand was made in Nassau's House of Assembly that the inquiry be reopened. The move was unsuccessful but those behind it insisted that they would try again at a later time.

There are many who still believe that further efforts will be made to reopen the case and some even predict that the mystery which began in 1943 will yet be solved with the murderer brought to justice. Unfortunately, however, whatever secret evidence Schindler guarded so carefully, has gone with him to the grave. He died on July 1, 1959, at his home in Tarrytown, New York.

3

THE DOUBLE

For nine years Adolf Beck of London lived and suffered in the sinister shadow of a "double," who, ironically, was not a double at all. Yet he was twice convicted of fraud and served more than five years in prison because many women, a handwriting expert of repute, and an experienced police officer mistook him for a notorious swindler and confidence man, whom he really did not resemble.

Unlike those whose cases already have been related, Beck did not win liberty and exoneration through the efforts of a single individual, but because three men—a brilliant lawyer, a distinguished journalist, and a shrewd inspector of Scotland Yard—joined in a relentless search for truth.

Though many years have passed since the end of Beck's long nightmare, his misfortune still is cited in England and in America as one of the most bizarre examples of mistaken identity, sheer stupidity and official incompetence. One chronicler of the case, H. B. Irving, epitomizes it in the words of Maurice Maeterlinck: "A thousand coincidences that might have been contrived in hell, blending and joining together to work the ruin of an innocent man."

Actually, Beck's troubles over many years had powerful impact. They led directly to the creation of England's Court of Criminal Appeal for which a long, persistent campaign had been fought. Because that court since has served to right many miscarriages of justice, the case of Adolf Beck has held

a significant place in the history of jurisprudence and is the
subject of many books by authorities on judicial progress.

To fully comprehend the situation in all of its amazing
complexities, one must first know of Beck's background and
follow him from his first entry upon a stage of trouble. Born
in Norway, the son of a captain in the merchant trade, he
first studied chemistry but later turned to music. Finally, he
chose to go to sea, impressed no doubt by his father's adven-
tures, and eventually decided to settle in England in 1865,
finding work with a ship chandlery firm.

Devoutly religious, he was softhearted and generous, a
kindly man who made friends easily. Those who knew him
said that he was incapable of an unfriendly act. Yet ill luck
pursued him and he was something of a ne'er-do-well. Of
medium height and good physique, with a carefully waxed
gray mustache, he was an imposing figure, always immaculately
dressed. Usually, he wore a tall silk hat, a long dark coat, and a
batwing collar with a neatly tied cravat. He was fond of
carrying his gold-mounted umbrella, but more often than not
it was in pawn.

Of a restless nature, he left England in 1868 for South
America where he tried unsuccessfully to become a singer
and soon found himself involved in a revolution in Monte-
video in which he was seriously wounded.

Seventeen years later, in 1885, he was back in London,
making and losing money in reckless ventures. However, life
in Victorian England was pleasant—at least until that fateful
Monday evening of December 16, 1895, when Beck stepped
casually outside the door of his flat looking for a newspaper
boy.

He had been there only a few moments when a well-
dressed, middle-aged woman, walking briskly down the street,
glanced at him and came to an abrupt stop. "What have you
done with my watch?" she demanded.

For an instant Beck stared at her in amazement. "Madam,"
he finally replied, "I do not know you—you are badly mis-

taken." For Beck this was the beginning of long and tragic trouble.

His answer fell far short of satisfying his accuser. When she persisted, claiming angrily that he had stolen her time-piece during a torrid love affair, he became incensed and threatened to call the police. Heated words followed and Beck finally demanded that she walk with him until they could find a constable.

They met one two blocks away and he insisted that the woman be taken into custody for annoying him. After some talk, the three went to the station house where the accuser soon became the accused.

The woman identified herself as Ottilie Meissonier and explained that she had first met Beck in Victoria Street less than a month before while she was on her way to a flower shop. He had approached her, she related, inquiring whether she was Lady Egerton and then apologized politely when he was told he was in error.

"We started talking," she continued, "and he told me that he was a cousin of Lord Salisbury. He said he had a large estate in Lincolnshire and employed ten gardeners. Somehow, I mentioned that I grew chrysanthemums in my garden and he asked if he might see them, so I invited him to call on me the following day."

A romance of sorts developed, she said, and her visitor, after casually mentioning an income of £180,000 a year, invited her to accompany him to the South of France, an offer which she readily accepted.

"When I told him that I would need some clothes," Miss Meissonier went on, "he wrote me a check for ten pounds. By this time I had shown him some of my jewelry and had told him that my watch was out of order. He said he would take it to a watchmaker and I also gave him a ring that needed fixing. After he left I discovered that my other watch was missing and later the bank returned the check with a note saying that it was worthless. I've been looking for him ever since."

Beck, still protesting that he had been mistaken for another, was held by police pending further investigation. It was not long before he faced swiftly mounting difficulties.

The police immediately turned their attention to a large number of complaints from other women who had been similarly duped by a suave imposter, who often posed as Lord Wilton and sometimes as Lord Winton de Willoughby. He won their confidence by boasting of his wealth and social standing, then swindled them of jewelry and money. Detectives had been looking for this man since the previous December of 1894 when Mrs. Fanny Nutt, a trusting widow, first had come to them with her story of deception. All of the victims agreed that the smooth-talking swindler was of medium height, with broad shoulders and a gray mustache, neatly waxed. In these respects, Beck fitted their descriptions.

For the next few days officers busied themselves rounding up these women. Twenty-two were finally brought to headquarters to view the prisoner. Of these, ten positively identified him. The others were uncertain, excepting one who said definitely that he was not the man. The police, however, were well satisfied that they were making no mistake.

Beck, nevertheless, might have proved his innocence had not an elderly Londoner, with a sharp memory, read newspaper accounts of Beck's arrest and recalled a similar wave of swindling operations eighteen years before and the conviction of the offender. He hastened to Scotland Yard to relate what he remembered.

Old records were quickly checked, disclosing that in May 1877 a man of many aliases had been sent to prison for five years for bilking women. This man had been sentenced as John Smith, although his true name was said to have been William Augustus Wyatt. However, he frequently pretended to be a Captain William and wrote romantic notes on stationery of the Army and Navy Club. After four years' imprisonment, he had written to the Home Office complaining that his sentence was too severe. It was subsequently shortened, permitting his discharge on April 14, 1881, at which time he disappeared after telling a friend that he was going to Germany.

The more the men at Scotland Yard delved into their files, the more convinced they became that Beck indeed was Smith, whose earlier exploits appeared to be identical with those that now concerned them. According to the records, there had been a Miss Ada Wooding from whom Smith had taken rings and coins after writing to her on crested paper, begging that she become his mistress. Mrs. Louise Leonard had suffered similarly, as had Louisa Howard and fully fifteen other guileless women. In every case there had been the same chance conversation on a street in the same neighborhood, followed by a visit to the victim's home, and the inevitable talk of romance.

Mrs. Leonard had finally brought about Smith's arrest. Recognizing him on a street corner, she had followed him for blocks until she met a constable. "That's the man who pretended to be Lord Willoughby," she told the officer. "Arrest him—he stole my jewelry."

Scotland Yard now wanted further proof that the man in jail was actually Smith. Poring through old reports, officers learned that an inspector named Eliss Spurrell had arrested Smith and had attended his trial after months of work on the case. Still in service, Spurrell was summoned to headquarters and told to look closely at Beck. Without hesitation, he declared that the prisoner was the man he had arrested eighteen years before and had seen many times in the courtroom.

"Are you positive that this man is Smith?" he was asked.

"I know what is at stake in my answer," Spurrell replied with an air of confidence, "and I may say without doubt that he is the man."

While some accepted the inspector's word as final, others insisted that one further point of proof was necessary—handwriting. Scotland Yard sent for a widely known expert, Thomas Henry Gurrin, who had played important roles in celebrated criminal cases in England and on the Continent. He was given letters sent by Smith to his victims and specimens of Beck's writing. Gurrin studied them carefully and finally reported that the writing was identical. The script, he noted, was of a "Scandinavian type" and that all of it showed evidence of an obvious attempt at disguise. The authorities now were fully satisfied that Beck was Smith.

Beck engaged a well-known solicitor to defend him. He was Thomas Duerdin Dutton, who for years had proved himself as able in investigating crime mysteries as he had in legal maneuvers. Dedicated to the cause of justice, Dutton proved to be one of the first of the three men who were to carry on Beck's long struggle for exoneration.

At the outset, Dutton asserted publicly that he could prove his client's innocence. He was obviously relying on sharp differences in the physical appearances of Beck and Smith, a vital factor in the case which did not seem to worry the police, although it has aroused the curiosity of writers to this day.

Beck's preliminary hearing took place in the Police Court in Westminster, and from the outset he fared badly. More than eight women followed each other to the box, identifying him as the suave confidence man who had decamped with their money and jewelry. The police asserted, more positively than ever, that Beck was actually Smith, and to support their conclusion, both Inspector Spurrell and Gurrin, the handwriting expert, testified at length.

It was during this testimony that Beck turned to his solicitor, whispering that he wished to make a statement to the court vigorously denying that he was the swindler of eighteen years before, but Dutton disagreed, explaining that this was unnecessary in the lower court; in fact, he was confident of winning a dismissal in spite of the prosecution's witnesses.

He had reckoned poorly, however, for the defendant was

finally committed for trial in Central Criminal Court on felony and misdemeanor charges. It was the first of many bitter disappointments that were to follow.

The trial opened on March 3, 1895, in Old Bailey. By a peculiar turn of circumstance, the presiding magistrate was Judge Forrest Fulton, who had prosecuted Smith in 1877, and who later became Recorder of London. The prosecutor was Horace Avory, who as Mr. Justice Avory in later years was regarded as the most famous, and the most feared judge of his day. Dutton, a solicitor, could not appear as defense counsel in the higher court but he counseled closely with Beck's barristers, Percival Clarke and C. F. Gill.

At the outset the defense suffered another serious defeat. Beck's lawyers had hoped to have him tried on felony counts of fraud, each of which mentioned that he had been previously convicted as Smith, a point which they believed could be effectively disproved. To this Avory, the prosecutor, vigorously objected, demanding that the accused be tried on the remaining charge, a misdemeanor, which did not involve the earlier crimes. He obviously wished to avoid that issue and to rest his case on the testimony of the women victims. The court ruled for Avory.

The prosecutor then called the first of the women to the box and she related her experience, blaming Beck. "Are you positive that the defendant is the man responsible?" Avory asked.

"He is the living image of the man who swindled me," she exclaimed, pointing angrily at the defendant.

Nine other women followed her with similar testimony, but some differed as to the swindler's voice. One said that she had been duped by a man with a "Yankee twang." Another asserted that her admirer definitely was not an Englishman. A third referred to a "Swiss-like" accent.

Defense counsel tried to capitalize on this conflict but since the Prisoners Evidence Act had not yet been passed in England, Beck was unable to go into the box and let his accusers hear his voice. Certainly, the testimony of some of his accusers would have been discredited. He did score, however, in an issue over a scar.

Several prosecution witnesses had told of observing a mark on the neck of the man who had defrauded them—a mark that they said could easily be seen above his high collar. During defense cross-examination of these women, the judge looked at Beck and remarked that no such scar was visible above his collar. Only when Beck opened and lowered his collar at the court's request could the mark be seen.

As the trial proceeded with frequent clashes between counsel, Beck suffered repeatedly in important rulings by the court. One of these came after Gurrin had testified that the defendant's handwriting proved his guilt and that it was exactly similar to that of Smith in the 1877 cases.

At the first mention of Smith's name, Gill jumped to his feet, challenging the statement as inadmissible, his purpose being to disassociate his client from Smith for all time, but Avory quickly interposed an objection to any discussion of this point.

Gill argued that he was well within his rights; that the accused was not Smith and that he should not be blamed for the acts of another. He was intimating—for the first time— that Smith, now probably back in England, was possibly the real offender in the present case.

In the end, the court ruled against Beck, declaring that the question of whether Beck was Smith was not admissible and likely to confuse the jury.

As soon as the government had closed its case, Gill called his first and most important witness, a man prepared to swear that he had met Beck in Peru in 1880, a time when Smith was in prison. Scarcely had the defense lawyer asked his first leading questions, indicating his purpose, than the prosecutor interposed an objection. Such testimony, he argued, would be irrevelant and misleading. Gill countered vigorously, insisting that his point was vital to the defense, but the court ruled against him and again Beck suffered a telling blow.

To Beck's counsel and other supporters, the judge's position seemed not only unfair but wholly inconsistent. The police, in preparing their case, had spared no effort in trying to establish that Beck was Smith, yet the man now on trial was denied an opportunity to disprove that theory.

Gill finally was obliged to rest his case on a flat denial of his client's guilt with strong emphasis on the fact that twelve of the twenty-two victims had failed to identify him. The jury, however, chose to believe the ten women whom they had heard. Beck was found guilty and sentenced to serve seven years in Wormwood Scrubs Prison. Adding to his troubles, he was given the same prison number as had been Smith's—D 523—with an additional W, which meant that he had previously been convicted of crime. In the eyes of the law, Beck now was Smith.

Without delay, Dutton, the solicitor, resumed the legal struggle for vindication. Satisfied that a flagrant miscarriage of justice had occurred, he drew on his long experience in criminal cases which had made him a familiar figure in the Westminster Police Court, known as a tireless worker for truth and fairness. He soon sent to the Home Office the first of a series of petitions setting forth that Beck and Smith were different individuals and that he could prove it. Beck, he declared, had been in South America from 1873 to 1884, part of which time Smith was in prison, a fact that he maintained could be established by four men who had known his client in Peru during that period. These four, he stated, had been present at Beck's trial and were eager to testify but had been prevented by the judge's ruling. One of them, he pointed out, had been an official under the Danish king and had been visited several times by Beck in Lima. Dutton offered to produce these witnesses for interrogation.

Weeks passed before the Home Office rendered its decision, bluntly refusing to engage in this phase of the case. "Even if the prisoner is not Smith," the Home Office contended, "the evidence of his guilt in the present case is quite overwhelming. He was identified by ten women whom he had defrauded."

There were significant references to the importance of the handwriting testimony and a curt refusal to inquire into Beck's claim of an alibi. Rather than listen to his supporting evidence, the Home Office pointed out that it would be difficult, if not impossible, to disprove his presence in South America.

Two years slipped by while Dutton continued his tireless but futile efforts to induce the authorities to reopen the case. He was rebuffed in a number of attempts to gain access to records of the Smith trial and the Home Secretary even refused to meet him.

The solicitor, however, was carrying on an inquiry of his own, probing here and there, wherever he thought he might find worthwhile information. It was not until early spring in 1898 that he came upon a vital fact that seemed too good to be true and he realized at once that at last he might hold the key that would unlock prison doors for Beck. It was a dominant point in Smith's description which, for some unaccountable reason, was not in the official records of Scotland Yard. If it could be followed to a successful conclusion, it would be incontrovertible proof that Beck was not Smith.

More hopeful than ever, Dutton pursued his inquiries, hastening to Wormwood Prison where he questioned officials on this new point of overwhelming import. To his delight, he received the answer he had wished for—the answer that proved his case!

Smith was circumcised. Beck was not!

Dutton's exhaustive investigation, delving deeply into every facet of the case, had uncovered a curious and surprising circumstance. Upon Smith's discharge from prison, Dutton learned, the authorities had sent his record with a photograph and description to Scotland Yard. But the fact of Smith's circumcision had been omitted. Dutton ascertained that the prison's medical officer had even certified to the circumcision. Had Dutton known of this, or even of the photograph, Beck's trial doubtlessly would have ended differently. Somehow, the matter of the photograph was overlooked by defense counsel —just how, has never been explained.

Satisfied that Beck's discharge would be only a matter of days, Dutton communicated at once with the Home Office, advising that now he was able to prove beyond the slightest doubt that his client was not Smith. It was May 25, 1898, more than two years after prison doors had closed behind the prisoner in December 1895.

Dutton waited anxiously for action but again he was destined for disappointment. The Home Secretary replied at length, admitting that he was convinced that the men were not the same—but he had more to say. "This does not prove," he emphasized, "that Beck was not guilty of offenses of which he was convicted." The Secretary agreed that Purrell, the inspector, had erred in stating that Beck was Smith, but he avoided any suggestion that the women accusing Beck might have been mistaken in their identification.

This decision, however, left one faint hope remaining. It concluded with the announcement that all of the records of the case, including Dutton's last communication, had been sent to Judge Fulton, who had presided at the trial.

After a time the jurist responded, admitting that while some doubt now existed that Beck was Smith, there was no official confirmation that the convicted man had not been circumcised. It was a point which the judge easily could have verified, if he had wished, but he chose to let the matter drop, merely pointing out that the defendant had been convicted on adequate evidence.

Weeks later Dutton was informed by the Home Office that it was not justified in interfering with the sentence and the only tangible result of the solicitor's convincing disclosure was a new cell for Beck and a new number. He was moved to

Fulton Prison and identified now as W 78, which actually meant that he no longer was considered to be Smith.

By this time the case had attracted wide attention throughout England and people were divided sharply in their judgment. By some, much was made of the fact that since Beck's imprisonment reports from women suffering at the hands of confidence men had ceased abruptly. Others offered to help the defense. The Danish Court official who had wanted to support Beck's alibi at the trial called at the Home Office, pleading for a reopening of the case. His request was ignored.

Beck, continuing to fight a seemingly hopeless cause, wrote to the authorities again and again. "It is only by the help and infinite mercy of God," he once stated, "that I am not now a lunatic from what I have endured."

In a later communication, he wrote:

"In whatsoever situation, misfortune or faults I may have had, I have never been guilty of obtaining anything by false pretenses, nor have I ever stolen the value of a halfpenny in my life."

Dutton stubbornly carried on new legal maneuvers but to no avail until the morning of July 8, 1901, five years after Beck had gone to prison. The Home Office suddenly announced that the prisoner would be released at once "on license," a procedure similar to the American system of parole.

Free at last, Beck set out to work for complete exoneration. In his absence his mother had died of a broken heart. Never affluent, his scant savings had been spent in the long legal fight but he soon won a new ally, the second in his trio of stanch, hard-working defenders. He was George Robert Sims, a distinguished journalist and playwright whose melodrama, *The Lights o' London* was credited with having earned him a fortune.

A large, muscular man with a Vandyke and a twinkling eye, Sims looked every inch the Bohemian and the bon vivant that he was. Fond of good food and drink, he was a conspicuous figure at the race tracks and at boxing bouts, a man whom everyone admired and wanted to know. At the height of his success, when four of his plays were running simultaneously in London's West End, a chance meeting with a journalist changed the entire course of his career. Suddenly fired with an urge to become a newspaperman, he turned his pen to a column which he wrote weekly for a popular publication, *Fun*. It was one of the first columns of its kind in England.

Later he joined the staff of *The Referee*, contributing a column in which he wrote in an original style of his thoughts and doings, his likes and prejudices. In this new field he rose rapidly and, at the turn of the century, he was ranked with W. T. Stead as one of the most popular and widely read journalists of the day.

Considering himself an amateur criminologist, Sims took up the cause of Beck with all of his characteristic enthusiasm and persistence. It soon gained many new supporters. Incensed at the injustice of it all, he wrote daringly of the flaws and blunders in the case. Often he excoriated Gurrin, the handwriting expert, declaring that he should have easily recognized that Beck in writing never crossed a "t" while Smith always did. Then he contacted one newspaper publisher after another, pleading for help. It was not long before the press had swung to Beck and many editors were demanding an immediate reconsideration of the entire affair. Some referred to it as a national scandal. The Salvation Army became interested and at long last Beck saw new hope for vindication. His luck, however, was soon to turn again.

Late in 1903 London was startled by the appearance of a confidence man who had swindled an unsuspecting woman, using methods precisely similar to those of the two earlier periods. As days passed, more women complained to the police and Beck's name soon was whispered about.

Search for the elusive culprit was still under way when Mrs. Pauline Scott walked into a police station on an April evening in 1904 to report that she had been fleeced by a man resembling Adolf Beck. "He said he was Lord Willoughby when he visited me at my invitation," she related, "and he explained that he could not remain very long because they were waiting for him at the House of Lords. I'm sure it was Beck."

She was given the address of the ill-fated suspect and told to stand by his lodgings until she saw him and could verify her suspicions.

Following instructions, Mrs. Scott took up her vigil and when Beck emerged from his flat hours later, she accused him of defrauding her. Again he protested but the woman called a constable who took the man to the station where he was positively identified in the presence of other officers.

More victims were summoned. One of them, Rose Reece, looked at the suspect and said she could recognize his nose "out of a thousand."

Beck stared at her in amazement. "Before God, I am absolutely innocent," he pleaded. "I've never seen any of these women before."

Dutton and Sims promptly rallied to his support but they were not prepared for what was to follow. The prosecuting authorities, completely ignoring all of Dutton's earlier disclosures, insisted again that Beck was Smith and no amount of argument could shake them from that opinion. To make matters worse, three more women came forward to identify the unfortunate man and to heap new accusations upon him.

On June 27, 1904, Beck faced his second trial, eight years after his first and only three years after his release from prison. The women testified against him, and Gurrin, the handwriting expert, once more linked him not only to the latest crimes but insisted anew that he was Smith.

This time the law permitted the accused to testify in his own behalf. Emphatically denying his guilt, Beck swore that he was attending to business matters in another part of London at the times he was alleged to have been with his accusers.

As before, the jury sided with the prosecution and Beck

was found guilty for a second time. The defense, however, had raised some doubt in the mind of the presiding jurist, Justice Grantham, and he announced that he would withhold sentence pending further inquiry.

While Dutton busied himself with legal maneuvers, Sims immediately took up his pen in a sweeping campaign to arouse public opinion in Beck's behalf. First in the *Weekly Dispatch* and later in the *London Mail* he published daring exposés, castigating the police and reviewing all of the evidence.

His articles, attracting wide attention, brought a third ally to the defense, Chief Inspector John Kane of Scotland Yard, who had become interested and decided to contribute his long experience and training to the cause. While Kane was heavily involved in other cases, word had reached him that Smith was back in London and was engaged in the jewelry business. Suspecting that this man might be back at his old tricks and that Beck again might be the sufferer, the Chief Inspector decided to investigate. He was still searching for Smith when the unexpected occurred.

Two sisters, Violet and Beulah Turner, unemployed actresses, walked angrily into a police station to report that three of their valuable rings had been stolen from their apartment by a confidence man with amorous ways. Luckily for Beck, Kane immediately gave his full attention to the complaint. One of the routine procedures naturally was to send a description of the stolen jewelry to pawnshops throughout the city.

Two days later a pawnbroker telephoned to the police that a stranger was in the place trying to dispose of the stolen rings and that he was being detained on a pretext. Kane, who had ordered that he be notified at once of such a situation, hurried to the shop, arriving there while the man was still bargaining for a better price. "What's your name?" he inquired.

"William Thomas."

"Thomas—nothing. You're John Smith and I'd recognize you anywhere," snapped Kane, who had attended Smith's trial and had an uncanny memory for faces.

Smith finally had overplayed his hand, recklessly resuming his old practices while Beck was in jail. At last he had done all that was needed to clear an innocent man.

Under Kane's sharp questioning, he reluctantly admitted his identity, explaining that he had gone to Australia after his release and had studied medicine. After practicing in America for a time as Dr. Marsh, he had returned to London in 1903.

Police sent for the five women who had identified Beck at his second trial. Two were abroad but the other three looked at Smith and readily admitted their mistake.

It was now apparent that the two men, strangely enough, resembled each other in only some respects and were decidedly different in others. While both were of medium, heavy build, of approximately equal height, Smith's hair and eyes were brown, while Beck's hair was grayish and he had brown eyes. Smith had a scar on his upper lip and a mole under his armpit. The other man had only a scar on his neck below the collar line and a small scar on his lower cheek. There were sharp differences in their ages. Smith was twenty-seven when he was first arrested. At that time Beck was thirty-six. Smith was known to speak English perfectly. Beck had a Nordic accent.

Such were the differences which many since have believed should have caused the police to have at least some doubt that Beck could have been the earlier offender. Nevertheless, they were thoroughly convinced and willing to take their case before a magistrate.

Days were spent in a hurried effort to locate the women who had appeared against Beck at the first trial eight years before. None could be found but detectives, led by the indefatigable Kane, did find one who had refused to identify Beck and therefore had not been called to the box. Escorted to headquarters and confronted with a row of prisoners in a police lineup, she pointed accusingly to Smith. Her identification was strengthened by the fact that Smith still was wearing a watch chain decorated with Egyptian coins, something that several of the victims had mentioned on previous occasions.

Gurrin, the handwriting witness, came forward and admitted that he had made a serious blunder. He explained that had he known of Smith's circumcision he would have withheld his testimony.

At long last the Home Office was thoroughly convinced. Beck's immediate release was ordered and he was granted a full pardon by the Crown.

On September 15, Smith appeared in Old Baily and pleaded guilty to stealing rings from the Turner sisters. He was sentenced to five years in prison after admitting his previous conviction in 1877, and telling police that he alone was responsible for the crimes of 1896.

Interest turned now to England's debt to Adolf Beck. The authorities first proposed that he be paid £6000, an offer which his three stanch defenders declared was far from adequate. What they wanted most and vigorously demanded, was an official inquiry into the entire case that would fix the blame for one of the most flagrant miscarriages of justice in English history.

While the authorities would have preferred to indemnify Beck and let the entire matter drop, Sims enlisted the support of the *Daily Mail*. In a new series of sensational articles, he again reviewed the case, concluding that only a far-reaching and fearless investigation would satisfy public conscience. His efforts even attracted the attention of the King of Norway, who conferred a high decoration upon Sims for his dedication to Beck, a native Norwegian.

Sims' demands echoed from one part of England to the other. The issue soon came before Parliament and the Home Office, reacting to mounting pressure, finally appointed a

Committee of Inquiry. Its members sat for five days reviewing every factor of the case.

Beck, who was questioned at some length, revealed his unusual philosophy and utter lack of bitterness, in one of his many statements.

"If there had been a Court of Criminal Appeal I should have been found an innocent man in 1896," he told the Committee.

"I think that is quite possible," replied Sir Richard Henn-Collins, who was presiding.

Beck smiled as he followed with this significant comment:

"If the establishment of such a court is the result of my being in the dock, then I shall know that God had placed me there for something, and I shall not regret that I have suffered."

The Committee's findings, however, were keenly disappointing. It found that the conduct of the police had been dictated "by nothing but a sense of duty and had been perfectly correct." The primary cause of all the blundering, the investigators stated, was the fact that prison authorities, in sending Smith's description to Scotland Yard upon his discharge, had omitted the one vitally important fact—his circumcision. The Home Office was blamed for decisions that were "defective," but Inspector Kane was highly praised for "intelligent work." The report concluded with a definite statement that there remained not a single shadow of doubt that Beck was completely innocent.

Still the case was not concluded. Dutton and Sims continued their pleas for adequate compensation. Others, among them many high in legal circles, renewed the agitation for establishment of a Criminal Court of Appeal, pointing out that Beck's misfortune demonstrated such a need.

Three years passed before their demands were answered. Beck finally accepted £5000 as a settlement for all his troubles but he did not have long to enjoy his vindication. After squandering all of his money, he died of pleurisy in Middlesex Hospital shortly before Christmas in 1909.

The case of Adolf Beck, however, is frequently recalled as a glaring example of human error, stupidity and stubbornness. It is probably no better characterized than by E. R. Watson, who called the affair a flagrant miscarriage of justice and "a sinister combination of unhappy coincidences such as seldom happen in the legal history of any country."

4

THE PHANTOM FORGER

Clifford T. Shepherd, a highly respected and successful businessman of Scotch Plains, New Jersey, arose early as usual on the morning of Tuesday, April 18, 1933, and prepared for a busy day. He had developed a lucrative enterprise as a professional fund raiser for needy churches and his yearly earnings had passed the $10,000 mark. His work took him to many cities where he had close friends. Every one held him in high regard, knowing that he often worked for little profit when he found a church in serious financial difficulties.

Late that afternoon he had returned to his boardinghouse earlier than usual and was standing on the front steps when a policeman appeared asking for his landlady, Mrs. Elizabeth Lester, a widow and mother of small children. "She's not in right now," Shepherd explained. "Is there anything that I can do? She runs this boardinghouse."

The officer explained that he was there to investigate a complaint by the woman's grocer, whose wife had accepted a $5 check from Mrs. Lester. When the bank returned the check because the account was overdrawn by thirty cents, the merchant in anger had notified the police.

"I'm sure this can be straightened out very easily," Shepherd assured the patrolman, who suggested that he accompany his landlady to police headquarters when she returned.

An hour later Shepherd, unsuspecting what lay ahead,

walked with Mrs. Lester to the station and remained outside while she entered to make explanations. As he stood there, a man brushed past him, stepped into the building, and complained that two customers, apparently man and wife, had given him a forged check for $35.

While this man was still relating details, he paused to look out of the station window. Suddenly, he pointed excitedly at Shepherd, exclaiming, "Look, there's the man now, standing outside—the fellow I cashed that check for."

An instant later he glanced at Mrs. Lester standing close by at the sergeant's desk. "And there's the woman who was with him. I want them both arrested."

From that moment Shepherd and his landlady were in serious trouble that plagued them for years. Though both vehemently denied the accusation and explained that they never shopped together, the police at once suspected that they were the pair sought for months on the complaints of storekeepers who had cashed worthless checks with cleverly forged signatures. Still protesting, Shepherd and Mrs. Lester were taken to jail and in the next few days fully a dozen merchants identified them as the guilty couple.

News of the arrests shocked the community where both the accused man and woman had many friends. Some doubted that Shepherd, with a career devoted to religious causes, had been leading a double life. Their promises of support, however, were of little help as authorities in neighboring cities called the Scotch Plains officers with orders to hold the two for similar offenses in their localities. But for these requests, the prisoners might easily have secured their release on bail. Under the circumstances there seemed to be no alternative but to remain in jail and trust a competent lawyer whom they had engaged, confident that they could prove their innocence.

The wheels of justice moved slowly while the authorities took their time in confronting the imprisoned couple with victims of forged checks from far and wide. Many were positive in their identifications; others were not so certain. Yet seven months passed before the two faced a jury and listened to the accusing words of a forger's victims. They were found guilty and, on November 22, 1935, Judge Adrian Lyon sentenced both Shepherd and Mrs. Lester to serve nine months in the Middlesex County Workhouse.

A day after their release and before they could even think of trying to resume normal life, they found themselves indicted by the Essex County Grand Jury on charges of passing five forged checks in East Orange. Both had previously been identified by victims in that community.

Since they had spent all of their money in fighting the first case, the luckless pair realized that now they were at the mercy of their accusers. Without funds for counsel, they decided against risking a jury trial, hoping that they might convince a judge in another county that they were victims of mistaken identity. The testimony of duped merchants, however, was overwhelming and Judge Daniel P. Brennan found both guilty. He sentenced Shepherd to serve eighteen months in the county jail at Caldwell. Mrs. Lester, because of her small children, was given a shorter term.

When they were finally released, the two faced ruined lives. More of their friends had turned against them; their reputations were gone. Shepherd's business had foundered and his wife, a missionary, had divorced him. Mrs. Lester was ostracized.

Shepherd, after serving thirty-four months in prison for crimes he had not committed, now faced a trying and uncertain future. Two months passed before he could even find a job and when he did it was as a porter in a cheap bar. He worked hard, with rehabilitation as his aim, but soon he faced new and unexpected difficulties.

In the city of Plainfield, a storekeeper had belatedly reported cashing a worthless check for a customer who had forged the name of William Brinkman, a well-known citizen. When his description of the culprit was found to match that

of Shepherd, the police communicated with the Scotch
Plains authorities and asked that the twice-convicted man be
arrested for a third time.

On the following day when the unfortunate Shepherd reported for work, a plain-clothesman was waiting for him.
Completely unnerved, he asserted that the charge was absurd
since he never had been in Plainfield. "My orders are to bring
you in," said the detective. "You can make your explanations
at headquarters."

Despite his protests, Shepherd was booked again, with the
notation that he was to be held for the police of the other
city. This time, however, he was more fortunate. He requested the officers to ascertain the date on which the Plainfield merchant had been defrauded. When the answer came a
day later, Shepherd easily proved that he was in jail at that
time and he was released. Nevertheless, an account of his arrest appeared in the newspapers and his townsfolk this time
were even more unfriendly in their comments than before.

A few remained, however, who doubted that the once-re-
spected businessman could really be a forger. One of them, a
member of the grand jury, suspected that Shepherd possibly
might have been mistaken for another. Curious, he sent for
the man and they discussed the matter.

"I've been arrested three times for things I didn't do,"
Shepherd said with justifiable bitterness. "Just how long I
can stand this, I really don't know. But what am I to do?"

"I wouldn't be at all surprised if you've got a double—and
you're paying for his crimes," the other suggested. "Why
don't you consult a good detective—someone with the Burns
people, perhaps. They represent the American Bankers Association."

The next day Shepherd was in New York, calling on
Horace A. Crowe, head of the Criminal Division of the William J. Burns International Detective Agency. His mentor
was the celebrated founder of that organization, whose early
years had been spent with the United States Secret Service.

Relentless in his pursuit of the guilty, Burns constantly admonished his men to protect the innocent. Crowe was one of the many in the world-wide agency who made his chief's orders his personal way of procedure.

The detective nodded occasionally as Shepherd related his many difficulties and it was obvious that an idea was clicking in Crowe's mind. After listening to the long and complicated story, he stepped into his record room, opened a tall steel file, and began thumbing through folders stuffed with circulars bearing descriptions of men wanted for forgery. Finally he came upon the one he wanted, a sheet pertaining to a man named Eugene Sullivan, a long-hunted fugitive known to the police as the "phantom forger."

Crowe scanned the printed lines, then looked sharply at Shepherd, eying him from head to foot. He and Sullivan appeared to be nearly as much alike as two peas in a pod. Both were of the same physique, heavily built. Sullivan was sixty-five. Shepherd was two years younger. The color of their hair and eyes was similar. Both were square jawed. Their complexions, features, and facial expressions were identical. "He really could be your identical twin," Crowe remarked. "I think I can see the whole thing now."

The detective then examined facsimiles of worthless checks for which Shepherd had been imprisoned and soon discovered that the names of payees corresponded with aliases known to have been used by Sullivan.

Satisfied that his early surmise had been confirmed, Crowe led Shepherd into another room and took his fingerprints. Placed side by side with those of Sullivan, they proved to be widely different.

"The answer to all your problems is quite apparent," Crowe said. "Now let's compare handwriting."

Shepherd sat down and penned a few lines. In no way did the script resemble Sullivan's.

"We'll consult an expert on handwriting," Crowe announced. "I'll send these two specimens to Albert Osborn.

He's one of the top authorities in this field in the country and his report will have professional status. Let's look at Sullivan's record."

As Crowe ran through a bulging file of complaints against the "phantom forger," Shepherd listened in amazement to the details of the other man's long career of crime. It had started early in 1925 when Sullivan, a native of Rapid City, South Dakota, first turned to forgery. A persuasive talker, with the appearance of a prosperous business executive, he had traveled from city to city, defrauding unsuspecting merchants with worthless checks.

Then somewhat of an amateur in this field of crime, he was apprehended months later in Detroit and sent to prison for five years. At once he became a model of good behavior, so convincing in his repentance that he succeeded in winning his release on parole after serving only two years.

With knowledge gained from seasoned prisoners, he returned to his evil ways. The police called his forged checks "real works of art" and his mode of operation as ingenious as it was successful.

Posing as a salesman for a mythical firm manufacturing check protecting machines, he would call on large insurance firms to demonstrate his product. In this way he was able to obtain a sample check or two which he promptly took to an unsuspecting printer, ordering a quantity to be printed with the firm name so that they might be used to prove the efficiency of his equipment.

Once supplied with the necessary blanks, he would number each check, date it with a rubber stamp, fill out the amount on a typewriter, and usually forge the signature of an officer of the company. Each check was made payable to one of the various aliases that Sullivan used and the finishing touch was supplied by the protecting machine which gave the paper a genuine appearance.

He was equally clever in converting his forgeries into cash. Experience had taught him that it was far safer to operate with a woman and so his wife, the mother of four children by a previous marriage, became his accomplice. They moved swiftly from city to city and from state to state, rarely remaining in the same place for more than a few days.

Never would they risk the chance of victimizing banks, which had been warned by the Burns Agency of their activities. Instead, they made friends with townspeople, familiarized themselves with the ways of small shopkeepers, and always selected their victims cautiously. Invariably, they operated on Saturday nights after banks had closed and before a check could be returned, they were on their way to new and fertile fields.

Together the two had used more than fifty aliases and were being hunted by police in a still larger number of communities. Their trail crisscrossed the country and for more than ten years they had eluded their pursuers.

When Crowe finally concluded his long account of Sullivan's criminal career, he told Shepherd that he would do all in his power to bring about the capture of the couple, explaining that up to this time he had not assumed a leading role in the pursuit, since banks, which the agency represented, had not been molested.

"You can count on us to get this couple," he told Shepherd. "You've been suffering too long on their account. It may take awhile, but we'll catch up with them. Just be patient."

Crowe at once assumed the leadership of the hunt. Checking time and place of the Sullivans' most recent operations, he contacted police in these cities, asking for any clue that might be helpful. Then he distributed new circulars in many states, describing the pair and calling for a closer watch than ever before.

For months Crowe was deluged with messages reporting that the elusive couple had been seen in one state and then in another. Clue after clue was followed without result. In some cases it appeared reasonably certain that the husband

and wife actually had been located but always they were on their way before they could be apprehended. In other instances, their identification proved to be false.

The first tangible lead finally came from the police in South Bend, Indiana, who reported that a man and woman, closely resembling the Sullivans, had been seen driving a large black sedan with New York license plates. Soon afterward, Crowe received a telegram from Milwaukee advising that the two were believed to be in Elmira, New York.

Police of that city went into action. While a search was under way, a druggist became suspicious of a check that he had just cashed for a man resembling Sullivan and followed his customer to the street, noting the license number of his car. Officers were notified and hours later Sullivan and his wife were captured. The tantalizing manhunt was at an end.

Milwaukee police, holding a number of complaints against the fugitive, insisted on bringing him to trial there and he was sentenced to ten years in prison. His wife, meanwhile, had been wanted by the authorities of Watertown, New York, where for once she had operated alone, and she, too, was sent to the penitentiary.

Shepherd was elated at the news. He went first to Watertown to interview Mrs. Sullivan and was impressed by her resemblance to Mrs. Lester. "It was easy to understand why one woman was mistaken for the other," he reported later. "They really do look very much alike and, strange to say, they dress much the same."

He traveled next to Milwaukee to meet Sullivan and was startled by their remarkably close likeness. It was obvious that in all outward appearances one easily could be mistaken for the other. Shepherd had never heard of Adolf Beck of London but if he had he would have been impressed by the striking similarity between his case and that of the ill-fated Englishman.

Shepherd's misfortune, however, differed in some respects. Not only had he served two prison terms for the other man's crimes, but his landlady, who looked like the forger's wife and accomplice, also was twice convicted and imprisoned. But they were not the only sufferers, as Shepherd learned long afterward. Three others, in different parts of the country, likewise had been mistaken for the elusive check passer and arrested while the police were hunting the "phantom forger," who for more than ten years had slipped repeatedly through a net literally spread across the continent.

As Sullivan and his double talked together in the Milwaukee prison, the convicted forger, who already had confessed to his long criminal career, recalled the specific offenses for which Shepherd had been arrested and convicted. Later Shepherd was shown copies of the checks for which he had been blamed and Sullivan identified them as those he had forged and cashed.

Returning later to Crowe's office, Shepherd happily recounted the details of his visit. "Sullivan seemed sincerely sorry for the trouble that he had caused me," the vindicated man related. "When I looked at him I really thought that I was seeing myself in the mirror."

With Crowe's help, Shepherd moved rapidly for official exoneration. Osborn, the handwriting expert, already had reported that the writing of the two men was different in every essential detail.

Shepherd's hopes for fast legal action, however, were soon dissipated as he learned to his dismay that the wheels of justice had moved faster against him than they would move in reverse. He called first on the New Jersey authorities and was given a cold reception. "They put a damper on my spirits right away," he said later. "Newspaper talk about a miscarriage of justice didn't set well with the prosecutor's staff. I was instructed not to talk to newspapermen and promised that everything would be handled quietly."

Crowe, meanwhile, had written to New Jersey officials informing them of his work and its results. "The evidence here," he stated, "conclusively shows that Clifford Shepherd is not guilty of cashing any worthless checks. It is my personal opinion that the State of New Jersey is under obligation to Mr. Shepherd and should compensate him not only for the embarrassment suffered but for the criminal record against him." He asked that the governor and the legislature be advised of the case.

Nothing was done. Despite his disappointment, Shepherd continued to call on New Jersey authorities, pleading for official action but he found that his efforts were to no avail. "I must have called on them no less than fifty times," he reported long afterward, "and each time I came away with only promises made with obvious indifference."

Two years passed. Mrs. Lester had remarried and with Shepherd petitioned for a pardon but the New Jersey Court of Pardons flatly rejected their applications without even giving a reason for its decision.

With difficulty Shepherd found odd jobs here and there, for, despite newspaper accounts of his exoneration, prejudices still lingered. But he was determined to continue his fight, no matter how long it would take.

He waited five years, then again petitioned for a pardon. Once more it was denied. Months later he learned that Sullivan had been paroled. An effort to bring him to trial in the cases for which Shepherd and Mrs. Lester served time had failed because of the statute of limitations. Sullivan, therefore, was free but the man who had suffered because of him still could not obtain a pardon.

Another five years elapsed and now, with a new Pardon Board in office, Shepherd decided to try his luck a third time. Again he was aided by Crowe and Osborn, who once more appeared before the Board with enlarged exemplars of the handwriting of the two men to illustrate how they proved Shepherd's innocence.

This time Shepherd was successful and on the Board's recommendation Governor Alfred E. Driscoll, on July 8, 1950, granted him an unconditional pardon. Fifteen years had passed since his first arrest and twelve since Sullivan's arrest and confession.

Shepherd's face beamed as he accepted the document that he had fought so long to obtain. "This is the most valuable piece of paper that I have ever received," he said.

Illness had prevented his one-time landlady from pursuing her plea for pardon but she announced that she would petition the governor at some later time.

As for "the phantom forger," he was never heard from again. Crowe and Shepherd hope that he learned the error of his ways.

5

THE STARS DECREE DEATH

For more than forty years Luke S. May has been known throughout the Pacific Northwest as "America's Sherlock Holmes." He has earned the sobriquet by unusual feats of crime detection, utilizing his wide knowledge of the natural sciences to unravel strange and baffling enigmas in criminal and civil cases.

To his laboratories in Seattle, Washington, have come law enforcement officers, corporation lawyers, and others from many parts of the United States and Canada, seeking his help in investigations requiring expert knowledge of chemistry, ballistics, physics, and other sciences. He has served three branches of the Federal Government—the Treasury, the War Department, and the Post Office.

Although May's work has sent many guilty men to prison, he is probably proudest of his achievements in using the sciences to prove the innocence of some who were falsely accused through incriminating circumstances and untested evidence. He pursues a policy of approaching every case with an open mind, relying for his conclusions solely on the findings of the laboratory. Science, he maintains, is the only key to truth and justice in criminal cases.

His records, including a number of celebrated cases, disclose how he often has utilized scientific study to reconstruct action in death mysteries. His success in absolving an innocent soldier of a murder charge is a good example.

The victim, a prominent merchant, had been found seated at the wheel of his automobile with bullet holes over his heart and directly through his back. When an autopsy surgeon found that the front of the man's shirt was frayed around the bullet hole while only a small, clean wound was visible on the back, he concluded that the victim had been shot from behind, probably from ambush.

Police soon discovered that there had been enmity between the dead man and the soldier. Finding of an Army rifle in the car beside the body strengthened suspicions and the serviceman was arrested as the killer, although he insisted that he knew nothing about the matter.

May, known as an authority on ballistics, was finally consulted. Under his strong microscopes, he examined the bullet holes. Powder marks on the front of the shirt and tiny fragments of torn fabric, invisible to the naked eye, convinced him beyond a doubt that the man had been shot from the front and not from the back as the police had supposed. It was obvious to him that the gun barrel had been pressed against the front of the clothing and that the case well might be one of suicide.

He then sought to verify this suspicion in the laboratory. First he prepared a dummy and then, picking up a rifle, he pressed the barrel on the spot identical with the wound of the dead man and fired. Close examination revealed the same kind of powder marks where the lead had entered and a similarly clean hole through the back. Now fully satisfied, he reported his findings which the police readily accepted and the case against the innocent soldier was dismissed.

In other mysteries, May's long experience in scientific crime detection has provided ample evidence to convict the guilty. In such a case he once used a tiny fir needle to help in weaving a web of evidence that sent the murderer of an eleven-year-old girl to the gallows. The child had been found some distance from her home in Battle Ground, Washington, her throat cut and her head brutally bludgeoned. Detectives, pressed for swift action, arrested a laborer against whom there was some circumstantial evidence. The man asserted his innocence and the police, recognizing their inability to prove their case, turned hopefully to May.

One of his first moves was to examine the child's clothing, inch by inch, under the microscope. This revealed a single fir needle caught in the hem of a garment. Magnified many times, it disclosed to the scientist that it was of a type peculiar to the area. May next turned to the clothing of the accused man and followed the same procedure. Inside the cuff of a trouser leg he found several fir needles of the same type.

Encouraged by these significant findings, May pursued an intensive inquiry into the man's movements and finally developed sufficient evidence to satisfy the authorities that they had a conclusive case.

When the trial finally opened, May appeared as a surprise witness, explaining to the jury with enlarged photographs of the fir needles how these minute particles had led to the development of convincing evidence. The accused man was found guilty and sent to the gallows.

A wiry, clean-shaven, baldish man, with a fringe of white hair and sharp, well-defined features, May greets his interviewer cordially but uses no unnecessary words in conversation. "No one commits a crime without leaving at least one clue to his identity," he once told me, "and frequently more clues can be obtained by careful scientific study. Interpreting these clues, however, is not always a simple matter. In scientific investigation, we develop facts and let them prove the truth."

As a schoolboy in a small Nebraska town, May showed an early interest in science and an avid desire to spend all of his leisure time in reading as much as he could absorb. At thirteen he already had decided to make scientific crime investigation his life's work and to become expert in as many scientific fields as possible. Chemistry and handwriting first drew his attention.

At seventeen, soon after he had moved with his family to Idaho, he received his first assignment in a case requiring him to pass judgment on a disputed document.

In 1919 he moved to Seattle and he has functioned there continuously in private practice, excepting for a single interruption in 1933 when he was drafted to reorganize the Detective Bureau of the Seattle Police Department which had been operating along "old school" lines. He installed a modern crime laboratory and trained men in its use. By introducing other new methods, he accomplished the seemingly impossible within a year. In that period the Bureau, under his direction, cleared up 1400 per cent more burglaries than it had in any previous year.

In what is regarded as May's most celebrated case he was called on by the authorities to solve a baffling mystery involving the death of a woman whose husband had been arrested as her murderer. The man was Dr. Fred Covell, a prominent and respected chiropractor of Bandon, Oregon, a devoted husband and the dutiful father of four children by a previous marriage.

It was Monday morning, September 3, 1923, that Dr. Covell, busy in his office, was called away from a patient to answer the telephone. Picking up the receiver, he quickly recognized the excited voice of his forty-six-year-old brother, Arthur, a helpless paralytic, bedridden for years and the sole occupant of an upstairs room in the large, comfortable Covell home. "Come home quick," Arthur Covell cried, "something terrible has happened to Ebba."

Knowing that his wife was subject to sudden illness and in a despondent mood, Dr. Covell pressed for details but his brother seemed too agitated to answer coherently, so the harried husband threw off his gown, reached for his coat, and hurried to his car.

The ride home, a considerable distance, seemed intermina-

ble despite the light traffic which enabled him to drive rapidly and to take short cuts with which he was familiar.
Nevertheless, it was fully half an hour later when he pulled
up in front of his house and hurried in. He found his wife
lying motionless across her bed. Anxiously he looked at the
glassy eyes and felt for her pulse. It did not take him long to
realize that she was dead.

"What in the world happened to Ebba?" he called frantically to his invalid brother.

"I haven't the faintest idea," the other answered, speaking
from his bed in the upstairs room. "Two of the children
found her lying on the kitchen floor. I told them to lift her
onto the bed as best they could. Then I called you."

Dr. Covell phoned for the family physician who arrived
soon afterward and examined the body. He could not tell
whether death was due to a heart attack or to other causes.
Her husband, recalling her melancholia, suggested that she
might have taken her life, yet the body showed no visible
evidence of poison and they could find none either in the
kitchen or in the bedroom. They looked in the medicine cabinet and found a half-empty vial of sleeping pills which
strengthened suspicions of suicide. Finally they notified the
coroner who, in turn, called the sheriff's office.

Since the cause of death could not be immediately determined, the body was removed to the coroner's office and Sheriff Ed Ellington of Coos County, who had reached the house
with his deputy, Sam Malehorn, began questioning the grief-
stricken husband and the two older children. Dr. Covell told
them that his wife had appeared to be in fair health when he
left for his office a few hours before he received his brother's
call. The two older children, Alton, a backward boy of sixteen; and his sister, Lucille, two years younger, were interviewed but they could only say that on entering the house
from play they had found their stepmother on the floor and
had called their uncle. The other children, somewhat younger,
had been away at the time.

Unexpected developments followed the coroner's order for a post-mortem examination which Dr. Covell and the authorities believed would verify their suspicions of suicide. To the amazement of everyone, the autopsy surgeon reported that Mrs. Covell had died of a broken neck. This positive conclusion, he said, was reached not only by himself alone but also by a consultant after he had made an incision which, he explained, had disclosed fractured vertebrae.

Almost at once suspicion turned on Dr. Covell, the authorities reasoning that being an experienced chiropractor with large, powerful hands, he would have been capable of inflicting such injuries in a way that would leave no external evidence. An element of time even strengthened their theory. While the exact hour of Mrs. Covell's death could not be accurately fixed, the coroner believed it would have been possible for her husband to have killed her before leaving for his office.

Interrogated along this line, Dr. Covell at first seemed so dumfounded at even being suspected that he could not take the officers seriously. It was not until they pressed their questions that he fully realized his predicament and began detailed explanations. He spoke tearfully of his devotion to his ailing wife and insisted that any thought of murder was absurd. He was certain that death must have occurred during his absence.

Still far from satisfied, the sheriff and his deputy withdrew, prepared to keep the husband under surveillance pending a coroner's inquest. When this took place several days later, the autopsy surgeon reported his findings. There was routine testimony concerning the finding of the body and the jury returned a verdict concluding that the fatal injury had resulted from causes "still to be determined." The authorities were called on to press a vigorous inquiry.

Dr. Covell was grilled for hours and once more his profession was emphasized in support of police suspicion. All of this he countered with ready answers except one. He could not account for his wife's broken neck but he surmised that it might have been sustained in a fall. The officers, however, were far from satisfied. They insisted—and probably rightly so—that a fall of such severity would have resulted in some external bruises. For this he could give no satisfactory explanation.

Meanwhile, feeling throughout Coos County was running high. The mystery of Mrs. Covell's death had become front-page news and people were sharply divided in their judgment. Friends and acquaintances of the husband were certain of his innocence. Others, quick to condemn, turned bitterly against him.

The next move was up to the authorities and they did not wait long after the funeral. Driving to the Covell home, deputy sheriffs met the husband and told him that he was under arrest.

In his jail cell Dr. Covell still protested his innocence and sent for a lawyer. Days of intensive investigation followed but the officers admitted that they were making no headway. They were certain that they had made no mistake, yet they agreed that it would be difficult to convince a jury. Sheriff Ellington and District Attorney Ben Fisher conferred again, wondering what their next move should be.

"I'm going to send for Luke May," the prosecutor finally announced. "He's cleared up other cases as tough as this. Maybe he can help us now."

The criminologist was contacted in his Seattle laboratory and soon was on his way to Oregon. But as he hurried southward in his car, he little realized how extraordinary a case confronted him—a case in which the stars and planets eventually were to play weird roles while a hypnotist cast a sinister spell with Svengali eyes.

Arriving in Bandon, May sat down with District Attorney Fisher and listened to details of the case he now was called on to solve. "We want the truth," Fisher told him. "If Dr. Covell is guilty we must develop sufficient evidence to convince a jury. If he's innocent, certainly we must know it and we must find the murderer whoever he is. Can you go to work right away?"

May agreed, explaining that his first step would be to question the man in custody.

A few hours later he was talking to Dr. Covell in his cell and when the interview had ended May felt satisfied that the accused man was telling the truth, but he knew, of course, that it would be necessary to support his judgment with scientific proof. To accomplish that he already had evolved a plan of action.

First he reported his belief to the district attorney who realized at once that he faced a new and perplexing problem. "If Dr. Covell didn't kill his wife, who could have done it?" he asked. It was not a simple question. The authorities already had eliminated the bedridden Arthur Covell, agreeing that it would have been physically impossible for him to have murdered his sister-in-law. They were equally convinced that the boy, Alton, was not involved and earlier inquiry had removed the possibility that a stranger could have been admitted to the house or broken in. How then had Ebba Covell come to her death? Had she actually been murderered or could she have died of an accidental fall? The two men wondered.

May requested that he first be given sufficient time to prove the husband's innocence. He then announced his intention of making a drastic move. Although Mrs. Covell's remains had been interred after funeral rites attended by a large number of the community's leading citizens, he declared that he intended to request a court order to exhume the body as soon as possible. He explained that he wanted to examine it himself, probably with a consultant. After that he would interrogate the children and then search the Covell home "from the basement to the roof."

The following day the grave was opened and the woman's body was moved to the coroner's office. May already had inquired into the manner in which the autopsy surgeon had reached his conclusions and now seriously questioned the findings. The surgeon, he was advised, had simply inserted a finger into an incision in the back of the woman's neck and had decided that vertebrae were fractured because the head moved forward. To check his doubts, May had sent for a noted authority on autopsies, a Dr. Mingus of Marshfield, Oregon, with whom he had worked many times and who had established an enviable record in Pennsylvania some years before.

In the autopsy room May began a minute examination of the corpse, working slowly with Dr. Mingus at his side. What they discovered came as a complete surprise. The neck definitely was not broken!

"Someone has made a very serious mistake," Dr. Mingus finally remarked after they had completely verified their conclusions.

As they went on with their work, May suddenly pointed to curious red splotches about the mouth and nose and on one cheek. "Peculiar these—they're definitely not bruises," he remarked. "Say, I think I know just what could have caused them—and you do, too. Let's check in the usual way."

Dr. Mingus, equally amazed, agreed. Working alone, they subjected the skin to various chemical tests and while these verified their earlier suspicions, they found themselves more baffled than ever. Finally they decided to keep this latest turn in their inquiry secret, while they sought an answer.

May next analyzed the contents of the dead woman's stomach and became satisfied that she had died a considerable time after her husband's departure for his office—another point supporting the accused man's alibi.

Shortly afterward May drove to the Covell home and began the thorough search that he had planned. He had not gone far before he made an amazing discovery. To his astonishment, he found evidence that eventually was to reveal Arthur Covell, the cripple, as an experienced astrologer and a hypnotist of extraordinary ability, exerting his strange powers from his bed, with an uncanny capacity to force his will on others to accomplish his evil purposes.

The detective's first surprising find was Arthur Covell's diary, written largely with the help of astrological signs and mysterious symbols. May had just begun to examine the cryptic writing, when he came upon a baffling entry. Though it had been made five days before Mrs. Covell's death, it recorded the writer's doings on the date of her demise—entries of his breakfast, his reading of newspapers, and like details. May's suspicions were aroused when he found no mention of the tragic happenings of that day.

Elsewhere about Arthur's room were curious charts and papers, describing the stars and interpreting them and their positions in terms of human destiny. There was correspondence showing that from his bed he had drafted the horoscopes of Hollywood celebrities and influential New Yorkers, sending them to these individuals in a continuous exchange of correspondence.

All of this May confided to the authorities and a new line of inquiry was begun. Two days later unexpected circumstances played into their hands. With Dr. Covell in jail, it had been necessary to move his invalid brother to the county farm since no adult remained in the house to care for him and he was unable to walk a single step. After this had been done, Deputy Sheriff Malehorn, who had been assigned to work with May, was informed that the cripple, before leaving home, had asked a neighbor to take a box of horoscopes with him for safekeeping. When this chest was examined it proved to be a Pandora's box, revealing the fantastic image of a man bent on wholesale murder with a sixteen-year-old boy as his tool acting under an hypnotic spell.

The chest was crammed with scribbled notes which at first glance appeared to be only vague plots for fiction stories but interspersed between the scrawled lines were the names of prominent people. Fastened to some of the notes were slips of paper bearing astrological characters and signs of the Zodiac, all written on a typewriter which the cripple owned. These were diversified with strange combinations of letters as if they were intended to form words and sentences.

May and the deputy, concluding that these involved a code, set out to find the key. It was a tantalizing task requiring days and nights of work but May, with much knowledge in this field, finally succeeded. What they revealed surpassed their wildest suspicions. The cryptic writing proved to be detailed instructions to the young nephew, Alton, in how and when to commit a series of cold-blooded murders!

In all, twenty-nine men and women, some of them prominent in the state, had been marked for death. In each case the lunar destinies of an intended victim were described with astrological readings that fixed the exact day and hour to strike. Different methods were indicated and minute instructions were provided should carefully made plans miscarry. And finally they came upon the horoscope of Ebba Covell with a note fixing the time for her to die! It was the exact day of the tragedy!

May lost no time in conferring with the officials and jail doors soon opened for the innocent chiropractor who had feared that he was doomed. Realizing that they had arrested a guiltless man, they moved fast to pursue their latest clues.

Before long they learned to their amazement that the invalid brother, besides plotting murder, had actually carried on a series of swindling operations. Working always from his bed, he had connived with a ring of confidence men to do his bidding in robbing unsuspecting victims. His scheme, utilizing his familiarity with astrology, was as ingenuous as it was corrupt.

In an endless chain of correspondence, the cripple had mailed to a long list of men and women horoscopes intended to show the precise time for them to make profitable investments. On the designated day, one of his accomplices would call on the individual as if by coincidence, offering sure-fire investments which, of course, were worthless. It was apparent that they were reaping rich harvests; for how long they had operated, the investigators could only guess.

On the basis of these new disclosures, Alton and his sister were brought before May and the officers for further questioning but it soon became apparent that they could not be made to divulge anything concerning their uncle's operations. They did admit a fondness for "Uncle Artie," as they called him, and seemed indifferent toward their father. Lucille, in fact, said she firmly believed he had killed their stepmother. The uncle, it already had been learned, often exerted his hypnotic powers over the two youngsters.

May and Malehorn went to the county farm to confront the crippled Arthur but they soon realized that they were pitting their wits against a stubborn, defiant man. He stared at them with his deep black, penetrating eyes and the two visitors exchanged knowing glances, realized that he was trying to hypnotize them.

"We know all about you," Malehorn began. "We've cracked your code. Now's the time for you to come clean. Come on—we're listening."

Arthur gazed at them but his expression did not change. "What are you talking about?" he asked with feigned innocence. "Are you suggesting that a poor invalid like me could do anything wrong—even if I wanted to?"

"None of that stuff," the deputy snapped; then for a few moments he stood silently, eying the bedridden man.

When he spoke again it was with slow, clipped words. "You murdered Ebba—we know that—you got Alton to do it for you. Now listen carefully—you plotted to kill E. J. Pressy, his wife and their three children. We know all about your plans to kill Ira Sidwell—we know everything about that. Now talk up."

A faint smile came upon the paralyzed man's face. He wet his lips and began to speak. "You've got me all wrong," he began, speaking softly with surprising calm. "Yes, I did write plots for killing people but I was only working my imagination overtime to keep from getting bored. I guess you'd call it fantasy. I just got a kick out of writing this kind of stuff out of my imagination, but really, I didn't intend it seriously. Why should I want to kill anybody. And how could I in my condition?"

"Then you actually did write all this stuff," Deputy Malehorn pressed.

"Only for fun like I told you—for my own amusement. It was my way of passing the time."

The two men questioned him for hours but he could not be shaken. Stubbornly he insisted that he had had no part in Mrs. Covell's death; that certainly he had no knowledge of how it had occurred. At last May and his companion withdrew, now thoroughly convinced of Arthur's guilt but satisfied that he was far from ready to confess.

After much discussion they evolved a plan calculated to wring the truth from him but first May wanted to continue his check of Alton's movements in the days preceding his stepmother's death. He already strongly suspected that the boy was seriously involved. Earlier days spent in interviewing Alton's friends had been to no avail and careful inquiry into his actions likewise had produced no incriminating information. Now the investigator resumed his task, more determined than ever, but considerable time was to elapse before he could uncover a worthwhile clue.

May began a systematic check of stores within a wide radius of the boy's home. The work was discouraging until at last he walked into a small grocery and began with the routine questions—did they know Alton Covell and had he made any purchases lately.

This grocer knew the lad and recalled his last visit well. "It was close to a month ago," he related, little suspecting the importance of what he was about to divulge. "He came running in here and bought a bottle of ammonia. As I remember it now, he seemed somewhat excited, but you know how kids are."

"Are you positive that he bought ammonia—not something else?" May inquired anxiously.

"Absolutely certain."

That was exactly what May needed to establish the missing link in his chain of evidence. He and Dr. Mingus had agreed that the reddish spots on Mrs. Covell's face had been caused by ammonia which, they knew, discolors the skin after death. They also knew that ammonia paralyzes the breathing apparatus in the human body and that traces of it disappear rapidly from the lungs. This had been their explanation of the woman's death and accounted for the absence of any other marks on her body. For a cunning murderer ammonia had proved an efficient and most deceptive weapon.

Now May was satisfied that Alton had played a part in his stepmother's death but what it was required a definite answer. Again he conferred with the sheriff and they decided to proceed with a scheme that both had been considering.

Taking newspaper editors into their confidence, May told them of Arthur Covell's admission that he had scribbled plans for wholesale murder, although he had denied any intention of carrying them out. The newsmen jumped at their chance, for here was an opportunity not only to cooperate with the authorities but to print a sensational story as well. CRIPPLED ASTROLOGER PLANS MURDER was one glaring headline the next morning. ARTHUR COVELL CONFESSES TO PLANNING MURDERS, another paper announced, with some stretch of the facts. These were precisely what May wanted.

He promptly took the newspapers to the Covell house and told Alton to read the headlines. Deliberately, the investigator concealed the news matter, for he wished the boy to believe that his uncle had confessed to the actual murder of Ebba Covell.

The lad, however, merely shrugged his shoulders, just as he had days before when he was queried about the ammonia purchase. "I told you I don't know nothin' about it," he repeated.

When further questioning proved to be of no avail, May notified the sheriff and the boy was led away to jail.

In the next few days May and Sheriff Ellington, working with a picked group of deputies, made more startling disclosures. They learned that for some time Arthur Covell, despite his infirmities, had exerted a strange hypnotic influence over his nephew—a power that actually compelled the youth to do the older man's bidding. Of late Alton had been sending secret messages to his uncle, his practice being to paste magazine pages together and to scribble notes on the margins of the glued leaves. Ellington found numbers of these in the cripple's room. All of them referred to the murder investigation and instructed Alton to say nothing to the authorities.

The sheriff also discovered that Arthur was sending notes to his nephew, hiding them in the cores of apples.

On the afternoon of October 9, more than a month after his stepmother's death, Alton Covell was brought to the sheriff's office and questioned again without result. Exasperated, May finally handed him a sheet of paper and a pen, telling him to return to his cell and write whatever he had to say. The youth was back in half an hour with a note which simply repeated his previous statements.

"Go back there again and think it over," he was told. "Think hard and see if you can't clear your mind of everything that's troubling you. Then you can start your life all over again—you're young and you have a long time ahead of you."

Alton returned to his cell. An hour later he sent out word that he wanted to see May and Ellington again. When they returned to the jail, the boy handed the two a carefully written note, one of the frankest and most extraordinary confessions they had ever seen. Brazenly admitting that he had followed his uncle's directions in snuffing out his stepmother's life with ammonia, Alton had written the following:

> I want to start and lead a clean life, and I want to be able to look back on everything I do and not be ashamed of anything I will do in the future. I don't know what made me do it. I can't understand why I done such a thing. I will see that it never happens again. I want to look back on a clear trail.
>
> I put ammonia on a rag and Ebba was standing by the stove. I walked up to her from behind and on the right hand side. I put the rag over her nose with my right hand and held her arms with my left. I held it on her nose for about three minutes after I let her down on the floor. There was a little ammonia left in the bottle and I threw it down into the gulch.
>
> Then I went and told my uncle that I had done it. Lucille and my uncle knew about the plan first. My uncle was the first to tell me. He told me to get the ammonia and how to use it.

The note was sent to the foreman of the grand jury and a group of officials, working with May, prepared to confront Arthur Covell with his nephew's statement. The party, comprising Sheriff Ellington, Deputy Malehorn, District Attorney Fisher, and May, had agreed to follow the same strategy that had wrung the truth from Alton. Fisher was chosen to be their spokesman.

"Your nephew Alton has told us everything," he began, as the men took their places around the invalid's bed at the county farm. "I'm not asking you any questions now. Just think it over—and write down anything you've got to say. We'll be back in a day or so for your answer."

Early the next morning the grand jury foreman was advised

that Arthur Covell had a written statement ready. He hastened to the farm, walked anxiously into the cripple's room,
and was handed a sheaf of papers. He scanned them eagerly
and read the following:

I make this a voluntary statement. I alone was the one
to plan the details and select the day. Lucille had nothing
to do with the plan or its execution.

Both Alton and Lucille were at all times under control
of my mind and will. My will was their will. They never
resisted my influence, but done without question as I
wished it done. They never argued, or thought if the action
was right or wrong, but my influence over both was so complete they seemed incapable to resist or think independently beyond my wish.

In regard to Ebba, soon after moving upstairs, I told
Alton I wanted her out of the way. I told him how to do
it without violence or bloodshed and with ammonia. I told
him I would choose the day, that I would not force him to
do it, and if he wanted to refuse it was all right with me;
but as I said this, I knew in my own heart he couldn't help
doing as I wanted.

My brother Fred is entirely innocent. Lucille is innocent
of any participation in the crime. Alton as an individual
is innocent. I forced my will on him and made him act
for me; in other words I used his body and his strength as
though it were my own; he had not the power of will to
resist me. I alone am guilty of the whole thing. I have
kept Alton under my control for a great many years and it
is this which makes him seem not bright, sometimes defi-
cient. My last instruction to him before we separated was:
"If you get in a tight pinch with this and there is no other
way out, it will be all right with me if you tell how I made
you do it. I do not want you to suffer for my sake." Hence
his and my statement.

Alton has a very mild nature, with nothing vicious in his makeup and if left to his own devices would be incapable of ever taking a human life.

(*signed*) Arthur Covell

At a later time the cripple explained how he had first become interested in hypnotism and in astrology. Working as a truck driver, he had stopped for repairs when a heavy wheel fell upon him, breaking his back and causing him to be a helpless invalid. Constantly suffering excruciating pain, he was attracted by a magazine advertisement offering a mail order course in hypnotism which was guaranteed as a means of relieving pain. Arthur took the course and after completing it turned to astrology which he studied intensively and finally turned his learning into evil ways.

Following the confession, additional guards were posted in his room and preparations were started for his trial, but events did not move as easily or as quickly as the authorities had expected.

Carried into court on a stretcher, the confessed murderer surprised everyone by pleading not guilty, explaining that he had admitted the crime only to spare his nephew. The trial opened a few weeks later and it was not long before Arthur's hypnotic spell on the children became apparent.

In turn, young Alton and his sister were called to the witness chair. As the prosecutor began his questions, the defendant was seen staring at them with his glaring eyes, obviously in a last desperate effort to silence them with his hypnotic powers. The two sat silently until in each case the district attorney stepped between them and their uncle. Only then did they begin to talk.

Alton not only repeated his confession in greater detail but volunteered new facts which made it evident that Mrs. Covell had become aware of the crippled man's machinations and that he, fearing exposure, had exerted his hypnotic powers on the boy to commit murder. This, May finally concluded, had motivated the crime.

Lucille, following her brother as a witness, admitted that she had overheard her uncle discussing murder plans with Alton and telling him the precise hour of the day that he was to act.

The defense made a stirring plea for sympathy, picturing the plight of a man with a broken back, and pleading for clemency.

At last the jury retired and Arthur Covell awaited its return with an optimism that amazed all who heard him. "The stars will save me," he told them. "The stars are in my favor, you'll see."

His faith in stellar intervention failed, however, for the jury returned a verdict finding him guilty of first degree murder and he was sentenced to the gallows.

While an appeal was pending, Alton was placed on trial and the jury, deliberating only forty-five minutes, likewise convicted him of murder. Because of his youth, he was sentenced to life imprisonment.

Higher courts finally denied the uncle's appeal and plans for the execution proceeded. Again he insisted that the stars would rescue him but the governor refused to intercede. When the time for execution came, guards lifted the condemned man into a wheel chair and led him to the scaffold. "I bear no ill will toward anyone," he said, as he stared at the noose close by. "All of you simply did your duty."

"Just why did you do it, Arthur?" an official asked him.

"I'm a cripple," he answered, "and I didn't want to be dependent on anyone. I killed Ebba so I could have full control over the children. She was always coming between us. Can't you understand?"

Minutes later he was strapped to a board to keep his body upright and carried to the trap. The hangman, working fast, proceeded with his grisly task.

6

THE REAL SHERLOCK HOLMES

Sherlock Holmes, with his unique powers of deduction, keen sense of observation and broad knowledge of many subjects, is a familiar figure to devotees of detective fiction. Far less known is the fact that Holmes's creator, Sir Arthur Conan Doyle, a physician as well as an author, did not confine his rare understanding of crime deduction to his writing. He actually utilized that knowledge in a number of celebrated cases in which his achievements rivaled those of the master sleuth created by his fertile imagination.

As Sir Arthur's stories of Sherlock Holmes attained worldwide popularity, he began to receive letters from many countries seeking his help in the solution of baffling crimes. These appeals continued for years in growing numbers, ending only after his death in 1930. Some were even addressed to "Mr. Sherlock Holmes" as though he were an actual person. Others were written to the fictional Dr. Watson, offering him varying sums of money if he would prevail upon Holmes to "get on the job."

From time to time an unusually intriguing case impelled Doyle to put aside his writing and turn detective himself. He was motivated not only by a natural fascination for perplexing mysteries but even more by a desire to see justice done and to uncover the truth. He was always a dedicated sympathizer of the underprivileged and acted vigorously against instances of injustice, persecution, or police incompetence.

When Doyle undertook a case he first would lock himself in his room for hours and seek a complete change in personality. Imagining himself to be Sherlock Holmes, he would picture his eccentric, pipe-smoking detective coming to grips with the problem. Then he would attempt to set down step by step the procedure that Holmes might follow.

Though both the author and his created character thus emerged into a single person, Doyle could hardly have looked less like the Holmes of his stories to whom he gave a thin, angular face, with a hawklike nose and penetrating eyes. Sir Arthur's physical appearance was exactly the opposite in almost every respect. Doyle, it is said, developed Holmes's physical image from that of a schoolteacher, Joe Bell, whom he adored and who had intrigued his young pupil by an almost uncanny facility for observing details.

Despite the mounting success of the stories which began with the introduction of Sherlock Holmes in A *Study in Scarlet* written in 1887, Doyle at times lost his zest for writing them. To his close friends he often confided a fear that he was "dogged with Holmes" for the rest of his life. He would tell them, too, that he actually had come to hate Holmes because of his popularity and, for this reason, he sometimes gave Dr. Watson an overamount of praise. In the author's mind, the two were living people.

To his intimates he also admitted that he would greatly prefer other fields of writing, but an eager public demanded more and more of the Holmes exploits and the writer complied. Not only did he wish to oblige his readers but he was mindful of the profits. It was said that he received at least ten shillings a word for a Sherlock Holmes story—far more than any of his other works yielded.

After his death a number of unpublished detective tales were found among his papers. Presumably, he was dissatisfied with them and had put the manuscripts aside, intending to revise them at some later time.

Of the real life cases to which he devoted his own detective talents, probably the most notable were those of Oscar Slater,* for whom Doyle won vindication and freedom after more than eighteen years in prison as a murderer, and George Edalji, a young lawyer and a clergyman's son, who was pardoned after three years of imprisonment.

While both cases exemplify the persistence and thoroughness with which Sir Arthur threw himself into investigations, the Edalji affair in particular was marked by such feats of crime detection as brought fame to Sherlock Holmes.

The tragic plight of George Edalji first came to Doyle's attention on a December evening in 1906, shortly before Christmas, at a time when the author was recovering from a severe illness that followed shock and bereavement over the death of his first wife. During this period he was paying only slight attention to his usually heavy mail which he had asked his secretary, Alfred Wood, to handle for him. When Wood found any correspondence which he believed would be of real interest to his ailing employer, he left it on the desk in Doyle's study.

It was on this night that the writer chanced to open a packet of newspaper clippings lying on his desk and to glance at them with only slight concern. All of them related developments in the Edalji case.

Suddenly Doyle found himself fascinated by this mystery which to him embodied many of the bizarre characteristics of his own detective stories. He read the stack of clippings avidly, weighing every paragraph over and over. Then he came upon a pathetic note written to him by young Edalji himself, then in prison, imploring Doyle to help him.

In the letter Doyle found what he believed to be a firm

* The case of Oscar Slater, likewise replete with dramatic impact, provides a separate chapter. It will be discussed in the following Chapter 7 entitled The Gilchrist Murder.

ring of truth and, aroused by the young prisoner's claims
of a cruel injustice, he promptly decided to look thoroughly
into the case. He little realized then that he was soon to put
aside all of his own professional work for eight full months,
paying all of his expenses in the hope of vindicating a man
he did not know and even would not meet until long after
his work was under way.

Although foreshadowed by a series of peculiar happenings
over a period of years, the events which seriously incriminated
Edalji actually did not begin to take shape until late in
February 1903 in an area of Staffordshire, some 135 miles
northwest of London. Morning after morning in and near the
village of Great Wyrley, horses, cows, and sheep were found
dying, victims of a mysterious and sadistic knife-wielder
whose procedure never varied. Apparently he enjoyed the
sight of suffering and never cut deeply enough to put the
animals quickly out of their misery but in every case caused
considerable spurting of blood. The mutilations angered the
entire area and the police were under severe pressure to capture
the culprit.

Thwarted at every turn, the authorities found themselves
still further perplexed by a deluge of jeering letters sent to
them, with signatures that proved to be either fictitious or
forged. One of these, which received more attention than the
others, bore what purported to be the signature of a boy attending the Walsall Grammar School, six miles from Great
Wyrley. However, after some inquiry, officers concluded that
the boy had had nothing to do with the letters, all of which
they believed had come from the same writer.

In one of them, the author referred glowingly to the sea;
then gloated over grim details of the mutilations. Identifying himself as a member of a gang, he indiscriminately named
a number of people as accomplices and told how they had
enjoyed taking part in the brutal butchery. Typical of his
accusations was this description of one whom he accused:

"He has eagle eyes and his ears is as sharp as a razor, and

he is as fleet of foot as a fox, and as noiseless, and he crawls on all fours up to the poor beasts."

Thorough investigation, however, proved that none of those named by the penman was in any way involved.

Continuing with his letters, the elusive writer finally had aroused the countryside with a chilling threat. "There will be merry times at Wyrley in November," he wrote, "when they start on little girls, for they will do twenty wenches like the horses before next March."

Search for the penman went on for months without result. The climax came early in the morning of August 18 when a boy, Henry Garrett, crossing a field on his way to work in the village colliery, heard the moaning of an animal a short distance away. He quickened his pace over slushy yellowish-red mud and soon came upon a pony, writhing in agony, its belly slit open apparently by a sharp blade in the hands of a fiend. The youth called for help and his cries brought a number of men employed at the mine as well as police who had been watching the area, some of them even assigned to guard the field itself.

Inspector Campbell of the Staffordshire County Constabulary looked at the pony and with sudden anger declared that he was ready to act; that he already had delayed too long and knew a man who now must be arrested; that actually all of his colleagues agreed with him as to the identity of the suspect. He led his men to the vicarage of Great Wyrley half a mile away where his suspect, the vicar's son, lived with his family, an unhappy group long shunned by their neighbors. Racial bigotry had haunted them for years, for the vicar was a Parsi, born of a sect in India, and was known therefore as a "Black Man."

That a man of his birth and skin color should hold an important position in the Anglican Church was something that the people of Great Wyrley simply refused to accept. His marriage to an Englishwoman, Charlotte Stoneman, had made no difference in their attitude.

The Reverend Shapurki Edalji's twenty-seven-year-old son, George, dark-skinned with bulging eyes, had been an honor student at Mason College and was recognized as a brilliant solicitor in Birmingham, where he practiced. The Law Society had awarded him prizes and his book on railway law had won wide recognition. Yet the townspeople held him in contempt. They said he was nervous, awkward, and unsocial; that he never noticed them in passing. Bitter prejudices had been aroused against him before when, in early boyhood, he had been suspected of subjecting his own family and neighbors to a fiendish reign of terror.

This had continued for three years beginning in 1892 when the vicar and his family received the first of a flood of poison pen letters which were alternately slipped under their front door or through their windows. All of them were filled with scandalous insults against the vicar, his wife and children. Similar letters, obviously from the same writer, went to neighbors and other clergymen in the area.

The Edalji family, however, was plagued in other ways. Spurious advertisements, bearing the vicar's name, appeared in newspapers, calling for merchandise. On one occasion old spoons, knives, and garbage were strewn about the lawn of the vicarage; on another, a large key, stolen from the Walsall Grammar School, was dropped on the front steps.

The police, moved by neighborhood prejudice rather than by any evidence, frankly admitted that they suspected young George Edalji of persecuting his own family, yet they offered no motive for such strange behavior. His parents ridiculed the idea, pointing out that some of the letters had been shoved under their door at times when George was in the house with them, but the argument made no impact on the authorities. In fact, Captain George Anson, Chief Constable of Staffordshire, openly accused young Edalji of all of this mischief and boasted of his hope that the youth could be sent to prison.

They still were trying to develop a case against the boy

when, at the end of December 1895, the nuisance stopped as abruptly as it had started. But the mystery and the suspicions it had aroused were not to be soon forgotten.

When the cattle slashing first began in 1903, the authorities at once turned their eyes toward George Edalji, recalling the poison pen letters of eight years before. They already had been watching his home for months when the incident of the mutilated pony occurred. And now Inspector Campbell was at the vicarage, demanding to see George's clothing and any weapons in the house.

The young solicitor already had left for his office in Birmingham. His mother and sister, who fully realized the meaning of the officer's visit, brought out a case of four razors belonging to the vicar. These were examined later and found to be free of bloodstains. The mother also produced George's boots encrusted with black mud, a pair of muddied trousers and an old house coat with stains which the inspector thought might prove to be dried blood from the dying pony. These were sufficient to serve the inspector's purpose. He held the coat to the window and eagerly pointed to what he insisted were horse hairs clinging to a sleeve. Mrs. Edalji angrily asserted that they were threads, and her husband who by now had joined his wife and daughter, supported her contention.

Ignoring them, the officer gathered up the coat and a matching vest and hurried to the office of the police surgeon, a Dr. Butter, who soon reported that he had found twenty-nine horse hairs on the coat and five on the vest. He declared further that one of several spots on a coat sleeve showed definite evidence of blood but whether it was that of the pony or from meat gravy he could not determine as the stains were old.

This was more than enough to satisfy Inspector Campbell. Without further deliberation, he decided that young Edalji was indeed the elusive slasher and should be apprehended. Obviously, he had no thought that his bungling in handling his latest "evidence" would be discovered by Conan Doyle at a later date and become a vital element in the defense.

Hours later George was arrested at his office in Birmingham despite his protestations of innocence. "This doesn't surprise me," he told the arresting officers. "I've been expecting it."

They quickly jotted down his words which were to be used later at his trial as evidence of a guilty conscience. Then he was asked to explain his movements on the night preceding the discovery of the mutilated pony.

"I got home from my office at half-past six," he began. "After talking to my family for a short time I walked over to the bootmaker's where I remained only a short time and started back for home. I knew that dinner would not be ready until nine-thirty so I walked around a bit. The walks were quite slushy as it had been raining. As soon as I returned to the vicarage we ate and then I went straight off to bed in the same room as my father where I had been sleeping for seventeen years. I did not leave the bedroom until twenty minutes to seven the next morning."

The Reverend Edalji later confirmed the statement, explaining that he was a light sleeper, that he had retired after his son, and as always kept his bedroom locked. It was absurd to suppose, he argued, that George could have slipped out between two and three o'clock the next morning—the time fixed by the police for the mutilation—without his father's knowledge.

Aroused townsfolk reacted angrily to news of the young man's arrest. Many said it should have occurred long before. The *Birmingham Express and Star* stated:

"Many and wonderful were the theories propounded in the local alehouses as to why Edalji had gone forth in the night to slay cattle, and a widely accepted idea was that he made nocturnal sacrifices to strange gods."

Talk of lynching moved the police to such precautions that the prisoner was escorted in a cab by officers to the courtroom. On the way, the machine was stopped by an angry mob and its door was torn off.

Two months later, on October 20, George Edalji was brought to trial in an atmosphere of racial hate. The county justice was known to have little legal knowledge and a barrister was engaged to counsel with him. Before the opening session had proceeded far into the case, the young defendant and his father learned to their amazement that the prosecution had completely reversed its theory as to the precise time of the pony slashing.

Up to the day of the trial, the police had insisted that the mutilation had occurred between 8 and 9:30 o'clock in the evening before it was discovered. This contention, however, had been upset by the statements of people who had seen young Edalji on his walk before dinner and thus confirmed a major part of his alibi. Further supporting his statement was the opinion of a veterinary who said that the animal was still bleeding when it was found in the morning and that the wounds could not have been inflicted before 2:30 A.M.

Faced with these contradictions, the prosecution, to the surprise of everyone, came forward at the trial with a new claim—George Edalji had slipped out of his father's bedroom between two and three o'clock in the morning, walked half a mile to the field where the slashing occurred, and returned home. The fact that officers were stationed about the area was completely ignored.

A constable testified that the defendant's boots fitted footprints leading to and from the pony. There was still more damaging testimony from a handwriting expert, Thomas Gurrin, who swore that George himself had written the anonymous letters accusing himself of cattle maiming.

The defense stressed what it regarded as a vital point—the mutilation of a horse after Edalji had been jailed, but the police countered with the claim that this was merely the work of a gang intent on confusing the case. The bootmaker whom the accused claimed to have visited on his night's walk, and others he said he had met, completely verified his statements.

Young Edalji and his parents waited hopefully while the jury deliberated. Little time passed, however, before it returned to the courtroom with a verdict—guilty. The defendant sank tearfully into his chair. "Oh Lord, have mercy on us!" his mother sobbed and then collapsed.

The court sentenced him to seven years in prison. Ironically, he was put to work making feed bags for horses.

While the authorities and prejudiced townsfolk hailed the conviction, there were many throughout Britain who believed firmly in Edalji's innocence and pointed to glaring weaknesses in the prosecution's case. Friendly lawyers took up his cause and as weeks passed the movement grew, especially after R. D. Yelverton, a former chief justice of the Bahamas, had assumed the leadership. Petitions bearing long lists of names were sent to the Home Office asking the government to intervene, but nothing resulted at the time.

Three years passed and then, late in 1906, the doors of Portland Prison suddenly swung open for George Edalji— without a pardon or even an explanation of his unexpectedly sudden release. Thoroughly confused, Edalji faced a dubious future. As a former convict, he had to remain under police surveillance and was barred from resuming the practice of his profession.

It was at this point that he wrote to Conan Doyle, reviewing his case and explaining his predicament. "What can I do now?" he asked. "Am I guilty or am I not? They just won't tell me."

The creator of Sherlock Holmes determined to find the answer as a matter of simple justice. "If he is innocent he must be pardoned," Doyle told his friends. "If he's guilty, he deserves every day of his seven years. If he's not guilty, he must have an apology, a pardon, and certain restitution."

Doyle determined to investigate in his own way even before meeting Edalji. First he inquired into the young man's background and found that Edalji had a previously unblemished record and had been regarded by legal associates as a brilliant member of the bar. He had won high honors in his classes. Everyone to whom Doyle spoke agreed that the young man never had shown the slightest sign of cruelty.

Doyle next undertook an intensive study of the entire transcript of the trial and as his work progressed he became appalled by the feeble nature of the prosecution's case and the obvious determination of the authorities to obtain a conviction regardless of the truth. Then he set about checking for himself every step of the procedures followed by the constabulary in its investigation.

Again emulating the strategy that Sherlock Holmes would have followed, he painstakingly examined the mud on Edalji's trousers which had been preserved as evidence and discovered that it was distinctly different in color and composition from the yellowish-red earth of the field where the pony had been found. He was convinced that it matched perfectly that of the village roadway, over which the accused said he had walked after a rain.

Doyle then turned his attention to the testimony of the constable who had sworn that George's boots fitted perfectly into footprints found in the soft ground around the dying animal. He pressed the officer for an explanation of his procedure.

The constable admitted, with no apparent show of embarrassment, that the ground had been trampled by police and sightseers alike, that he had taken one of Edalji's boots and pressed it into the earth beside one of these prints. He had measured the two impressions and judged them to be the same.

Grasping his opportunity, Doyle fired more questions. "Did you make a cast of the prints?"

The constable shook his head.

"Were they photographed?"

"No."

"Why didn't you dig up a clod of earth and get a perfect impression?"

"The ground was too soft in one place and too hard in another, sir."

Then Doyle inquired how the footprints had been measured.

"With a stick, sir—and a little piece of straw."

Doyle pressed further, inquiring about the horse hairs which the police claimed to have found on Edalji's coat. Delving deeply into the procedure of Inspector Campbell who had taken the coat from the vicarage, he learned that the pony had been destroyed and that the officer, cutting off a strip of hide, had wrapped it into a bundle with the coat and taken it to the police surgeon who had discovered hairs on the sleeve.

After further inquiry along other lines, Doyle arranged for his first meeting with Edalji in the lobby of the Grand Hotel in Charing Cross. There the writer readily recognized the young man, standing alone with a newspaper held close to his eyes. "Don't you suffer from astigmatic myopia?" Sir Arthur asked, much as Holmes himself might have inquired of one whom he noted was nearsighted.

"I do," Edalji replied with some surprise, not knowing that the author, as a physician, had devoted much time to a study of the eyes and once had considered practicing as an oculist. "How did you know?" the young man inquired. "I've been to two ophthalmic surgeons and they can't fit me with glasses. I'm really half-blind."

"Wasn't this brought out at your trial?"

The vicar's son shook his head sadly. "I begged my lawyer to summon an eye specialist as a witness," he explained, "but my legal advisers said the case against me was so weak it wouldn't even be necessary."

Doyle at once grasped the importance of the point. He already had surveyed every foot of the ground where the mutilation had occurred. Now he realized that a man with Edalji's handicap would be more than half-blind in full daylight with still less vision at night; that to commit the crime laid to him he would have been compelled to grope his way over a wide expanse of railway tracks, to hurdle hedges, overcoming a maze of wire entanglements—a feat difficult enough even with normal sight.

Satisfied as he was of his own judgment, Sir Arthur still was anxious to verify his conclusions. He sent Edalji to a noted eye specialist, Dr. Kenneth Scott, who found the young man's vision to be even far worse than Doyle had believed; actually, he was unable to recognize a person at six yards' distance.

Although thoroughly convinced of the enormity of the injustice that had been done, Doyle was determined to conclude his inquiries with the thoroughness of Holmes. He took a train to Great Wyrley, examined the vicarage and after questioning the Reverend Edalji for hours, he went away satisfied that the son could not have left his bedroom unnoticed on the night in question.

Doyle now at long last believed that the time had come for a major move to gain public support. Early in January 1907 the first of a series of his articles dealing with the case in every detail appeared in *The Daily Telegraph* under the title of "The Case of Mr. George Edalji." As his startling disclosures unfolded, he bore down hard on the elements of prejudice, likening the case to that of France's Captain Dreyfus who had been made a scapegoat largely because he was a Jew. Edalji, he charged, was being similarly persecuted because he was a Parsi and a "Black Man." All England, he declared, had abhorred such elements in the Dreyfus affair. How, he demanded, could a similar injustice be tolerated in England?

He excoriated the Home Office for only releasing Edalji from prison without granting him a pardon after the entire case had been exposed. "Evidently the authorities were shaken and compromised with their consciences," he charged.

"After three years they turned the victim loose; but without pardon. Serenely they cried, 'Go free,' while adding, 'You're still guilty.'

"Now the door is shut in our faces and we turn to the last tribunal of all, a tribunal which never errs when the facts are brought before them, and we ask the public of Great Britain whether this thing is to go on."

As he had expected, "the last tribunal of all" reacted with resounding indignation. Almost overnight, the case of young Edalji became a *cause célèbre*. Leading figures in British life joined Doyle in demanding justice and in castigating the police.

To *The Daily Telegraph* came a flood of letters from agitated readers, commending the exposé and supporting Doyle's call on public opinion.

Sir George Lewis, a widely known criminologist, joined the outcry and pledged his help. Like many others, he demanded to know who was responsible for the "free but guilty" decision of the government.

No explanation came from the Home Office but Herbert Gladstone, the Home Secretary, the son of England's "Grand Old Man," did announce that the case would be investigated. He was careful to explain, however, that legal difficulties stood in the way. A Court of Criminal Appeal had not yet been created, although for years its need had been argued. However, Gladstone offered to appoint a committee of three open-minded men to make an exhaustive study of the matter in all of its ramifications and to recommend what should be done.

Doyle, who confidently believed he knew the identity of the guilty person, was satisfied with this offer. In it he saw an opportunity to present all of the evidence that he had accumulated.

In the ensuing weeks, as he busied himself assembling his voluminous reports, there was a startling new development. Doyle suddenly found himself deluged with anonymous letters identical to those that had reached the authorities before—letters purporting to come from the slasher, boasting of his deeds in his strange, sadistic vein.

Day after day Doyle's mail contained several such messages and finally he received a threat. "I know from a detective in Scotland Yard," this letter read, "that if you write to Gladstone and say you find Edalji is guilty after all, they will make you a lord next year. Is it not better to be a lord than to run the risk of losing kidneys and liver?" The writer concluded, as he always did, with a flat assertion that Edalji was guilty.

In another letter, still accusing the vicar's son, the penman wrote:

"The proof of what I tell you is in the writing he put in the papers when they loose him out of prison where he ought to have been kept along with his dad and all black and yellow-faced Jews. Nobody could copy his writing like that, you blind fool."

Doyle set to work on the letters, examining them meticulously. He studied the script, the use of words and the vile implications; then he undertook to compare them with the anonymous notes written from 1892 to 1895, and with those received after the cattle slashing began, eight years afterward.

When his arduous work was over he had reached definite conclusions. "I am satisfied," he announced, "that the anonymous letters of 1892 to 1895 were the work of two persons—one an educated man, the other a vulgar boy. The letters of 1903, I am convinced, were written by this same boy, now a man probably in his twenties. And I am satisfied that he also slashed the cattle. The educated man, I am satisfied, can be eliminated. He was probably somewhat unstable."

"But how do you reach such conclusions?" some of his associates asked.

Sir Arthur, in reply, began reading some of the 1903 letters. "Note this," he said. "The writer makes at least three allusions to the sea. He recommends an apprentice's life at sea. Considering the long gap between the two series of letters, is it not reasonable to suppose that he had gone to sea and now returned."

"And what else?" someone else pressed.

"Now," Doyle resumed, "let's consider the role of the Walsall School in all of the letters. In the earliest batch the headmaster receives an insulting letter and a key stolen from the school is dropped on the Edalji stairs. Eight years pass and the forged signature of a boy at Walsall School appears on one of the second run of letters. Then, in 1907, I receive a letter berating the headmaster of the same school. What does all that mean to you?"

He went on to explain that pursuing this theory he had launched an inquiry at Walsall School, searching through the records for the name of a boy attending there in the late nineties—a boy who was vicious, hated the headmaster, and actually had gone to sea.

He discovered that in fact there had been such a boy at that time, a lad to whom Doyle gave the fictitious name of Peter Hudson, confiding his true identity only to the highest authorities. This lad had been expelled at the age of thirteen because he was unmanageable, forged letters and delighted in the use of a long, sharp knife. It was his habit, on the way to school, to rip the cushions in the railroad coaches until the horse-hair stuffing emerged.

After Peter Hudson had engaged in a feud with a class-mate, Sir Arthur learned, Peter had flooded that boy's family with bitter anonymous letters. And this was between 1892 and 1895.

After leaving Walsall, the records showed, Peter had been apprenticed to a butcher who taught him how to use a knife on animals.

But Doyle learned still more. Near the end of December 1895, Peter Hudson had been sent to sea. For ten months in 1902 he worked aboard a cattle ship where he learned to handle livestock. He returned home the following year and was living near Great Wyrley at the time of the cattle slashing and the second wave of letter writing.

While many an investigator might have considered his work completed at this point, the author of Sherlock Holmes moved still further. By persistent inquiry he learned that a Mrs. Emily Smallking had visited the Hudson home after Peter's return. "It was at a time when resentment against the slashings was at its height," Doyle related to his friends. "Mrs. Smallking mentioned these goings-on to Peter, who smilingly stepped to a closet and displayed a large-sized horse lancet.

"This is what they kill cattle with," he informed his visitor who eyed the instrument with disgust.

"Put it away," the woman admonished. "You wouldn't want me to think you're the guilty man, would you?"

Peter Hudson made no reply.

In a way that he never disclosed, Doyle obtained the lancet and sent it to the Home Office with a bulky packet of reports disclosing all that he had uncovered. Included with a sketch of the instrument, was this significant comment:

"It is very sharp yet it could never penetrate more than superficially. I submit this very large horse lancet, obtained by Peter Hudson from the cattle ship, as being the only kind of instrument which could have committed all the crimes."

His reports concluded with the true name of Peter Hudson and Sir Arthur waited anxiously—and hopefully—for action by the investigating committee.

Months passed before a public announcement came from that body and the Home Secretary. Doyle and his colleagues read it and were stunned. The committee had concluded that George Edalji had been wrongfully convicted of mutilating cattle but—and the concluding lines were frustrating.

The government's investigators declared that they saw no reason to doubt that Edalji had written the anonymous letters and that "assuming him to be an innocent man, he had to some extent brought his trouble on himself." For these reasons, the committee found, he would be granted a pardon but no compensation for the three years which he had spent in prison.

There was a furore in the House of Commons and bitter criticism of the committee. The Law Society immediately readmitted Edalji to legal practice and *The Daily Telegraph* raised a substantial sum for him. Still Doyle refused to let the matter drop. After excoriating the Home Office and publishing more articles in the press, he obtained specimens of Peter Hudson's writing—just how, no one ever knew. These he sent with a number of the anonymous letters to Dr. Lindsay Johnson, then recognized as one of Europe's most outstanding handwriting experts, and who had figured prominently in the Dreyfus trial. Johnson examined the letters for weeks and finally concluded definitely that Peter Hudson was the writer. These findings went to the authorities who merely answered that they were not concerned with Peter Hudson either as an anonymous letter writer or as a suspect in the cattle maiming case. With that the matter was closed so far as the committee was concerned. There it has remained ever since. For reasons that were never disclosed, the government chose to drop the matter and, of course, the true name of Peter Hudson was never made public. And Doyle, in view of this policy, likewise kept the name securely locked in his files. He obviously did not want to risk a libel suit.

Despite his disappointment and frustration, Doyle's experience did end on a happy note—at his wedding to Jean Lackie, on September 18, 1907. While a throng of well-wishers milled about the gay couple after the ceremony at St. Margaret's in Westchester, a frail, dark-skinned young man elbowed his way to the groom and warmly shook his hand. He was George Edalji, come to offer his congratulations and best wishes.

7

THE GILCHRIST MURDER

After sixteen years in prison under life sentence as a murderer, and at one time facing execution, Oscar Slater had all but abandoned hope of ever establishing his innocence. Frustration and the physical strain of work on the rock pile day after day had taken heavy toll of both his mind and body.

In his despair he first rejected the offer of a friendly convict, on the eve of his discharge, to smuggle out a message to Conan Doyle, but he finally accepted. It was the summer of 1925. Already Doyle and a few others of influence had spent years in earnest but futile efforts to undo the wrong they believed had been done to Slater.

With the stub of an indelible pencil Slater wrote a note on a narrow strip of glazed, transparent paper picked up in a prison shop. Then he rolled it into a tiny pellet which he passed to his friend at a meeting of the prison debating society.

When time came for the outgoing prisoner's release, guards who knew of his friendship for Slater searched him suspiciously from head to toe. They examined the lining of his coat and even slit open the leather handle of his valise. The note remained concealed in his mouth.

When Doyle received the message and learned how it had been sent to him, he felt renewed zeal for a struggle he had dropped reluctantly as hopeless nearly ten years before. His campaign soon became a bitter political issue throughout Scotland but long years were to pass before success would be attained. They were marked by Doyle's repeated disclosures not only of police corruption and incompetence but of deliberate efforts to fasten the guilt on Slater, regardless of facts, evidence, and truth.

The murder for which Slater was sentenced to death occurred in Glasgow on the rainy night of Monday, December 21, 1908. Criminologists have filled entire books with the strange and conflicting details of the crime. The victim was an eighty-two-year-old spinster, Marion Gilchrist, who lived alone except for a young housemaid, in a six-room second-floor flat at No. 15 West Princes Street, an address which became well-known throughout the British Isles.

Miss Gilchrist was regarded in the neighborhood as a recluse and only a few friends knew that over the years she had collected a fortune in precious stones and had them made into earrings, brooches, and other jewelry, which she was in the habit of hiding about the house. A few suspected that she had profited by trading in jewelry and by investing her profits in securities.

At seven o'clock on the fatal night, Miss Gilchrist's trusted servant, twenty-one-year-old Helen Lambie, a girl of splendid reputation, went out to buy a newspaper, as was her custom at that hour. She left the aged woman sitting at the dining-room table and carefully closed both the flat door with its double lock and the street entrance. In her pocket she carried two keys, one for each of the door locks.

A few minutes later Arthur M. Adams, a musician occupying the flat directly below with his family, heard a loud thud and three distinct knocks from the room above. He sprang to his feet, for he recognized the knocking as a signal arranged long before with Miss Gilchrist should she need help whenever left alone.

Adams hurried out and found the street door to the upper flat open. He ascended the stairs and rang the bell. Receiving no answer, he returned to his family who insisted that he try again. Failing a second time to get a response, he was hurrying down the stairway when he encountered the Lambie girl returning with the paper. She unlocked the upper door of the flat and was surprised to see a man walking out at a leisurely gait from the direction of the spare bedroom. He brushed by her, then quickened his pace, and abruptly broke into a run as he reached the street.

A moment later Adams heard the anguished screams of Helen Lambie and ran back upstairs. In the dining room he found Miss Gilchrist on the floor dead, lying on her back with her head battered almost beyond recognition. The room was spattered with blood and it was evident that she had been beaten unmercifully. The two horrified people, suspecting robbery, hurried out for help, Helen summoning her mistress's niece, a Miss Birrell, living close by, and Adams sending for a doctor and the police. Neither observed any trace of the man they had so recently seen leaving the murdered woman's home.

Officers soon reached the scene and concluded that the woman probably had been beaten to death with the leg of a chair which lay close to the body. Searching the flat for clues, they found that the killer had not disturbed an array of valuable jewelry lying on tables in the spare bedroom but had forced open a wooden box containing papers. Its contents were scattered about the floor.

While robbery first had been discarded as a motive, detectives were less certain an hour later when the girl discovered that a large crescent-shaped brooch, set with diamonds, was missing from its usual place on a bedroom table. As the case developed, this little item became a major issue.

Other mysterious factors, particularly the manner in which the murderer had gained entrance to the flat, soon confronted the police. Though Miss Lambie insisted that she had never seen the stranger before, detectives reckoned that the aged spinster must have admitted him since there were no signs of forceful entry and the upper door of the flat was double-locked when the girl returned.

Who was this visitor, obviously the murderer, and by what ruse had he gained entrance to the flat? Or had he engaged in secret dealings with the victim—transactions involved in papers of which he now desperately wished possession?

These questions baffled the police as they set to work broadcasting detailed descriptions of the man and of the missing brooch, the only possible clues at the time, and called on the public for help.

Helen Lambie pictured the man as of decidedly foreign appearance, dark complexioned with dark hair, about twenty-five, tall and clean shaven. She said he wore a long gray overcoat and a cap. These details later played an important part in the case as events developed.

Adams, the only other person known at the time to have seen the stranger, agreed as to his general build but insisted that he was unable to provide more specific details since he was nearsighted and had caught only a passing glance as the man hurried into dimly lighted Princes Street.

Within hours police were deluged with conflicting reports from citizens that the wanted man had been seen in one part of Glasgow or in another. Officers scurried through the city, following lead after lead, only to find themselves frustrated at every turn. Pawnshops were visited in the vain hope that the brooch might be uncovered and thus provide a clue to the killer's identity.

Detectives still were groping for a clue two days later when a new witness appeared, fourteen-year-old Mary Barrowman, a precocious child, who informed the police that she had passed Miss Gilchrist's home at the moment of Helen's return and had seen a man hurrying away. Her description of him differed somewhat from that already given by the maid, but she stressed the stranger's "upturned nose" and his foreign appearance.

By now the brutality of the crime against an eighty-two-year

old woman had aroused indignation throughout Glasgow and
police were exerting every possible effort to penetrate the mystery. Four days passed before they found what appeared to
be an important clue. It came from a man who visited the
Central Police Office. He introduced himself as Allan M'Lean,
a dealer in bicycles.

M'Lean asserted that he was a member of the Sloper Club,
a social group of sorts, and he told of a new member, a German named Oscar Slater, who, he said, had been displaying
a pawn ticket for a diamond crescent brooch, offering it for
sale.

"When I read about the murder of this old lady," M'Lean
told the police, "I got to thinking right away about this
brooch and I'm quite sure it was pawned about the time of
the murder. This chap Slater is about thirty-seven. He fits the
description of the man you're looking for, but I'm not sure
that his real name is Slater. I understand he's gone by
several other names. Slater seems to be the last name he used
—and I can tell you exactly where he lives."

Spurred by this new and startling information, officers hastened to the address given them by M'Lean, a flat in a
modest residential district. To their disappointment, Slater
was not there but neighbors were eager to furnish information which strengthened police suspicions. The detectives were
informed that Slater had moved away only three hours before
with a woman not his wife, although his lease would not
expire for another seventeen months. He had occupied the
flat as "Mr. Anderson" and although he posed as a dentist,
he was actually a gambler who spent much of his time at
cards and other games of chance. Recently, the neighbors
said, he had spoken of going to America.

This was sufficient to spur an intensive city-wide search for
Slater. It was at its height when police received definite information on two vital elements of the case, either of which
should have induced them to at least reconsider their course,

but with an aroused public clamoring for an arrest, they were loath to turn away from a likely suspect.

This information disclosed that Slater had pawned a crescent-shaped diamond brooch on November 18, more than a month before Miss Gilchrist's death. Moreover, a new witness had been found who swore that Slater had dined with him at about the hour of the murder.

Despite the fact that the pawned brooch was the most incriminating factor in the case against Slater, the police now continued stubbornly on his trail, still firmly convinced that he was the murderer, who must be apprehended in complete disregard of the newly discovered contradictory facts.

The hunt for him was still under way when detectives learned that Slater and his woman companion were aboard the luxury liner *Lusitania* bound for New York. They had sailed December 26, five days after the crime. Here was ample evidence, the authorities reasoned—if they reasoned at all—that the wanted man had deliberately fled the country. At once he was declared a fugitive from justice, no longer referred to as a suspect but as the actual killer.

Glasgow authorities went into conference, then cabled New York police to apprehend Slater on his arrival. Significantly, the cable was sent on December 29, three days after the officers had received positive information that Slater had pawned the missing brooch long before the murder.

On Saturday, January 2, 1909, New York detectives swarmed aboard the *Lusitania* as it entered the harbor. In a matter of hours Slater was in the Tombs. In his pocket they found a pawn ticket for a diamond brooch. It bore a date which verified the fact, previously disclosed, that the pin had been pawned long before the slaying of Miss Gilchrist. Slater stated that he knew nothing of the crime, that he never had heard of Marion Gilchrist, and did not even know that he was wanted.

News of his capture was cabled at once to Glasgow and jubilant police responded with a request for his immediate extradition. American authorities, however, were not to be hurried. They demanded evidence justifying Slater's return—at least a fairly definite identification of the prisoner as the man observed leaving the murder scene.

It did not take Glasgow long to meet the challenge. On January 13, 1909, Helen Lambie, little Mary Barrowman, and Adams—accompanied by Glasgow detectives—were hustled aboard a steamer bound for New York. While the promptness of their action met with general commendation in Glasgow, there were a few skeptics who doubted its wisdom. They pointed to a published report that the Lambie girl questioned whether she could recognize the man she had seen leaving the Gilchrist flat, and that Adams, because of his poor vision, was practically worthless as a witness.

Nevertheless, an extradition hearing began soon after the arrival of the party. It opened in an atmosphere that reflected again the determination of the Glasgow authorities to fasten the crime on Slater, regardless of truth or evidence. The two girls were called as star witnesses and, as Conan Doyle was to learn much later, the stage was carefully set to facilitate their identification of Slater. Before the "show up" with other prisoners, they were permitted to stand in a hallway and look on as Slater was led in handcuffed to a guard. There could be no mistake as to his identity.

In such a setting, it was obvious that both girls should point out Slater, but Helen Lambie did explain that she could not be positive, although she did believe that she could identify Slater by his build and walk. She admitted that she was unable to recognize his face. Mary was indecisive and somewhat confused, but said she "thought" he was the man she had seen leaving the flat on the fatal night of December 21, 1908.

Much was made of a little metal hammer found in Slater's luggage, although a chemist who examined it reported that it showed no trace of blood or of having been cleaned in recent months. His findings were ridiculed by the Glasgow detectives who said they only proved Slater's "cunning" as a murderer.

The case dragged on for weeks until Slater, confident that proving his innocence would be a simple matter, agreed to return home voluntarily and face trial. He did not know what had been going on in Glasgow during his absence.

Day after day the press there, reacting to police information, had been reporting that new evidence was piling up against Slater. He had become known as "The Great Suspect" and public opinion already had found him guilty. A barber had told of seeing fingernail scratches on Slater's face after the murder. Someone reported that he had turned from poverty to wealth overnight. There were other rumors equally prejudicial and no one seemed interested in trying to verify them.

The day of Slater's return to Glasgow took on a festive air what with crowds lining the dock as he disembarked, all eager for a look at "The Great Suspect." Detectives soon were searching his baggage which had been sealed in New York. In a trunk they found an overcoat and cap which fairly well matched the descriptions given by the girls. The small tack hammer in his suitcase became an important clue, suddenly accepted as the murder weapon, despite the negative findings of the chemist.

The trial, which opened May 3, 1909, and lasted for four days, has been described by impartial observers as a farce. Helen Lambie now was positive in her identification, explaining that in New York she had been unable to carefully observe the prisoner's face. Mary this time was certain that the defendant was the man she had seen.

Other witnesses swore that they had observed Slater loitering outside of the Gilchrist home for days before the tragedy. The Crown made much of Slater's way of life, his gambling and his illicit love affair, as well as his alleged flight from Glasgow. Even the little tack hammer was shown to the jury as the instrument of death, but the chemist whose examination had produced negative results, was completely ignored. The exhibit, nevertheless, made a strong impact on the jury.

The once-important missing brooch was not even mentioned and the prosecution failed to make any showing that Slater had had an association with Miss Gilchrist or that he even had known her.

In the face of this situation, the defense counsel, A. L. McClure, tried his best to present his client's case. He stressed the weaknesses and inconsistencies in the identifications, inquiring why Helen Lambie now was so positive though she had been uncertain at the hearing in America. He emphasized Slater's alibi, even introducing the testimony of a friend, Duncan Mac Brayne, who said he had met the defendant at 8:15 on the night of the murder and had talked with him for a time.

Slater's mistress was called to the stand and further strengthened his alibi but the prosecution, in cross-examination, weakened her testimony materially by forcing admissions as to their illicit relationship.

Then McClure made a decision which many regarded later as a serious blunder. He refused to allow the defendant to testify in his own behalf, although Slater repeatedly had pleaded for a chance to take the stand. The lawyer, no doubt, was swayed by the belief of courtroom observers that acquittal was a certainty.

It took the jurors only one hour and ten minutes to find Slater guilty of murder, although they were far from unanimous, only nine of the fifteen members having voted for conviction. Five had cast ballots for "not proven" and one for acquittal.

In the prisoner's dock, Slater arose and dramatically asked leave to address the court. "You are convicting an innocent man," he exclaimed, then dropped back into his chair. A few moments later Lord Guthrie adjusted the black cap on his head and sentenced Slater to the gallows. The execution was set for Thursday, May 27, 1909.

Glasgow hailed the trial's end as a triumph for justice. The press generally agreed but there were two important exceptions—and in these well-known writers strongly stressed glaring flaws in the prosecution's case, raising serious questions about the verdict. The articles soon fanned new doubts about the case and petitions demanding clemency were circulated. Professors, doctors, and university officials joined the 20,000 signers enlisted in house-to-house canvasses.

Meanwhile preparations for the execution went ahead. A portable scaffold was being erected and Slater, resigned to his fate, requested that a photograph of his mother and sister be buried with him.

The unexpected came two days before the date set for the execution. Slater was called from his cell and informed that he had been reprieved, his sentence now being life imprisonment. This move immediately spurred new interest in the case and the ranks of Slater's supporters grew rapidly.

William Roughead, a distinguished Scottish criminologist, undertook a study of the entire affair. In April 1910, he published a long review of the full transcript, pointing out in an introduction all of the striking inconsistencies in the case. His conclusions attracted wide attention and Conan Doyle became seriously concerned. His analytical reading of the trial transcript in Roughead's book convinced him that much of the testimony was false and misleading, that there was strong reason to question the truth of Helen Lambie's sworn testimony, and that there were glaring irregularities in the trial proceedings.

With his usual dedication to the underprivileged and his interest in "lost causes," Sir Arthur Conan Doyle went into action. As in the Edalji case, he dropped all of his other work to delve deeply into this new mystery. He first discussed the intricacies of the case with Slater's lawyers who explained that they had undertaken the defense with reluctance because they believed their client was "a blackguard."

"Never mind his character," Doyle interrupted heatedly. "If he is innocent he must be freed."

Then he pledged himself to join Roughead as a partner and the pair made many visits to Glasgow and Edinburgh, examining witnesses, sifting scores of rumors, and checking the truth of many conflicting reports.

Again emulating the procedures characteristic of Sherlock Holmes, Doyle probed every facet of the case. With Roughead, he searched the Gilchrist home for days for new clues and studied the physical evidence still held by the police. In the end, thoroughly convinced that a tragic blunder had occurred, Doyle wrote a short pamphlet, *The Case of Oscar Slater*, which created a sensation when it reached the bookstands. In its clear perception, deductive reasoning, and step-by-step analysis it could have been another Holmes story. The public read it avidly and new supporters came forward by the thousands.

They were impressed by Doyle's incisive exposé of police bungling and the unanswered questions that he posed. "Why had Helen Lambie shown no surprise when she found a stranger in the flat?" he demanded. "Was it because the man was not a stranger and because she had readily recognized him? Had not Miss Gilchrist known him and readily admitted him to the flat?"

Miss Gilchrist's windows, he pointed out, were double-locked, convincing him that the man either had been admitted by the aged woman or possessed a key to the place.

He stressed the fact that the murderer obviously had moved swiftly into the spare bedroom after killing his victim, lighted the gas, and rifled the private box of papers without disturbing the jewelry on the dresser table. "Were the papers the object of his visit and why?" Doyle asked. "Why had the police ignored this factor? And was the crescent brooch taken only to mislead them into a theory that robbery was the motive?"

"It is an atrocious story," he told a group that had called

on him to discuss the matter. "I have come to understand the wickedness of the whole affair and I am determined to do everything I can for this man, though I do not even know him."

Within days Doyle was receiving scores of letters from all parts of Scotland and England, urging him to press for a reconsideration of the case. One member of the convicting jury wrote that he was now convinced of Slater's innocence. All of this received wide publicity but the Secretary for Scotland, refusing to be influenced, ruled that there was no justification for further official action.

The decision served to intensify Doyle's determination to prove Slater's innocence. He was still hard at work when he was informed that an inspector who had worked diligently on the case, John Thomson Trench, was thoroughly dissatisfied with the manner of its handling and seriously doubted Slater's guilt. Long conferences between Doyle and Trench followed, during which the inspector pointed to grave blunders in police procedures, supporting the claim that the authorities were determined to convict Slater at all costs. He unhesitatingly verified previous reports that Marion Gilchrist's niece had told him that Helen Lambie actually had named the mysterious visitor to the aged woman's flat.

With his customary attention to every detail, Sir Arthur undertook a long and painstaking investigation of all that Trench had told him. More witnesses were questioned and new evidence was analyzed. The result was a secret inquiry ordered by the Glasgow authorities into Trench's charges. When it was over, Trench, with an unblemished record of many years of service, was summarily dismissed from the force. He was later arrested on a false charge of receiving stolen property and obliged to face a jury trial which resulted in quick acquittal. Brokenhearted, he died a few years later.

It was at this point that Conan Doyle, frustrated and dejected, realized the futility of his work and agreed with others that nothing more could be done. He resumed his writing and other endeavors until 1925 when he received the smuggled note from Slater, pleading for help. Fully a decade had passed but the prisoner's pitiful plea again moved the author into action. Doyle realized that public opinion must be aroused anew, since many had forgotten Slater or at least dismissed him from their minds. He recognized further that to accomplish this purpose, he must launch an entirely new inquiry into every facet of the case, starting again at the beginning and probing every element involved. William Park, a widely known Glasgow journalist, proved a ready partner.

Utilizing developments in Doyle's renewed investigation, Park wrote a new book, *The Truth About Slater*, a stinging exposé that tore the case apart. Written to impress the average reader and with an introduction by Sir Arthur, it created a nation-wide sensation.

As Doyle continued delving into the case, friendly editors gave their help, reporting each new disclosure with Sir Arthur's interpretation of its importance. He learned that Miss Gilchrist had expressed fear of robbery at the hands of someone with whom she was acquainted. The murderer, he reasoned, was not a stranger, since Helen Lambie had expressed no surprise when she saw him leaving the house. It was his theory that the man had come for important papers, possibly a note for a large loan.

Doyle also concerned himself with the circumstances under which Helen Lambie and Mary Barrowman had changed their testimony at the Glasgow trial where they were positive in their identification of Slater. Doubting their story that they had not discussed the case on their trip to America, he ascertained that they had shared the same stateroom on the steamer.

Months were spent in a desperate effort to ascertain whether Slater ever knew the murder victim. In the end Doyle satisfied himself that the prisoner not only had never seen her but never had been in her flat.

The hammer, found in Slater's luggage and used by the

prosecution as an incriminating exhibit, was subjected to careful study. Doyle, with considerable difficulty, located the chemist who had pronounced it free of bloodstains. This man declared that he had been eager to testify in Slater's behalf but had not been summoned.

As one disclosure followed another, editors of law journals joined in the crusade for justice but Doyle was not content until he had enlisted the support of Ramsay MacDonald, then leader of the opposition party, who agreed that Slater had received "a most horrible injustice."

Sir Arthur was pressing hard for high government intervention when a new and unexpected development shook the country. It was a published interview with Helen Lambie, then married and living in the United States—an interview which has never been denied so far as is known. In it, Miss Gilchrist's former maid, reportedly admitted that she had told the police the name of the man she recognized walking from the Gilchrist home after the murder and that he was not Slater.

"I knew the man in the hall," she was quoted as saying. "I told the police his name but they said it was nonsense; that I must have been mistaken. Slater looked rather like him and so I was led to identify him instead."

She concluded with the reported admission that the police had paid her £40.

Doyle, elated over this disclosure, decided that Mary Barrowman must be found and interrogated. With Park and others he began a search and how they finally located her would make a Sherlock Holmes story in itself.

Now in full womanhood, she spoke freely, telling how she had been coached day after day to make her identification of Slater positive rather than merely testifying that he "looked like the man" she had observed.

Ramsay MacDonald now demanded immediate action, threatening to take the floor in Parliament if something were not done at once. Apparently, the government had heard enough. A few days later Sir John Gilmour, the Scottish Secretary, announced that he had authorized Slater's release "on license" but his statement carefully avoided any mention of an injustice.

Soon afterward, prison gates swung open and Slater, after more than eighteen years, walked out into the free world. To Doyle he wrote a note in which he said: "You breaker of my shackles, you lover of truth for justice sake, I thank you from the bottom of my heart."

The controversy, however, was far from ended. Neither Slater nor Doyle was satisfied, for "release on license" meant that Slater must report regularly to the police. More than that, the government had withheld what both men wanted most—complete vindication.

Sir Arthur decided to center his efforts in London at the highest official level. At his expense he printed new pamphlets presenting the situation in cold, blunt facts and explaining what he still believed remained to be done. Ramsay Mac-Donald supported him through the opposition. Doyle pressed directly at the government and finally succeeded in having Parliament pass a bill authorizing an appeal to the highest courts. Eminent counsel was engaged for the defense and Doyle paid the fees.

The hearing opened June 8, 1928, almost twenty years after the murder of Marion Gilchrist. Again all of the mysterious details of the case were exposed to public view and there was much new evidence of Slater's innocence, gathered by Doyle through relentless detective work.

The final result was the court's decision that Slater's conviction should be set aside and the government awarded him £6000 "in consequence of your wrongful conviction . . . and subsequent imprisonment." No effort was ever made toward apprehending the actual murderer. The name given to the police by Helen Lambie was never revealed and many surmised that the authorities were eager to drop the case, fearing public resentment that would result from any further disclosures of their bungling.

As for Conan Doyle, the real-life Sherlock Holmes, he had won again though he admittedly was disappointed that the slayer was allowed to remain at large. During the sixteen years of struggle his hair, like Slater's, had turned from dark to grayish white.

8

HOMER S. CUMMINGS TURNS DETECTIVE

On Monday morning, February 4, 1924, the people of Bridgeport, Connecticut, picked up their newspapers and read the first details of a shocking and mysterious murder. One of the city's most popular priests, Father Hubert Dahme of St. Joseph's Roman Catholic Church, had been fatally shot the previous evening on a downtown street corner by an assassin who fled from the scene and disappeared. An all-night search by special details of police had failed to uncover a single clue.

Father Dahme had been in the habit of taking a nightly stroll, the weather notwithstanding, and usually he passed the same locality at about the same time every evening. It was exactly 7:45 o'clock that Sunday evening when several men and women at the intersection of High and Main Streets saw the priest approaching and then a man who quickened his steps from behind, drew a revolver, held it close to Father Dahme's head and fired. Father Dahme fell forward on his face and the gunman, running up High Street, was lost to sight among the passersby.

The priest died an hour later at St. Vincent's Hospital without regaining consciousness.

While the accounts of witnesses differed in some details, mainly in descriptions of the murderer, all agreed that he was young, of medium build, and that he wore a gray cap and a three-quarter length brownish overcoat with a velvet collar.

The ruthless nature of the attack and the community's high regard for the murdered priest spurred police to intensive action. Every man on the force was alerted to look for suspicious characters. A description of the killer was distributed over a wide area extending far beyond Connecticut and roadblocks were set up. A large reward was offered for information leading to the assassin's capture. However, all measures failed to produce the slightest trace of the fugitive.

The motive for the crime was a mystery. Some theorized that it might have been prompted by a fancied grudge; others that it was the act of an anti-Catholic fanatic and that Father Dahme had simply chanced to come along as the victim. Yet it appeared logical to assume that the killer was familiar with the priest's strolls and had deliberately waited for him that evening.

Days of far-flung police activity continued without result. Literally scores of suspects were picked up for questioning and soon released. There was only one possibly valid clue to the crime, the bullet extracted by the autopsy surgeon from Father Dahme's brain.

Then an unexpected turn came late one night that February. A patrolman, walking his beat in Norwalk, a small community fourteen miles from Bridgeport, came upon a young man standing on a street corner. He was wearing a cap and a long overcoat. His manner, plus attire that tallied with descriptions of the slayer, alerted the officer and after brief questioning, the suspect was taken to the station. There he was searched and a revolver was found in a trousers pocket. Four of its chambers were loaded. One was empty.

The man protested his innocence and identified himself as Harold Israel. He said he had been discharged from the Army a short time before and, being penniless, was planning to hitchhike to his father's home in Pennsylvania. Questioned about the revolver, he said that he had used it for target practice along with two friends whom he named, but he had difficulty in explaining why he was still carrying the weapon.

While officers busied themselves in rounding up eyewitnesses to the murder and in checking essential details of Israel's statements, he was taken before a judge on a charge of carrying concealed weapons and sentenced to five days in jail. This also served as a means of holding him pending further investigation.

Israel's account of where he had previously lived was readily verified by two friends, roommates whom he had left when his funds were gone. His importance as a suspect was heightened somewhat when several of the eyewitnesses identified him positively as the man they had seen running from the scene of the shooting, although others were either in doubt or flatly denied recognition. One woman, apparently prompted by religious prejudice, declared after noting the suspect's name that while she had not seen the fugitive closely, she was certain that "he had walked like a Jew."

Although Israel, under continued police questioning, still protested his innocence, a new and unexpected development added strength to the case against him. A waitress, Nellie Trafton, had been brought to police headquarters with a surprising story. She had become acquainted with the suspect while working at a lunch counter in the building where he had formerly lived but recently she had taken a similar job in another eating place only a block from the murder scene. Shortly before the killing, she said, she had seen Israel walking by this place in the direction of the corner of High and Main where Father Dahme was shot. Miss Trafton was certain that Israel was the killer and to support her belief she related that some time before he had displayed a revolver and told her that he intended to kill someone.

Impressed with the importance of her statements, detectives led Miss Trafton before a line-up at headquarters. Without hesitation, she pointed to Israel.

Convinced of the man's guilt, the police pressed him hard for a confession. A grilling began at noon, continued through the night and far into the following day. Hour after hour, with only a few brief intervals for rest, Israel was questioned by the officers, alternating in pairs.

Israel, at first defiant, parried all queries and repeatedly asserted his innocence, but as dawn broke, his answers began to be confused and contradictory.

By four o'clock that afternoon he was showing plain signs of distress. He squirmed nervously in his chair, twisting his hands and biting his lips. It was clear that he could not much longer endure the ordeal.

However, the questioning went on relentlessly, to be halted abruptly as Israel suddenly jumped to his feet and in a tone of frantic despair poured out the words for which the police had been waiting. "All right, I did it," he gasped. "I can't stand this any longer. I'll tell you everything you want to know."

His admission of guilt was set down on paper and he readily signed his name. The police, although pleased with their success, desired detailed verification of what they had heard. They first asked Israel what he had done with the empty shell. "You'll find it on a shelf in the toilet room where I used to live," he told them. "That is, unless someone has taken it since I left."

Officers hastened to the place and found the empty cartridge precisely where Israel said he had left it—an important exhibit for the prosecution.

That night the prisoner was taken in handcuffs to the scene of the murder where he proceeded to reconstruct the course of his flight as he had described it—a route previously detailed by eyewitnesses. He even picked out a curb where he said he had stumbled—a point frequently mentioned by those who had seen the fleeing gunman.

On the following day Israel was taken before a city magistrate who, after routine procedures, held him for trial in Superior Court. All Bridgeport relaxed with the reassuring news that the wanton killer of Father Hubert Dahme had not only been captured but had confessed the crime.

The police moved fast to reinforce the confession with an air-tight case. They sent to Boston for a widely known ballistics expert, a man with long Army experience and more recently in an important position with an arms manufacturing concern. He came to Bridgeport, studied the evidence in the hands of the authorities, and reported that the lethal bullet had come from Israel's revolver.

Those findings already had been made an important factor in the coroner's verdict, which cited salient points as sufficient to establish Israel's guilt beyond a doubt. Identification of the prisoner by four eyewitnesses and his own confession also were emphasized.

Apparently it remained only for the police and the state's prosecutor to join forces in preparing their case for a jury trial. Throughout Connecticut the guilt of Harold Israel was generally accepted and speculation turned only to his punishment, a life sentence or the electric chair. Perhaps only a very scant few had read the confession with a degree of skepticism as to whether Israel actually was the killer—but even these would have been hard pressed to explain their feelings.

One man who held some doubts was none other than the state official whose duty it would be to direct the prosecution —Homer S. Cummings, then state's attorney for Fairfield County, a decade later to become United States Attorney General under President Franklin D. Roosevelt and win a national reputation as one of the country's most outstanding legal authorities. Cummings, with the keen perception of a brilliant lawyer, probably felt that the case against Israel might be "too perfect." Moreover, he was known for his meticulous ways in verifying every fact in every matter that came before him. Some insisted that he possessed "a sixth sense."

Aside from his concern with the law, Cummings had devoted himself for years to intensive studies of crime detection. He had written extensively on criminology and had participated brilliantly in the solution of crime hysteria. He was credited with a major role in expanding the program of the FBI.

Cummings had come to the view that every facet of the Israel case should be painstakingly scrutinized rather than accept the apparent guilt of the man. While many a state's attorney, involved as he was in a multitude of cases, would have assigned the task to his investigators and deputies, Cummings chose to carry on the inquiry by himself, regardless of the time and effort involved. It was a conclusion that the police had difficulty in understanding.

To members of his staff the prosecutor's plan came as no surprise. He was known to them as a man who insisted always upon determining the truth, regardless of whether it would lead to conviction or to vindication. Through the years they often had heard him quote to them from the Code of Ethics:

"The primary duty of a lawyer exercising the office of public prosecutor is not to convict but to see that justice is done."

The words had become Homer Cummings' own personal philosophy as state's attorney. "It goes without saying," he would tell his associates, "that it is just as important for a state's attorney to use the great powers of his office to protect the innocent as it is to convict the guilty."

With the Israel case approaching trial, Cummings was once more to put these words into practice.

"I'm going to dig into this case from the moment that the crime took place," he told his men. "I'm going to do it personally and with your help when it's needed. I'm starting with a thoroughly open mind—without any preconceived opinions in spite of the confession and the evidence. The conclusions will be based on my own independent findings."

Whether Cummings then foresaw the tremendous task before him no one ever knew. For more than three months he worked incessantly, usually alone, both day and night. Through this period he discarded the role of prosecutor to become a skilled, hard-plodding detective to whom hours of exhausting leg work were only a matter of duty. By day he moved from one part of the city to the other, locating witnesses and interrogating them; by night he often visited the scene of the murder, studying the High and Main Streets area and retracing the course taken by the fleeing gunman under the exact lighting conditions as of that fatal Sunday evening. His work had barely started when it brought the first surprise.

Cummings' initial move was prompted by his desire to know more about Israel's mental stability and his emotional condition at the time of the confession. He summoned three noted physicians—Drs. John C. Lynch, John H. Finnegan, and Frank W. Stevens—and gave them detailed instructions.

For three full days these men subjected the prisoner to intensive psychiatric examination. Only hours after they had begun their work Israel retracted his confession and reasserted his innocence!

Asked why he had admitted guilt, he explained that at the time he was utterly exhausted by prolonged police questioning, that it was the only way he could find surcease from incessant interrogation. "I was so tired that I was ready to admit anything," he told the doctors. "And anyway, everything seemed to be against me. But, believe me, I didn't kill the priest." It was a statement that Israel was to repeat many times as the inquiry progressed.

The medical men submitted a significant report. They agreed that Israel was of low mentality and easily susceptible to suggestion. His confession, they concluded, came at a time when he was nervously and physically exhausted and therefore was of no value. In fact, it was their belief that he could be made to admit almost anything under the pressure of continuous questioning and suggestion. They noted, also, that Israel in his admission of guilt had disclosed nothing beyond facts already known to the police and suggested in their interrogation.

Now still more eager for the truth and increasingly dubious

of Israel's guilt, Cummings turned to the bullet which he regarded as the crux of the case and he determined to inquire into the findings of the ballistics expert. His first step in this regard was to make a personal inspection of the toilet room where an empty shell, supposedly from the lethal bullet, had been found. There, to his surprise, he came upon a second shell.

His curiosity aroused, Cummings called on the accused man's two companions who explained that they, with Israel, were accustomed to discarding empty cartridges in the room after target practice.

This led the prosecutor into a searching review of ballistics, a subject with which he already was familiar. He examined the two empty shells and found that they had been exploded by a trigger point that was unusually dull while the trigger point of Israel's revolver was exceedingly sharp, an important point that he carefully verified by firing test shots from the weapon.

Cummings was convinced now that the ballistics phase of the case demanded still more study and he seriously questioned the bullet report given to the police. He interviewed one of Israel's companions, Charles Cihal, who explained that at Israel's request he had taken the accused man's gun to a carpenter shop to have its trigger point sharpened.

While many an investigator would have considered his work in this area of the case completed, Cummings proceeded further. He already knew that of the various eyewitnesses to the murder, only one, Ralph Esposito, had been able to describe the killer's gun. He had told detectives that he believed it was "one of those black pistols." Testifying at the coroner's inquest, he said he was certain that "it did not shine." Israel's revolver was nickel-plated. To thoroughly convince himself of Esposito's error, Cummings carried the gun to the scene of the killing. There, at the exact hour of the murder, he took it in his hand—and it gleamed.

He decided next to call on not one but six of the most

qualified ballistics experts that he could find in New England. When they assembled in his office in Bridgeport, he handed them the deadly bullet, Israel's revolver, and the empty shells.

The six spent several days in technical studies and practical demonstrations. They interviewed the police expert to learn how he had reached his conclusions concerning the bullet. He had superimposed enlarged photographs of the one in evidence and of those he fired as tests and had found "certain lines of similarity." His findings, however, were completely rejected by Cummings' experts. They declared that the slug taken from the priest's head could not have been fired from Israel's gun.

After his ballistics panel had returned to their homes, Cummings applied himself to studies and experiments of his own. His work extended even beyond that so carefully carried on by the group of specialists and served to confirm in his own mind that the original comparisons given to the police were in error, that the Israel revolver definitely had not fired the fatal shot. Cummings felt that he had reached the turning point in the case but he regarded his investigation still far from finished. Turning to the eyewitnesses who had identified Israel and those who could not, he summoned them one by one, and interviewed each for hours. Several who then were positive that Israel was the man they had seen in flight, admitted to doubts when they first had viewed him in custody. These witnesses included one who had stood closest to Father Dahme and still could not recognize the accused. Another insisted that the slayer's cap was black; all of the others said it was gray.

Once more the prosecutor returned to the murder scene in early evening, placing himself in the exact position fixed by each of the witnesses. He finally left, convinced that most of them could not have seen what they described; that even a friend could not be recognized under similar conditions.

He visited the restaurant where Nellie Trafton worked and

while patrons looked on curiously, Cummings stood on the precise spot from which she claimed to have seen Israel walking toward the murder scene. He soon discovered that because of the position of the front window and the large lettering on its pane, it would have been impossible for her to recognize any passerby. Moreover, he learned that the waitress had not reported her experience until after a reward had been offered and then had formally claimed it.

In Cummings' judgment it was now time to interview the accused man himself. He was especially anxious to learn more of Israel's alibi and to check it thoroughly. If it could be verified, the prosecutor believed this would be the final step in proving the prisoner's innocence. Israel had insisted that he was attending a motion picture show at the Empire Theatre at the exact time of the killing; in fact, he said that he entered the movie house at 7 P.M. and did not leave until after 9.

"What pictures did you see—can you remember?" Israel was asked.

"That's easy," he replied unhesitatingly. "I remember them well—*The Mystery Girl, The Leather Pushers, Fighting Skipper,* and *Ghost of the Dungeon.*

"What picture was on when you walked in?"

"*The Leather Pushers.*"

"What came next?"

Israel named the film.

"And what was showing when you walked out?"

"*Ghost of the Dungeon.*"

Cummings sent for the manager of the Empire and asked that he bring his time schedule for the showing of the feature and the short subjects with him. The two compared Israel's statements with theater records and found that they coincided perfectly. "There just isn't as much as two minutes difference," the show man finally stated. It was obvious that Israel could not have anticipated such questions. His alibi was completely verified. Now it was up to Cummings to take official action.

First he spent days in assemblying the results of his prolonged investigation, preparing them for an official statement to the court. Three months had passed since the murder of Father Dahme and people were asking why the trial had been delayed, especially in view of Israel's confession. They learned the reason on the morning of Tuesday, May 27, 1942, a day that created a sensation in Bridgeport.

Homer S. Cummings, as state's attorney for Fairfield County, walked into the courtroom of Superior Judge L. P. Waldo Marvin and asked leave to read a statement. He explained that it would be lengthy and of surprising content. The court told him to proceed and Cummings began reading from a heavy sheaf of papers.

It proved to be one of the most amazing statements ever read in a Connecticut courtroom—a statement that has been preserved and often referred to as an outstanding example not only of Cummings' rare talents as a prosecutor and as a detective, but as an illustration of his firm belief that law-enforcement officials must seek the truth whether or not it leads to convictions.

Facing Judge Marvin, Cummings opened his lengthy presentation with a factual review of the circumstances of the murder itself. He reviewed the earliest statements of the witnesses as they were made to the police, carefully indicating the points of agreement and those of conflict. He read every word of the coroner's findings, citing the ten damning points by which that official had fastened the guilt on Israel.

He turned then to his decision to undertake a personal investigation of the entire case and as he proceeded with his clear, analytical statement, moving from one area of the inquiry to another, his voice sometimes rose as he sought to emphasize what he regarded as a vital point. On occasion he paused, reading slowly to stress his words.

"The case against the accused seemed overwhelming," he

said, referring to his study of the coroner's report. "Upon its face, at least, it seemed like a well-nigh perfect case, affording but very little difficulty in the matter of its successful prosecution. In fact, if Your Honor please, it seemed like an annihilating case. There did not seem to be a vestige of reason for suspecting for a moment that the accused was innocent. The evidence had been described by those who believed in the guilt of the accused as one hundred per cent perfect.

"Despite these facts, however," he went on, "there were many people who, without any particular assignable reason, felt that the accused was innocent and that he had been the victim of a most extraordinary combination of circumstances.

"My own view necessarily was that if the facts stated were subject to verification, the accused was undoubtedly guilty, but there were sufficient circumstances of an unusual character involved to make it highly important that every fact should be scrutinized with the utmost care and in the most impartial manner. It goes without saying that it is just as important for a state's attorney to use the great powers of his office to protect the innocent as to convict the guilty."

His personal inquiry, he stated, had started on the day that Israel was held for trial in the higher court. He reviewed quickly the wide scope that his work had covered and the meticulous care with which he had studied testimony, interviewed witnesses and interrogated many others involved.

He reported to detail the conclusions of the physicians whom he had asked to examine Israel. It was their opinion, he emphasized, "that any confession made by the accused was totally without value and they were of the opinion also that if they care to subject the accused to a continuous and fatiguing line of interrogation, accusation, and suggestion, in due time he would be reduced to such a mental state that he would admit practically anything that his interrogators desired."

Cummings next reviewed the testimony of the eyewitnesses, moving from one to another, pointing out weakness and contradictions in their statements. One of them, he said, had insisted that the fleeing assassin had a peculiarly long nose—a feature quite contrary to Israel's appearance.

He related how he had stood at the murder scene, trying to picture himself in the person of each of the witnesses to determine how accurately they could have described the man they saw running. He finally concluded that their accounts could not be correct.

Then, to support his conclusion, he told the court of a novel experiment of his own planning. On a day when a large crowd had gathered in front of the courthouse, expecting the trial to begin, Cummings and two deputy sheriffs had scanned the faces of the curious to see if any resembled Israel. One deputy picked out seven men; another eight. Seven of those selected by the two officers were the same people.

On another day, while Israel was in jail, Cummings had walked into a courtroom and observed a man closely resembling the prisoner, seated in a forward chair. On his lap were a gray cap and a velvet-collared overcoat, similar to those which witnesses had said they had seen on Israel.

Of the vitally important death bullet and its study by experts, Cummings spoke at length, discussing the technical points with unusual simplicity so that they might be understood by anyone. After relating the conclusions of the ballistics experts whom he had assembled, he told of his own studies made in the hope that one less familiar with the intricacies of the subject could readily follow their deductions.

He informed the court how he had conferred with the man who made the bullet studies for the police and how this man had demonstrated his findings by superimposing a photograph of the lethal bullet against a picture of a bullet fired from Israel's gun.

"I worked on that superimposing for two hours one day," Cummings stated. The police expert who was with him finally had succeeded in making the bullet markings coincide.

"I am free to say," Cummings declared, "that I am unable to make any such deduction. It seemed obvious to me that instead of demonstrating that the mortal bullet had been fired through the Israel revolver, it demonstrated that the mortal bullet had not been fired from the Israel gun."

This conclusion, he told the judge, was shared by the six experts he had summoned, all of whom agreed that the fatal pellet had come from some other weapon.

Cummings still was unwilling to drop this phase of his presentation. Obviously, he wished the judge to be convinced and he probably feared that the court would consider the conflicting opinions as simply another instance of disagreement between experts.

In consequence, he followed with an explanation of elementary facts much as a ballistics professor in a criminology class would give to beginners. First he explained to the judge in simple terms the existence of grooves in a revolver barrel and of raised lines between the indentations that are known as "lands." He pointed out how these "riflings" left their marks almost like fingerprints on fired bullets. To illustrate, he exhibited enlarged photographs.

From this beginning, he followed with pictures of bullet markings from Israel's weapon and from others. Then he exhibited a photograph of the lethal bullet enlarged to heroic size, carefully pointing out the lack of any similarity, which he attributed, in part, to his discovery that Israel's revolver, badly in need of repair, had a rusted barrel which would have a "choking effect" when fired.

He moved now into more technical details, explaining that in testing the defendant's gun he had found that it frequently missed fire. He said that many times he had pulled the trigger, holding the weapon at the same angle as did the killer, and that it had missed fire eighteen times in succession.

"These circumstances," he concluded, repeating his earlier argument, "amount to a demonstration that the bullet which killed Father Dahme did not pass through Israel's revolver."

Referring again to the judgment of the six experts he had summoned, he said firmly: "In the face of such an opinion it would be preposterous to contemplate a trial and, moreover, it would be an injustice even to longer suspect Israel of murder."

Cummings, however, was not yet ready to submit his case. He spoke again, and at length, of the conflicts in the statements of witnesses, explaining to the judge why he discarded as valueless the account given to the police by waitress Nellie Trafton.

Nearing the conclusion of his long presentation, he put great stress on the support of Israel's alibi by the manager of the motion picture theater.

Then he paused for a moment and formally moved for a dismissal of the case—in legal parlance he "entered a nolle."

While Cummings may have expected that Judge Marvin would take the motion under advisement, he did not have to wait for a decision.

"The court has given very close attention to the state's attorney," the judge began, "and followed the presentation of the case as closely as it could. It is perfectly evident that a great deal of painstaking care has been expended on this case and that the attitude of the state's attorney's office has been what it should be, one of impartiality and a desire to shield the innocent as well as a determination to prosecute those who are guilty.

"The court cannot help but feel," he continued, "that after the care that has been expended by those who are well qualified and the careful and exhaustive review of the case and the statements that are made, that the recommendation of the state's attorney is one that should be approved and carried out. I feel that the state's attorney's office is entirely justified in the recommendations that have been made and it is so ordered."

Homer S. Cummings bowed his thanks and prison doors

soon opened for Harold Israel, the man who once had confessed that he was a murderer.

Who killed Father Dahme is still not known but an innocent man was spared from either execution or life imprisonment.

Though years have passed since Israel's exoneration, Cummings' notable statement to the court has been reprinted in
important legal volumes long after his death on September
10, 1956. He had served six years in the Roosevelt cabinet.

The statement comprises a lengthy chapter in the *Journal of
Law and Criminology*, published by the Northwestern University Press for the American Institute of Law and Criminology.

To fully appreciate its impact and significance, a few lines
from an introduction written in that book by Superior Court
Judge William M. Maltbie of Hartford, Connecticut, should
be quoted. Judge Maltbie concluded his preface to Cummings' statement with these words:

"His statement is interesting because of the nature of the
case: it is valuable because of the methods followed by him
in analyzing the evidence, because of the suggestions it con-
tains for other prosecutors, but more because of the splendid
exemplification of that cardinal principle which Our Code of
Ethics states as follows: 'The primary duty of a lawyer exercising the office of public prosecutor is not to convict but to
see that justice is done. . . .'"

9

THE COURT OF LAST RESORT

A small group of dedicated men, working unofficially and without pay or profit, is credited with having done more to right miscarriages of justice than any other body with like purpose in the country. It was distinctly unique and wholly without counterpart.

It called itself The Court of Last Resort, a name befitting its aims and functions. For years its members, all occupied with their own affairs, traveled back and forth across the continent, investigating seemingly hopeless cases of individuals who pleaded their innocence from behind prison bars. Truth was their objective and when it verified an error in the law's procedures, members of The Court were relentless in enlisting official aid to undo a wrong.

To this little group of volunteers, all experts in the field of crime detection, scores, perhaps hundreds of unfortunate men owe the freedom they enjoy today. In all respects, The Court commands a place as the most unique and effective organization of its kind ever created to serve the ends of justice.

The idea was that of the famous author of detective stories and creator of Perry Mason, Erle Stanley Gardner, a long-time resident of Southern California.

At a time when he was a practicing attorney, Gardner was enjoying an adventurous camping trip into Baja California with his close friend, Henry Steeger, head of a large New York publishing house which includes *Argosy* magazine as one of its many enterprises. Fresh in Gardner's mind were the details of a case he had just concluded—a case in which he saved an innocent man from the gallows. As the lawyer lay in his sleeping bag gazing at the stars, he became absorbed with thoughts of freedom and of those who are unjustly deprived of it.

Wondering what could be done in an organized way to rescue men like his recent client from mistakes in the administration of justice, he hit upon the plan which was to become one of his major interests for many years.

He confided his idea to Steeger who responded enthusiastically, not only offering the pages of *Argosy* as the medium through which to expose such cases but volunteering to defray the expenses of investigators who would be needed to carry on the project. And so The Court of Last Resort was born in 1948. It operated until a few years ago when increasing demands on their time forced its members to bring the project to an end.

It was their intention that The Court should really comprise the rank and file of the American people. In their concept it would be a court of public opinion which would react to the disclosures of truth made through impartial investigations.

Returning from their camping trip, Gardner and Steeger soon enlisted the cooperation of three outstanding authorities in crime detection. This formed the nucleus of the group which was to be aided as situations developed by other experts.

One of the three was Dr. LeMoyne Snyder, a physician and an attorney, who had distinguished himself in the field of legal medicine. Another was a famous detective, Raymond Schindler, whose work on the murder of Sir Harry Oakes in the Bahamas has been detailed in an earlier chapter of this book. The third was a pioneer in the development and use of the lie detector, Leonarde Keeler, who died in the early period of The Court's operation and his place was taken by

Alex Gregory, a keen, experienced investigator, thoroughly familiar with the use of the polygraph.

Soon two others were recruited as ace investigators to carry on the hard-plodding, day-to-day work in The Court's many and varied cases. They were Tom Smith, who retired in 1948 as superintendent of Washington State Penitentiary at Walla Walla; and B. J. (Bob) Rhay, who had worked at the prison as a sociologist and who, at this writing, is its superintendent.

As different in appearance as in background, they functioned as a remarkable team. Smith, short, chunky, and slightly stooped, had shown an instinctive insight into crime and penology that compensated for his lack of college education. He was known for his unusual powers of observation and deduction.

Rhay, tall, slender and erect, had joined the prison staff after receiving degrees at Whitman College in Washington. Resigning to serve The Court, he had kept his post until the outbreak of the Korean War when he joined the Army Air Force and piloted a fighting plane. On his return to civilian life, he resumed his previous work until 1955, when he was appointed assistant superintendent of the penitentiary and later became its top man.

There were others, as requirements developed, but through the years leadership remained with Gardner in California and Steeger in New York, the two working together from opposite sides of the continent, always ready to drop their personal affairs to travel from one place to another by train, automobile, or plane as necessity and circumstances demanded.

It was obvious that such a project, from its beginning, would bring appeals for help from many in scattered parts of the country. The response surpassed all expectations. Every case received the most exacting attention and when preliminary inquiry established that prolonged investigation was justified, workers for The Court moved rapidly, regardless of difficulties. Not until all of the necessary facts were assembled did Gardner and his colleagues call on local and state officials for action. In most instances, public opinion, mobilized through the pages of Steeger's magazine, became a powerful and effective ally.

Volumes would be required to record all of the brilliant achievements of The Court through its years of service. An illustrative case is that of Silas Rogers, a young Negro with an unblemished record, who spent two years in the death house at Virginia State Prison in Richmond, living in the shadow of the electric chair, while members of The Court combed the country for a key witness, the one person in the world who stood between life and death for Rogers. Their only description of this man was that "he looked like a mechanic." He was finally located after nearly a year of untiring search and his testimony, together with many startling disclosures brought to light by skilled investigators with the aid of a conscientious chief of police, resulted in freedom for the condemned man and a pardon almost ten years after his arrest.

The crime of which Rogers was convicted and sentenced to death occurred in Petersburg, Virginia, on a Sunday morning, July 18, 1943, when a policeman, Robert B. Hatchell of that city, was shot and fatally wounded while he and other officers were pursuing the fleeing driver of a supposedly stolen automobile.

Shortly after 7 o'clock, Hatchell and his partner, Corporal W. M. Jolly, starting out on their morning rounds in a radio prowl car, were halted by a traffic light. Looking ahead, they observed a large red sedan with North Carolina license plates approaching the intersection from the opposite direction, its brakes grinding as it came to an abrupt stop. Almost instantly the officers realized that the machine fitted the description of a stolen car for which they had been looking. "We'll turn when the light changes and stop them," Hatchell told his partner, who was driving.

As the police car changed its course, the officers noted that the other machine, driven by a Negro with a white cap, had stalled and that a passenger in Army uniform had jumped out and was pushing it into motion.

Circling through a nearby service station, the policemen caught up with the red sedan and Hatchell called to the driver to pull to the side of the road and stop. Instead, the machine lurched forward, racing ahead with the prowl car in fast pursuit.

The chase continued through the streets of Petersburg as the sedan, gaining a speed of more than sixty miles an hour, ignored stop signs and red lights as it zigzagged recklessly in its driver's frantic efforts to elude the police. Suddenly it swerved into a sharp right turn that took it within a few feet of a dead-end barrier, perilously close to the edge of a steep bluff. The police car, close behind with its siren screeching, was about to close in when the driver of the machine ahead, with amazing skill, maneuvered his way into a narrow walkway between the St. Petersburg Hospital and the barrier, where it came to a sudden halt.

The two officers stopped their car and jumped out, Jolly hurrying toward the stalled sedan and Hatchell running after its driver who was dashing wildly toward the rear of the hospital, obviously making for a densely wooded ravine at the foot of the embankment.

Jolly found two soldiers sitting in the back of the machine and handcuffed them without difficulty. A few moments later he was joined by his partner who had lost sight of the driver in the open area behind the hospital and was returning for help.

Reasoning that the fugitive probably had descended into the ravine, the officers rapidly moved their manacled prisoners into the prowl car and started off, swinging into a nearby street that took them to the open area of the hollow from which they could see anyone dropping down the slope.

They had barely reached this point when Hatchell caught sight of a man making his way through the thick shrubbery below. As he left the car and started in pursuit, his partner picked up his microphone and radioed headquarters for men to come for the soldiers.

He had scarcely finished his message when two officers, Seward and Lockett, who had been attracted by the police siren, dashed to the scene in their patrol car and were told the cause of the trouble. Both men hurried after Hatchell to offer help but returned in a short time, informing Jolly that they had observed tracks leading into the gulch but could find no trace of the fugitive. Hatchell, they said, chose to remain behind to continue the search. Being off duty, Lockett and Seward waited until a patrol wagon arrived for the prisoners and then started for their homes.

Jolly, now alone, circled the area to be on hand if needed but when more than twenty minutes passed without sight of Hatchell or even a call from him, he became worried and hastened on foot to the hospital. There an attendant told him that a short time before he had heard two shots, fired in quick succession, apparently in that vicinity.

The officer, now fearful of serious trouble, started for the bluff but he had gone only a few paces when a nurse hurried out excitedly, calling that she had just seen a man, apparently wounded, lying on the ground close by.

Jolly made for the spot, close to where the soldiers' car had stopped less than half an hour before, and found his partner lying unconscious on the walk, bleeding profusely from a bullet wound in his left hip. Hatchell was carried into the hospital where he died a short time later without regaining his senses. Examination showed that the bullet had plowed into his abdomen, causing severe internal hemorrhages.

At headquarters, outraged police flew into action, eager to avenge the wanton killing of a popular officer but they were taken to task some time later by many who believed that in their excitement, important routine procedures had been overlooked. A description of the Negro driver was broadcast with orders for his capture as the murderer but for reasons that were never explained no one called for an organized search of the ravine. The two soldiers were booked without charge pending further developments.

Circumstances of the murder remained a mystery. Whether Hatchell had been shot in a pistol duel with the fugitive or had been killed by him after his capture were matters of conjecture. There was no trace of the death weapon nor was it ever found. Hatchell's service revolver was missing and officers theorized that it had been used against him.

Obviously, the first task confronting the police was to capture the missing driver but almost three hours of intensive search had passed before Silas Rogers walked into the trap. It was then that Policeman Curtiss R. Mason of Colonial Heights, on the lookout for the hunted man, sighted a Negro on the north end of the Appomattox Bridge on the road into Petersburg. Mason noted that he resembled the fugitive in a general way and that he was wearing a white sailor's cap and a tan shirt. He was carrying a small bundle.

The officer stopped him and announced that they would proceed at once to police headquarters.

"What have I done?" the startled Negro demanded. "I'm bumming my way to New York to report to my draft board."

"Maybe you are," Mason retorted, "but you look a lot like the man we're looking for—the man who just killed an officer. If you're not him, you can explain everything to the chief."

A short time later Rogers, vigorously protesting his arrest, gave the authorities a detailed account of his recent movements. A pleasant-looking young man, then twenty-one, he said that he had once been a jazz musician and had never been in serious trouble. A hurried check of police records confirmed that statement.

However, the two soldiers already had told their story and it was as different from Rogers' as day is from night. They insisted that they had been picked up in Raleigh by Rogers who told them that he had stolen the red sedan. He was driving them into Petersburg, they said, explaining that they last saw him when he jumped from the stalled machine near the hospital and left them stranded.

At no point did Rogers' statement coincide with that of the other two. "I've come from Miami," he told the police, with an apparent eagerness to explain his movements. "My twin brother, Paul, and I have been doing odd jobs for a man who runs a hotel there. When I got an induction notice from my draft board in Long Beach—that's on Long Island—I decided to get there by riding blind on the railroad. I'd done that before.

"I left Miami on Friday, the sixteenth of July hoboing on the Florida East Coast train. At Savannah I sneaked aboard a northbound Seaboard Air Line freight that took me to Hamlet, North Carolina. I got off there and managed to find a safe place on the *Silver Meteor* right between the diesel and the baggage car. Everything was going fine until trainmen saw me as we were moving into McKenney and they said I'd have to get off at Petersburg. It was early when I left the train here so I went to the Dunlop Street Station, washed up and changed my shirt and pants. I put the soiled ones in a paper bag; that's what I was carrying when I was arrested. I guess you know the rest."

The police, frankly admitting that they did not believe Rogers' explanation, pressed for specific details, obviously hoping to disprove his statements. He told them to interview two men who had told him to leave the train at Petersburg. One was the conductor; and the other was a workman with whom he had had some conversation at the station. "This second man," Rogers stated, "told me not to try to get back on the train because there were a lot of railroad detectives around the yards at the next stop and they'd be sure to take me in."

"Who was that man—what did he look like?" the officers inquired.

Rogers shrugged his shoulders. "That's what I can't answer

very well. He was a friendly guy and he looked like a mechanic."

Pressed for the precise time of his arrival at Petersburg, Rogers said that it was well after 7:30—a time that would definitely support his alibi.

The officers, however, were still strongly inclined to believe the soldiers and, thinking that Rogers could be induced to confess, they began a vigorous grilling. It went on relentlessly for hours at a time without result but some of their "persuasive" methods did not come to light until long afterward.

When two days passed with Rogers still insisting on his innocence, detectives started out to inquire into his account of the train ride and to look for the individuals he had mentioned. They finally located three men whose statements only partially verified his story. One was the conductor, W. R. Bright, who recalled having ordered a hobo to leave the train but he had not taken careful note of the man's appearance and therefore would be unable to recognize him. Another was the station porter who had observed a man climbing down from the *Silver Meteor* but when he looked at Rogers at headquarters he could not identify him. A third man said positively that the prisoner was the man he had seen sneaking aboard the Florida East Coast train at Miami. No trace could be found of the individual Rogers had described as "looking like a mechanic" and the search for him was abandoned.

Although this investigation did support Rogers' account to some degree, the authorities were more convinced than ever that he had not told the truth and that, in fact, he was the murderer. The Commonwealth Attorney, Oliver A. Pollard, busied himself preparing for the trial and since the accused could not afford to engage counsel, the court appointed Robert H. Cooley, a Negro lawyer, to defend him.

The trial, held before Judge H. T. Wilson, was of short duration. The two soldiers, Privates James M. Jordan and

Charles Stephens, became the state's star witnesses. Under oath, they repeated the story they had told earlier to the police and pointed accusingly at Rogers as the man who had taken them into his car at Raleigh and driven them to Petersburg. The jury appeared to be deeply impressed.

Rogers, testifying in a frantic effort to save his life, denied everything that the servicemen had said and insisted that he could prove his alibi. In detail he repeated his account of the train ride from Miami, emphasizing his arrival in Petersburg at a time somewhat later than the pursuit of the red sedan had begun.

His lawyer, in closing argument, reviewed the defendant's straightforward statements covering his movements on the morning of the murder. Referring to the conflict in testimony, he stressed the element of reasonable doubt, insisting that it should be considered in the accused man's favor.

The jury, however, after sitting for two days, chose to believe the soldiers. Convicted of murder, Rogers was sentenced to the electric chair and moved to the death house at the penitentiary in Richmond.

In desperation he wrote to his few friends pleading with them to intercede but there was little that they could do. Fortunately for the condemned man, a reporter on the staff of the *News Leader* in Richmond heard of Rogers' repeated claims of innocence and decided to inquire into the case. Before long he became aware of the possibility of a miscarriage of justice and wrote a long article, pointing out a number of significant discrepancies. His account attracted the attention of a few lawyers who agreed that the matter of Rogers' guilt required thorough and impartial investigation. Volunteering their services, they filed a succession of appeals which stayed the execution.

Months had passed when Rogers, still living in the shadow of death, received a letter from his brother. In it was enclosed a clipping of the article in the Richmond newspaper. The prisoner read it over and over, lingering on the words, and at last he decided on a course of action. Inmates had told him a few things about The Court of Last Resort and with faint hope he mailed the clipping to Erle Stanley Gardner along with a letter appealing for help.

Gardner, busy with his own affairs on his Southern California *rancho*, read the newspaper story and found himself intrigued by many of the elements involved. He sent it to Steeger in New York and together they soon started the customary preliminary inquiry to determine whether Rogers' case warranted an exhaustive investigation in depth that would involve heavy expense and the services of skilled men for a considerable time.

Before long they concluded that the plight of the convicted man in Virginia was indeed a subject to seriously concern The Court. Rhay and Smith were detailed to conduct the investigation.

As they undertook their assignment, they began by familiarizing themselves thoroughly with the trial transcript. After ascertaining that Rogers never had been in trouble, they took a plane to Richmond for a long interview with him and the more they talked the more convinced they became that the vital key to the case lay with the man who "looked like a mechanic"; that somehow he must be found. The police had done their utmost to locate him in the hope of disproving Rogers' alibi. Now Smith and Rhay took up the search to help the man in the death house.

They began by enlisting the help of officials of the railroad line operating the fast *Silver Meteor* on which Rogers claimed to have been "riding blind baggage." They obtained the names of everyone known to have made up the crew on the run involved. Some already had left the company's employ and moved to other areas; others were quickly available for questioning.

Moving from place to place, the investigators sought to locate every railroadman who had been aboard the train at the time of Rogers' ride and especially to ascertain the identity of the "mechanic" who, it developed, could not have been a member of the regular crew. Two or three recalled having seen a man of his description but no one knew who he was, nor could anyone explain why he had been on the *Silver Meteor*.

As the inquiry went on, a few meager clues developed but they led only to disappointments. Relentlessly, the two men kept at their task, encouraged by offers of help from a few who recognized the importance of the search. Smith and Rhay knew that the odds were heavily against them but they were determined that the all-important witness must be found no matter how long it might take.

Their work on other aspects of the case was uncovering a number of surprising facts. They learned that police had found many fingerprints on the car that the soldiers claimed had been driven by Rogers. The steering wheel, especially, was well finger-marked. Experts had spent days comparing these with Rogers' prints. None of them matched.

Then they started looking into the conduct of several officers during the long hours when Rogers was being pressed for a confession. The prisoner already had given the investigators an almost incredible account of police brutality. The men from The Court were convinced that every detail must be checked and when they had completed this phase of their work they were satisfied that Rogers had spoken only the truth; that he not only had been severely beaten about the body and threatened with death but had been knocked to the floor many times by detectives who struck him over the head with the butts of their revolvers as they insisted that he tell them where he had hidden the murder weapon.

How desperately some of the Petersburg officers had tried to "persuade" Rogers to confess is still recorded in the files of The Court of Last Resort in this notation:

"The present Petersburg chief of police, Willard E. Traylor, then a sergeant, told us [The Court] that when he reported for duty that morning Rogers' entire back was covered with blood and that he himself was threatened with firing for asking why Rogers was beaten. Judge H. T. Wilson, who had presided over the trial, denounced the police vehemently for this beating."

Chief Traylor, who verified these facts, volunteered his help to Rhay and Smith and soon became one of their most valuable aides. Fully convinced of Rogers' innocence, he turned over to them vital records of the police investigation which they had tried unsuccessfully to obtain. He also became absorbed in the frustrating hunt for the missing "mechanic" and spent much time in sifting the mass of conflicting reports that were coming from many areas.

On the basis of evidence already uncovered, The Court had succeeded in having Rogers' execution deferred but he remained desolately in the death house, praying that the key man would be found.

Nearly a year of persistent search had passed when the two investigators, working closely with Traylor, stumbled on their first promising lead. It was one of those strange freaks of circumstance such as a writer of fiction might conjure in a mystery novel. They were told of someone who had heard of a conversation between two railroadmen, E. D. Foxworth and Robert D. Murray. These two had been amusing each other with tales of hobos riding the trains when Murray casually related how he had put one off of the *Silver Meteor* on a Sunday morning months before at Petersburg.

Days later Foxworth's mind turned to the story of the hobo. Suddenly he recalled vaguely the details of a newspaper item telling of the prolonged hunt for the vital witness. Realizing the significance of what he had heard, he decided that he must tell someone of it.

Grasping the importance of their information, Smith, Rhay, and Traylor soon located Foxworth who offered to cooperate and told them that Murray, a diesel supervisor, moving from one train to another, lived in Hamlet, North Carolina.

Hours later the three investigators were on an eastbound

plane. Luckily Murray was at home and he explained that while he never had heard of Rogers, he would give all possible help. He was taken at once to the Virginia penitentiary and the condemned man was called from his cell.

For minutes the railroadman stared silently at the prisoner, who returned Murray's gaze with a curious look, not suspectint that his life perhaps depended on what this stranger would say.

At last Murray looked up exclaiming: "That's him—the man I put off the train at Petersburg—almost a year ago." Recalling associated incidents, he was able to fix the time and Rogers' own statement in that respect was verified. The long-hunted key witness at last had given the condemned man an airtight alibi. The state's case collapsed like a pricked balloon.

Oliver Pollard, who had prosecuted Rogers, conceded that the identification made by the soldiers must be false and that Rogers had told the truth. No motive for the testimony of the servicemen was ever fully established though there were many surmises.

On the basis of these developments, the Virginia State Board of Pardons commuted Rogers' sentence to life imprisonment, ruling that still further investigation was needed before it would recommend a pardon.

Rogers was taken from the death house and the men working under Gardner and Steeger plunged into a remaining mass of details that called for still more painstaking inquiry.

Months before Smith had evinced interest in the expertness with which the man driving the soldiers had zigzagged in and out of traffic at high speed, finally maneuvering the car into the narrow walk by the hospital. "That was no ordinary driver," he had remarked to Rhay. "That man must be an expert."

Rogers, however, had told them that he had never driven a car and did not know how. The statement, of course, called for verification and Smith knew just how to proceed. He sent letters to the authorities in every state in which Rogers had

ever been—New York, Florida, and New Jersey—inquiring
whether a driver's license had ever been issued to him or if he
ever had been seen driving a machine.

He waited anxiously for replies. One by one state officials
responded that they had no record of Rogers either being
licensed to drive or of even having been issued a student
driver's permit. Neither had anyone ever seen him at the
wheel. One more important point was scored.

They turned next on another tack, eager to further disprove
the soldiers' story. The service men, once asked how they
could so easily identify Rogers with whom they said they had
ridden on a dark night, replied that they had observed his
features clearly many times when they lighted his cigarettes.

Rhay pursued this seemingly inconsequential fact. In a
short time he had proved to his satisfaction that Rogers did
not smoke and never had. He also learned, quite accidentally
—and significantly—that although the soldiers had testified to
being held in jail during the trial, they actually had been guests
at Peterburg's best hotel, with the city paying their bills.

Still The Court's detectives were not finished. Their per-
severence uncovered the independent work of another dedicated officer who, like Traylor, believed in getting the truth regardless of consequences. This man, Detective E. M. Parrish,
had arrived at headquarters on the morning of the murder
shortly after Rogers' arrival there as a suspect. Unable to stand
by while the prisoner was being beaten, Parrish had walked
out determined to look over the murder scene by himself and
without authority.

Concluding that the killer would have fled in a direction
opposite to the Appomattox Bridge where Rogers was found,
Parrish had calculated the fugitive's possible running speed,
and, with another officer, had set out in the hope of intercept-
ing him. On their way, they met pedestrians who reported
having seen a man slinking through vacant lots toward a railroad bridge. The officers took off in that direction and saw a
tall Negro hiding behind a pile of ties. Drawing their guns,

Parrish and his companion started after him but he started running. Together the policemen fired twelve shots at the fleeing figure but he dashed into a wooded area and could not be found. This man, they agreed, probably was the murderer of Policeman Hatchell but the officers in charge of the case evidently were content to proceed against Rogers on the statements of the soldiers without further inquiry.

With Parrish's disclosures, Gardner and Steeger, as well as Smith and Rhay, agreed that they had gathered sufficient evidence to establish Rogers' innocence beyond any doubt. They sent to Governor John S. Battle a fully documented history of their investigation and asked for a pardon.

The response came early in March 1953 when the Virginia Governor announced that he was granting Rogers an unconditional pardon. Hours later Rogers walked out of the penitentiary a free man. Nearly ten years had passed since his arrest.

The murderer of Policeman Hatchell has never been apprehended but an innocent man was saved from the electric chair through the efforts of The Court of Last Resort, with the aid of an honest, conscientious chief of police.

10

BORN FOR TROUBLE

One of the hundreds of reports in the bulky files of The Court of Last Resort opens with this statement:

"The murder of Maurice Pederson, retired saloonkeeper, set off the most bizarre series of events ever recorded in American police records."

The statement may be a bit exaggerated, but this case did include almost every element of drama and misfortune that could be crammed into the life of a single individual.

This person was Clarence Gilmore Boggie, an old-line logger in the Pacific Northwest, who apparently was born for trouble. Adversity constantly dogged his footsteps, for he emerged from one serious difficulty only to become involved in another. The murder of Maurice Pederson was but one chapter in the strange and troubled life of this unfortunate man.

When Erle Stanley Gardner and his associates first learned of the case, Boggie already had served more than ten years of a life sentence as the murderer of Maurice Pederson, a crime which he insisted he had not committed.

Pederson, a seventy-eight-year-old recluse, had been beaten to death in his shack in Spokane on Monday, June 26, 1933, by a man wielding a homemade bludgeon—a round rock wrapped tightly in burlap with its ends twisted and sewed together for a handle. The crime was mysterious in many ways.

The shack had been ransacked on the preceding Saturday by someone apparently searching for papers without thought of robbery. Pederson told friends that he knew who was responsible but did not want to notify the police.

On Monday morning neighbors, first attracted by sounds of a violent struggle and later by loud moans, found Pederson lying on his front porch brutally beaten and near death. Several women who had seen the assailant running from the place, chased him for several blocks until he disappeared in a wooded area.

Pederson died in a hospital a short time later and the police went into action. Hours afterward they apprehended a suspect and neighbors said he resembled the fugitive. One woman was certain that she had seen him loitering in the area some time before the attack. This man, however, declared that they were mistaken and said he had been miles away during the fateful morning hours.

His explanation was investigated and police announced that night that he had been released after his alibi had been verified conclusively.

Weeks passed without tangible clues and the murder finally was recorded as another unsolved crime.

Two and a half years later, through strange and unexpected circumstances, the finger of guilt suddenly pointed at Boggie. A former convict, held in an Idaho jail for robbery and suspected of a more serious crime in another state, had sought to ingratiate himself with the police by telling them that he could solve the Pederson murder. He declared that his one-time friend, Boggie, had boasted of the killing and had given him a pair of overalls and shoes, explaining that he had taken them from the victim.

Spokane authorities, elated by this disclosure, grasped the opportunity to clear an unsolved crime. Boggie, then in jail for another offense of which he claimed he was innocent, later was taken to Spokane where he tried vainly to explain that he knew nothing of the Pederson killing. Nevertheless, he was

identified by several women as the fleeing slayer, although two
of these witnesses previously had accused the earlier suspect
who had been released because of his alibi.

The positive identification of Boggie by these women was
strengthened materially when the accused man admitted own-
ership of an overcoat which Pederson's daughter readily recognized as her father's.

There was other incriminating evidence—the overalls and
shoes mentioned by the Idaho informer, who told detectives
that they could be found in the storeroom of a Spokane lodging house where Boggie often stayed and left his belongings.
These articles, recovered by police, were recognized by friends
of Pederson as his property. Added to this were statements by
neighbors of the murdered man that they had seen Boggie
loitering about the victim's shack a short time before the killing.

Such was the evidence massed against Boggie when he was
brought to trial and the prosecution made much of his two
previous convictions. Despite his vigorous assertion that he
was not in Spokane at the time of the murder, he was convicted early in December 1935 and sent to the Washington
State Penitentiary. There he gave all of his tobacco rations to
fellow prisoners who typed his letters to congressmen and
other officials pleading for help. No one seemed to be interested.

The tide began to turn in 1945, after more than ten years,
when Tom Smith became warden of the prison. Like his
predecessors, he listened to Boggie's long, fantastic story of a
life of trouble and regarded it as unbelievable. However, he
was impressed by the man's record of perfect conduct and his
help in solving some of the prison's mechanical problems. A
sympathetic person, Smith extended Boggie's privileges, permitting him to contact visitors more readily and to write to
more people for assistance.

The Reverend William A. Gilbert, rector of St. Paul's Epis-
copal Church in Walla Walla and a volunteer prison chaplain,

finally became interested in Boggie's case. He inquired into some of the details and satisfied himself that the man had spoken truthfully. The entire case, he decided, should be brought to the attention of The Court of Last Resort.

Being a man of action, the chaplain drove to Gardner's *rancho* in Southern California, taking with him the prisoner's lengthy letters and documents. These were studied by the two men for hours and Gardner agreed that the matter warranted his attention. In fact, he promised to go at once to the prison.

Brushing aside his own affairs, Gardner boarded a plane for the Northwest and interviewed Boggie in the penitentiary. They talked for an entire day but before the visit had ended Gardner's interest and curiosity had been aroused by one of the most fantastic life stories he had ever heard. Not only had Boggie discussed his trial for the Pederson murder, but he had related amazing details of a turbulent life that seemed wholly incredible. He even admitted having served two previous prison terms but insisted that he was not guilty of either crime. In one case, he said, he had been pardoned.

Gardner decided that this should be a major case for The Court's attention and Raymond Schindler, the agency's ace detective, soon was on a plane en route to Walla Walla.

In the prison reception room Schindler sat for hours listening to Boggie. After taking careful notes of the many complicated and essential facts, he decided to begin his inquiry from the start of Boggie's troubles rather than concern himself at once with the Pederson murder as a single episode.

In essential details, this was Boggie's story:

His first serious difficulty had occurred in Oregon years before when he was arrested for a bank robbery which, he declared, he did not even know had taken place.

Out of work and penniless, he was camping under a highway bridge when he saw a coat tossed from a car speeding across the overhead span. With no thought that the men in the machine were bank robbers, he grabbed the coat as a windfall and was trying it on when police, pursuing the bandits, caught sight of him and hurried to investigate. The coat pockets were stuffed with stolen currency.

Despite his explanation, Boggie was arrested, convicted and sent to the Oregon penitentiary where he remained for several years until, by good fortune, the robbers were captured and he was exonerated. A full pardon by Governor Julius Meier followed but Boggie was not out of trouble long.

He found a job in a logging camp and when it ended he moved to Spokane to look again for work. There, in a cheap Skid Row rooming house, he made friends with derelicts and former convicts. One of them he knew as Blackie, a hard character whom he had met in the Oregon prison and who later was to involve him in the Pederson murder. This man introduced him to a friend named Wallie and the two suggested that he accompany them to Missoula, Montana, where jobs were said to be plentiful. Neither explained what kind of jobs they had in mind and Boggie, always naïve and trusting, little suspected that they regarded him as a "dumb logger" who would fit well in their evil plans.

The departure was delayed for various reasons and Boggie, again without money, decided to start out alone, after first arranging to meet the others in Mullan, Idaho.

He hitchhiked out of Spokane and many miles away was given a long ride by an old prospector in a battered coupe. Near Coeur d'Alene the car broke down and Boggie, eager to lend a helping hand, volunteered to repair it—a good deed that was to repay him manyfold in later years.

Pushing the machine into a nearby service station, he borrowed tools, restored it to running order, and finally reached Mullan with his benefactor.

He met his friends and two strangers who had driven with them from Spokane. Boggie greeted them warmly and climbed into their car, not knowing that it had been stolen at gunpoint in a holdup and that its owner had been left tied to a pole. Only long afterward was he told that the bandits had eluded pursuing police in a gun battle in which a fifth member was wounded and abandoned.

After a short stay in Montana, the men drove back to Idaho and in a small town the car was left in Boggie's care while his companions started out on what they said was a business errand. On their return he learned that they had robbed a store and he flatly refused to accompany them further. Blackie angrily drew a revolver and compelled him to take the wheel.

They had traveled only a few miles when they were overtaken by pursuing police and arrested for both robberies. Boggie pleaded that he had had no part in either crime. The old prospector and the service station attendant, he explained, could easily establish his alibi for the first holdup. The police were not impressed and he was taken to jail at Saint Maries while Blackie and the others were held in Coeur d'Alene.

A few days later Boggie made a serious mistake. Believing that he could locate the two men as alibi witnesses, he escaped from jail but his search for the pair was futile. He hitchhiked to Portland, Oregon, and was soon apprehended as a jail breaker. Taken to Idaho for trial, he was convicted as an accomplice in the Mullan holdup and sentenced to a year in prison. What he did not know was that his erstwhile friend, Blackie, hoping to avoid extradition to Washington for a kidnaping, had told the authorities that Boggie was the murderer of Maurice Pederson. To strengthen his story, Blackie emphasized the shoes and overalls which he said Boggie had given him with the admission that they had been taken from Pederson.

Spokane authorities, advised of these developments, reviewed the cold records of the Pederson murder, more than two years before, and waited patiently for Boggie to be returned to them as soon as he had finished his prison term.

Despite his protests, Boggie was finally transferred to Spokane and charged with murder. A lawyer, engaged by his mother, did his best but he could not overcome a strong case presented by the prosecutor. Boggie was sentenced to the penitentiary for life.

This, in brief, was the involved, almost incredible story that challenged Raymond Schindler's skill as an investigator. Traveling constantly from one place to another, through three states, he verified bit by bit many of the essential facts. With the help of the Reverend Gilbert, the prison chaplain, he even succeeded in locating the prospector and the service station attendant in Idaho, and they supported Boggie's alibi for the first holdup near Mullan.

The detective then turned his attention to the Pederson murder, fully realizing that he would be obliged to delve into a crime more than twelve years after it had been committed. Some of the important witnesses had moved; others had forgotten vital details, but Schindler had not worked long before he was startled by strange circumstances and irregularities.

He learned to his surprise that witnesses who had seen the killer fleeing from the murder scene had readily identified Boggie more than two years later, although he differed widely from their original descriptions. They had pictured the fugitive as a large, heavy-set man with bushy hair and a fast gait. In no way did Boggie fit these details. He even walked with a decided limp. None of the eyewitnesses had seen the murderer's face and when they were called to look at Boggie, he was made to stand before them alone, rather than in the customary police lineup.

Schindler interviewed Pederson's daughter, Mrs. Emma L. Rolfe, who had told a judge in an earlier *habeas corpus* hearing that she was certain Boggie was not the murderer. Still of the same opinion, she recalled her father's last words, whispered to her as she leaned over his hospital bed a few moments before he died.

"Who did it?" she asked him.

"It was that porter who works for———," he answered feebly, naming a relative as the man's employer. The porter's name was given to the police but this was completely ignored. The reason was never learned.

Poring over every page of the trial transcript, Schindler discovered that one of the prosecution's most damning points concerned the overcoat that police had found in a room formerly occupied by Boggie. Pederson's daughter had identified it as having belonged to her father.

Boggie's explanation seemed almost impossible to believe. He told the investigator that he had bought the coat in a Portland pawnshop under peculiar circumstances. He had walked into the place at a moment when a customer, trying to pawn the garment, was arguing over money with the shopkeeper. Boggie had interrupted impatiently, offered the owner one dollar, and had bought the coat while the pawnbroker looked on bitterly over the loss of business.

Realizing the importance of verifying this statement—if, indeed, it could be verified—Schindler started out to find the owner of the store. Accompanied by Gardner, he followed a cold trail that took them south into Oregon and back again to Washington. When they finally had located this man after days of travel, he recalled the incident well and corroborated everything that Boggie had said. Another vital piece of prosecution evidence was exploded.

Schindler next chose to concern himself with two other important pieces of evidence in the prosecution's case—the overalls and shoes, supposedly belonging to Pederson, which Blackie claimed to have received from Boggie. After pursuing this tack for a considerable time, the detective established to his full satisfaction that the murdered man never had owned the overalls or the shoes, which were many sizes too large for him.

Although convinced by now of Boggie's innocence, Schindler was unprepared for his next disclosure. His attention had been drawn to the trial testimony of one of Pederson's neighbors who had identified Boggie as the man she saw running from the scene of the murder. Something in the manner of her examination in the courthouse had aroused his suspicions and he determined to satisfy his curiosity. He located this woman and was stunned by what she told him.

She related that she and her young son had seen the killer running from Pederson's home and had tried to follow him. The boy had almost forgotten the incident in the intervening years when he was visited at his school by an official a few days before Boggie's trial opened and told that he was wanted as a vital witness. He was advised that he should positively identify the defendant.

The lad demurred, stating that he had not seen the killer's face and therefore could not truthfully identify Boggie. Tempting rewards were suggested—a day out of school, witness fees, and the unusual opportunity of sitting in the witness chair in an important murder trial. The boy remained obdurate despite his visitor's persistence.

He was told again, more pointedly than before, that he was to swear that he had seen the fugitive's face and recognized the man on trial. In fact, he was assured that no public official would ever ask a boy to swear falsely in a courtroom. Still the youth refused and he was finally warned to say nothing of the interview to anyone.

That night, disregarding the warning, he told his mother what had occurred and she went with him to the official's office, bitterly accusing him of wrongdoing. Obviously, the boy was not called to testify.

Schindler asked for a chance to interview the boy but was told that he had died during Army service.

His mother had still more to tell. She advised Schindler that shortly after Boggie had been brought to Spokane to face trial, she had seen a prowler acting suspiciously about the Pederson house. This was only a few days after several weapons, closely resembling the oddly made bludgeon used in the murder, had been found in a nearby vacant lot. She had telephoned this information to the police but was curtly told, she said, that the murderer (Boggie) was already in custody.

Schindler still had much more to do. Boggie had claimed an alibi for the Pederson murder, insisting that he was in Portland, Oregon, when it occurred and that several people he would name could prove it. This, too, was corroborated.

It soon came time for the investigator to submit a complete report to the members of The Court of Last Resort. Gardner and Harry Steeger flew to Spokane where they met their investigator and the three presented their facts to the State Attorney General, Smith Troy, who listened attentively and declared that if Boggie was innocent he should be freed. Ed Lehan, one of Troy's ablest assistants, was assigned to study the reports and to undertake an inquiry of his own.

Some time later, Troy, satisfied that justice had miscarried, called on Governor Monrad C. Wallgren, with Steeger and Gardner to present a definite recommendation for pardon. The governor, equally anxious to see justice done, promised to study all of the findings and to investigate for himself.

He was seriously considering the matter when the Seattle *Times* unexpectedly became interested. One of its star reporters, Don Magnuson, who later became a member of the House of Representatives, had read accounts of the case in Steeger's *Argosy* magazine and concluded that Boggie was newsworthy. He wrote a number of articles for the *Times* and they attracted wide attention.

Before the series had been concluded, Magnuson listened to a surprising story that came to him over the telephone from a reader. This man advised the reporter that he was fully familiar with the Pederson murder; that, in fact, he knew the name of the killer. He had been unaware of Boggie's conviction and had wondered through the years how the actual murderer had escaped capture.

Realizing that he may have come upon the most sensational disclosure in the entire investigation, Magnuson hastened to meet his informant and listened to facts even more amazing than some which Schindler had unearthed.

This man, a former Spokane merchant, related that a

short time before the murder, a stranger had come into his store several times and that on one occasion he carried with him a bludgeon similar to the one with which Pederson had been murdered—a weapon commonly known as a sap.

On reading of the crime and seeing a newspaper reproduction of the weapon, the storekeeper had realized the importance of what he knew and had promptly called the police, telling them where this person could be found. Detectives had questioned him and learned that he had been near Pederson's house on the morning of the tragedy, though they were unable to establish his presence at the exact time of the killing.

This was the suspect, Magnuson learned later, who had been released by the police because he had an alibi. And the newsman's surprise grew even greater when he discovered that this was the same man who had been identified at the time of the murder by one woman who, two years later, had pointed to Boggie in court as the man she had seen running from Pederson's shack.

Informed of these developments, Gardner and Schindler hastened to Seattle, determined to find this man though years had passed since he had been permitted to slip away from the authorities. It was a difficult trail to follow and clues were few. With the help of Magnuson and his newspaper colleagues, they did trace him to Arizona but he had vanished there and months passed before he was finally located in jail at The Dalles, serving time for a minor offense.

As might have been expected, he denied all knowledge of the murder, although he did admit having been near Pederson's house some time before. However, after hours of grilling, he made a surprising admission which corroborated one of the most vital points in Boggie's behalf.

He told the investigators that he had been in Spokane weeks before the murder and had stolen an overcoat belonging to Pederson. "And what became of it?" one of the interrogators demanded.

"I sold it to a man in a Portland hockshop," he answered.

It was obvious that by a one-in-a-million coincidence he had sold Boggie the exact coat that had helped to send the unfortunate man to the penitentiary.

Members of The Court, gratified by their accomplishment, looked hopefully for action by the authorities against this man but they were bitterly disappointed. A short time later it was officially announced that there would be no prosecution. The reason given was that it would be impossible to obtain a conviction since several vital witnesses had died and others could not be located.

There were those who listened to this explanation with raised eyebrows, commenting that it was typical of the complacent attitude of some authorities toward reopening old cases in spite of serious errors. At all events, the law had spoken the final word and the prisoner was freed some time later. Nevertheless, The Court of Last Resort investigators did proceed with an extraordinary experiment that still further supported Boggie's innocence.

The man who had given the Seattle *Times* its original clue was taken to Spokane where police spread out before him an odd assortment of bludgeons, all somewhat similar to the murder weapon and he was asked if he could pick out the one he had seen in his store. He eyed them all closely, silently examining one after the other.

"Take your time," one of the officers told him. "See if you can possibly recognize the one you saw."

Tense moments passed and at last the man's hand fell on a single weapon. It was the exact one that had killed Maurice Pederson!

"How could you tell?" someone asked.

He quickly pointed to a peculiarity in the handle, an identifying mark that the police had overlooked.

It appeared now that Clarence Gilmore Boggie's innocence

had been fully established. Lehan, the attorney general's deputy, reported his final conclusions to his superior who, in turn, informed Governor Wallgren.

Late in December 1948 the governor signed a pardon that sent Boggie back into the free world after thirteen years in prison. The Court of Last Resort had spent fully three years and thousands of dollars in bringing about his vindication.

The investigation previously had won a pardon in the Montana holdup case and Boggie now returned to his old haunts after having been pardoned three times in three states for crimes of which he was completely innocent.

He resumed his former occupation, boasting that his long imprisonment had not impaired his strength or deprived him of his skill as a logger. Some time later he married a woman who had befriended him while he was in prison.

Swinging his ax in a lumber camp months afterward, he was stricken with a fatal heart attack. Boggie had been born for trouble but he died a free and happy man, thanks to The Court of Last Resort.

THE KLAN AT WORK

Visitors to Statesville Penitentiary in Illinois were accustomed to hearing the name of "Big Jim" Montgomery. "He don't belong here," some inmates said. "He's a lifer and he's been framed," others insisted.

While such talk had persisted for more than twenty years, it was rare in any "Big House" where traditionally every man is concerned only with himself and his own hope for freedom; where stories of innocence and deliberate "frame-ups" come from almost every cell. The other fellow's troubles are his own.

In Statesville, during this period, there was a constant, earnest solicitude for Montgomery, a stocky Negro, powerfully built, with the shoulders of a wrestler and a round, fleshy face. Quiet and reserved, he was not especially popular with the convicts and when he talked to them it was mostly about his own case. Yet of all the prisoners, he was singled out by them as their *cause célèbre*, a symbol of vicious persecution and injustice.

From time to time lawyers and friends of inmates, curious or sympathetic, left the penitentiary determined to inquire into Montgomery's fate and to learn the reason for such unusual and widespread interest. They ascertained that he had been a factory worker in Waukegan, Illinois, that he had been a law-abiding member of his community, and had owned two houses, one of which he rented while he occupied the other with his wife.

At thirty, all that he had worked for suddenly collapsed. It was then that a sixty-two-year-old white woman, Mamie Snow, had gone to police headquarters, bruised and battered, charging that Montgomery, whom she knew, had raped her in a cemetery.

Officers found him sitting quietly in front of a restaurant drinking a bottle of soda. Despite his protests, he was rushed to jail and later booked for rape. Days afterward the grand jury returned a formal indictment.

The trial had taken exactly twelve minutes. After Mamie Snow, the only witness, had identified Montgomery as her assailant, the prosecution rested. Neither the defendant nor his lawyer had said a word and the jury promptly returned a guilty verdict. He was sentenced to serve the remainder of his life in prison.

Such were the salient facts gleaned by those who inquired about Montgomery. Some who occasionally pressed with further questions, wondering whether a mistake might possibly have occurred, were ridiculed by the authorities who declared assuredly that "Big Jim" deserved his punishment; that there was no doubt of his guilt.

Long tedious years of mental torture dragged on for Jim Montgomery. At first he wrote scores of letters, pleading with officials to reopen his case; to at least investigate a number of points which he declared would easily prove his innocence. To his dismay he learned long afterward that the prison authorities had refused to mail his correspondence and that it had been destroyed.

His wife, convinced of his innocence, did her best for him. With few friends and only limited funds, she had pleaded desperately for a parole or even a shortening of his sentence. Rebuffed at every turn, she became seriously ill and was obliged to sell their property to meet bare living expenses.

As letters reached Montgomery with news of his wife's

increasing troubles, his anguish at times became almost un-
bearable, yet there seemed nothing more that could be done.
It was little solace that he had the sympathy of his fellow
prisoners and that they had made his case their cause, for
nothing ever came of promises made by visitors who offered
to intercede.

Montgomery's twenty-second year in prison had passed
when another ray of hope pierced the darkness of his life.
By now his black hair was turning gray and his once plump
face was drawn and flabby. By chance a widely known
Chicago attorney had visited the penitentiary in behalf of
several clients and had heard the incessant claims of prisoners
that an innocent man named Montgomery had been
"framed."

Luis Kutner, a relentless crusader for civil rights and a distinguished champion of the downtrodden, had listened cyni-
cally at first, for in his long legal career he had learned that
few men in prison ever admit their guilt. But as Kutner, on
frequent visits to the institution, heard the same talk from an
increasing number of inmates, he was moved to satisfy his
curiosity and decided to at least make some initial inquiries.
He chose to begin by interviewing the man.

Their first talk, lasting several hours, was the beginning of
an investigation that extended over three years during which
Kutner spent thousands of dollars of his own funds, besides
losing an estimated $100,000 in fees for legal services that
he had no time to render.

It was Montgomery's good fortune that a man of Luis Kutner's background, experience, and dedication to equal justice
had chosen to delve into the case, for this lawyer had become
nationally known through his success in exonerating hundreds
of men and women falsely accused of crimes in which they
had no part.

His concern with fair play began in 1922 at the age of
fourteen when he was arrested while angling for goldfish in a
Chicago park. A thoughtless patrolman locked him in a base-

ment cell of the police station and forgot to tell the sergeant. Two days later the boy, frightened and starving, was found by a janitor and sent home to his harried parents. Young Kutner decided then and there to become a lawyer and devote his life to fighting injustice.

Today, in his early fifties, Kutner is a powerful man, built like a fullback. Immaculate in appearance, his eyes sparkle and a neatly trimmed mustache adds a touch of distinction to his well-shaped features. By wrestling he keeps physically fit and finds relaxation at the piano, in painting, sculpturing, and writing poetry. He is a visiting associate professor at Yale Law School and for years has been president of the Commission for International Due Process of Law. Recently he won the commendation of lawyers by publishing a new book, *World Habeas Corpus*, which realistically presents the need for security of the individual against arbitrary detention and proposes an international court to deal with such cases.

Little, if any, of this background was known to Montgomery when he first met Kutner face to face in the prison reception room but he soon discovered that his visitor was an unusual person. Kutner lost no time in coming directly to the point.

"Well, Montgomery," he began, "I hear you don't belong here."

"That's right, Mr. Lawyer," the other answered, speaking quietly and without emotion. "But you know, color is evidence."

"Tell me all about it—from the beginning. I'm here to listen."

Montgomery began his story.

It had its beginning in 1923 during the heyday of the Ku Klux Klan, then a powerful organization operating openly and encouraged by police and prosecuting attorneys in some states. Waukegan, Illinois, where Montgomery lived and worked, was a hotbed of Klan strength and Negroes were not wanted there.

Montgomery related that in many instances some unscrupulous police officers and deputy sheriffs were in the habit of "planting" half-pint bottles of whisky in Negro homes which would be raided soon afterward. The liquor, then confiscated, would be used as evidence of bootlegging and the innocent householder would be sent to jail. It was one way of trying to keep Waukegan an "all-white town."

Militantly championing fair play, Montgomery decried such tactics and tried his best to arouse his people to resistance. Actually, he was calling on a small group of Negroes, without influence or money, to fight the powerful, hate-mongering Klan.

A devout churchgoer, he found it necessary to carry on much of his campaign alone, for most of his Negro neighbors were either too frightened to join him or too busy trying to earn a living. Montgomery was in better circumstances than most, for as a skilled worker for a steel and wire fence company, he earned a little more than $3000 a year—a good salary in those days.

The Klan soon found a way of bringing his drive for justice to an abrupt end. Police raided his flat in his absence and when Montgomery and his wife returned they found their home a shambles. Furniture was smashed, ornaments were broken, and most of their possessions were ruined.

While many a Negro in Waukegan would have accepted such an outrage as beyond redress and quietly moved away, Montgomery chose to assert his rights and refuse to be intimidated. The next day he called on the police chief and the state's attorney, threatening a civil action for damages to property and for trespassing. The authorities offered to pay him $600 and he accepted their check.

Montgomery did not suspect his doom was sealed for the Klan's plot against him was set to go into operation in less than two weeks. He did not learn the details until many years had passed. Thousands of Klansmen gathered at a picnic on a farm near Waukegan, determined to find an effective way of punishing Montgomery. A Negro with a sense of justice was not wanted in the town.

The Klan worked fast. On the following day Mamie Snow, who was known to be mentally deranged, walked into police headquarters and told the officers that Montgomery had raped her. She pointed to bruises on her head and face, declaring that he had inflicted them during a struggle.

Montgomery was arrested a short time later and although he vigorously denied any wrongdoing, he was held in jail while officers spent days coaching his accuser, who suddenly had become uncertain that he was actually her assailant. Three weeks passed and Montgomery's lawyer obtained his release by *habeas corpus* proceedings. Both hoped that the case was closed. They were sadly disappointed.

On the following day Montgomery was rearrested and Mamie Snow now asserted in his presence that she was positive in her identification.

"Now let me tell you what happened before my trial," the prisoner went on, as Kutner sat before him taking many notes. "I had a Negro lawyer named Horn—Chester C. Horn it was —and the Klansmen told him that if he even tried to have me acquitted he would be tarred and feathered. They threatened me with the same treatment if I testified and to prove that they meant business, the police beat me in my cell and pressed lighted cigarettes against my arms and legs. That's why I didn't even try to tell my story in court, and what's more, you ought to know . . ."

"Know what?" Kutner pressed. "Tell me everything—I'm listening."

"It was right after my lawyer had gotten me out on that writ. One of the police came to tell me that I'd be turned over to the Klan and lynched. 'Just like they do in Georgia,' he said, and he explained that he belonged to it himself."

Montgomery then related details of his twelve-minute trial, stating that the jurors had been selected before he even was brought into the courtroom.

"Now that's my story, Mr. Lawyer," he finally concluded, "and I hope you believe me. Just remember, I've been here for twenty-two years. Isn't that too much for something I didn't do?"

Kutner was impressed not only by the prisoner's attitude but by the manner in which he told his story. "It was a most unique situation," he recalled long afterward. "In the first place, I sat down with Montgomery because this was the first time that men in prison had ever told me of another inmate about whose case they felt so deeply. Ordinarily they are so concerned with their own troubles that they don't bother with those of anyone else. In this instance, it was very different.

"When I first met Montgomery and listened to his story, I was struck by his quiet dignity and the absence of the usual 'hang dog' look. He had a way that took me completely by surprise."

Although the lawyer was convinced that the man had told the truth, he realized that all of the facts required verification; that it would be necessary not only to check every detail since the arrest but to delve far into the background.

All attorneys, whether in civil or criminal practice, must be investigators. Many engage professionals for this type of work. Kutner, however, operates differently. Trained and skilled in crime detection, he always has insisted on personally carrying on his own inquiries, even to the most tedious and time-consuming leg work. And experience has taught him that on occasion harsh measures, sometimes even rough, must take the place of suave persuasion. The Montgomery case, he soon discovered, was one of these, yet he was not prepared for situations that would develop or for the shocking disclosures of racial bigotry and deliberate persecution that were to come.

First Kutner familiarized himself with the records and with the transcript of Montgomery's trial. Then he interviewed the prisoner's lawyer, who readily admitted that Klansmen had threatened him with a "tar and feather party" if he dared to make a single move to save his client. That corroborated one facet of Montgomery's story.

Through secret channels of his own, Kutner located a witness to the secret picnic of the Klan and was told at firsthand how the hooded men had vowed vengeance on the Negro.

With motive thus established, the attorney turned next to a point in the trial transcript that had aroused his curiosity and suspicions. Mamie Snow, sworn as the star witness for the prosecution, had been asked the simple question:

"Were you raped by Montgomery?"

Her reply was "Yes." The state abruptly closed its case. To Kutner's amazement no medical testimony had been offered to support her charge. Mamie Snow must be found and interrogated, Kutner reasoned. However, he soon learned to his dismay that she had been committed to an institution for the insane soon after the trial and had died there.

Delving further, he was advised that after first hearing the woman's accusation, the police had sent her to Victory Memorial Hospital in Waukegan for a medical examination. Kutner, curious that the history of the case contained no reference to the doctor's findings, decided to investigate in his own way.

He went to the hospital and, after identifying himself, asked to see the records pertaining to Mamie Snow. His request met with blunt refusal—the case was already more than twenty years old. No one knew where such records might be stored, and no one had time to look. It was as discouraging a reception as Kutner had received in his years of legal practice.

Determined, he returned to the hospital day after day, at different hours, repeating his request to different clerks. Always the answer was the same—until more than a week later when he encountered a young woman who listened attentively, then glanced furtively about to make certain that no one was within hearing distance.

"Come back tonight after nine," she whispered, "and I'll

let you into the basement. That's where we keep the old records."

Carrying overalls in a bag, the lawyer did as he was told and was escorted down a back stairway into the basement. There before him stood stacks of barrels and boxes crammed with papers. He now faced a needle in a haystack search, with no clue as to where to start. He decided to begin at the farthest end of the cellar and examine every record in every barrel. At four o'clock the next morning he left and returned home for a few hours' sleep. He had scanned hundreds of documents without success.

He was back the next night and the next. Eight nights of tantalizing search had passed with the contents of many barrels and crates still to be examined. Not until the tenth night, long after midnight, did he strike pay dirt. He had come to a heavy carton labeled DRUG BILLS and was about to ignore it when a strange impulse induced him to look inside. To his surprise, it contained reports of medical examinations—and from the year 1923!

Now Kutner worked at feverish pace, scanning one paper after another. At last he found the object of his hunt—a document bearing the signature of Dr. John E. Walter. It stated that he had examined Mamie Snow and had found no evidence of rape! Obviously the record, blasting the state's case against Montgomery, had been suppressed and carefully hidden!

The lawyer put his prize in his pocket and hurried away.

Locating Dr. Walter was not an easy task. The doctor had retired years before and no one seemed to know where he was. It took Kutner weeks to trace him to a suburb where he found a stubborn, gray-haired man, now seventy-six years of age, still afraid to talk about the case.

"I've come to find out everything that you can tell me about your examination of Mamie Snow in 1923," Kutner explained. "An innocent man's liberty depends on you."

Dr. Walter stared silently at his visitor and shrugged his shoulders.

"Come, come," the attorney insisted. "You're the man who can prove the innocence of a prisoner who's been locked up for twenty-two years for something he didn't do. Certainly you're going to help."

Again the other shrugged his shoulders. "Not me," he finally said, with a cold, determined look.

Exasperated, Kutner related the entire situation, beginning with his first meeting with Montgomery and finally coming to his recent discovery of the hidden record. Still Dr. Walter refused to talk.

Kutner, however, was not to be thwarted at the door of his goal. If extreme measures were necessary now, he was prepared to use them. "I'm only asking you to help another human being," he coaxed in a final plea.

"I've got to live in this town, man," the medic finally blurted. "And besides, don't go wasting your time. This man Montgomery is a nigger."

The lawyer no longer could keep his seat. Springing from his chair, he seized the aging doctor by his coat lapels, pulled him from behind a desk, and shoved him against a window. Pointing angrily to the sidewalk below, he curtly informed Dr. Walter that he would not hesitate to throw him out.

Pale and trembling, the physician jerked himself free and reluctantly promised to cooperate. Taxing his memory, he recalled that Mamie Snow had shown no signs of rape and confided that he had been greatly relieved at not being summoned to testify at the trial.

"You weren't alone when you examined her," Kutner pressed.

"There was a nurse with me, of course. I'll tell you her name but you'll have to find her. I have only a vague idea where she might be now."

That started the attorney on another search, a long one, for in more than twenty years the woman had been forgotten by many of her friends. Kutner remained stubbornly on the trail, following meager clues, until someone gave him an address in the most dilapidated quarter of Waukegan.

He finally knocked on the basement door of a filthy shack near ruin and was admitted by a wrinkled, toothless woman, trembling as with palsy. Before him was a scene of squalor such as he had rarely seen. A rotting floor was strewn with medicine bottles and the stench was almost beyond endurance.

With difficulty he explained his mission, trying to turn the woman's memory back into the past. More than an hour elapsed before she could even recall the case of Mamie Snow, but at last she verified all that Dr. Walter had said and offered what help she could give.

Jubilant, Kutner returned to his office and moved to other factors of the case. A week later he learned to his dismay that the nurse was dead. Now he would be obliged to depend only on Dr. Walter and there was little certainty that the frightened, aged man would keep his word.

Much work still remained. Kutner knew that motive was a vital element in the case, that the Klan plot must be proved beyond the slightest doubt. How to do it was a problem. The man who had attended the picnic of the plotters obviously could not be called to court. How then could his story be corroborated?

After much thought and deliberation, the attorney concluded that ends sometimes justify the means. He evolved a plan that called for strong and courageous men—men whose proven loyalty to him could be depended on. He found their names in his files of the innocents whom he had freed in previous years.

Then he sent for three of the most stalwart and unfolded a daring scheme. He spared no words in explaining the risks involved and asked if they would help. "I won't blame you if you refuse," he told them. "Think before you answer."

Not a man hesitated.

The time was set for two o'clock in the morning four days hence. The place was the headquarters of the Ku Klux Klan in Waukegan. There, if Kutner's reasoning was correct, he should find some documentary evidence of an organized plot against Jim Montgomery.

Long after midnight, under cover of darkness, the lawyer and his volunteers assembled close to the offices of the Klan. Following plans that had been carefully made and well rehearsed, one of Kutner's former clients took his post at the north end of the building. Another stationed himself well to the south.

Signals were exchanged. Then, with a hurried glance in all directions, Attorney Kutner and the third man forced their way into the place and cautiously began to search the files.

An hour passed, then two and more as the men worked fast against the approach of dawn. Then, suddenly, they came upon what they wanted—an old document with precise directions for executing the diabolical plot against Jim Montgomery.

Kutner was elated but he had still more to do. He now must learn more of the circumstances under which Mamie Snow had finally made positive identification of the man she accused.

By uncovering hidden records and interviewing officers long retired, he finally came upon surprising facts. Only a day after the woman had made her charges, she was confronted with Montgomery in the jail and asked if she could identify him. "No, I cannot," she answered. "I am not going to lie." The same reply came a day later in the district attorney's office, yet at the trial she had sworn that he was her attacker.

The final disclosure was made in the institution where Mamie Snow had died hopelessly insane. It was a document revealing that she had gone to her grave chaste—a virgin. She was a member of a religious cult that made chastity mandatory.

Kutner now abandoned his role of investigator and resumed

the functions of a lawyer. Confident that at last he had accumulated all of the necessary evidence, he petitioned for Montgomery's release on a writ of *habeas corpus*. The hearing was set for June 27, 1949, before Judge Michael L. Igoe of the United States District Court in Chicago. More than three years had passed since Montgomery and the lawyer first had met in Joliet. Ironically, the judge who had tried Montgomery, the state's prosecutor, and the complaining witness all were dead.

The courtroom was crowded when Kutner entered, carrying bulging briefcases, and walked briskly to his place before the bench. After a few formalities he was on his feet, launching an argument that continued for hours.

First he explained how he had become interested in the case. Then, without restraint, he began tearing away the veil of mystery and intrigue. He spared no one, naming police and prosecuting officials as he went on, exposing what he characterized as a plot inspired by racial bigotry and executed by authorities in connivance with the Ku Klux Klan.

He took the judge through every step of his investigation, detailing his procedures and explaining the significance of what he had uncovered. The suppressed medical report of Mamie Snow's examination was exhibited as were the records of the Klan. It was a daring exposé in which Kutner frequently reverted to his role of master detective.

At one point Judge Igoe interrupted to inquire how the lawyer had gained possession of the secret documents of the Klansmen. Kutner did not hesitate to answer:

"We stole them, Judge."

A faint smile came on the jurist's face but he made no comment.

Kutner resumed his presentation, interrupted occasionally by the state's attorney with repeated demands that the case be transferred to a state court but Judge Igoe was adamant and motioned to defense counsel to proceed.

Long afterward Kutner came to a sudden pause. As spectators exchanged puzzled looks, he called out in loud, clear voice:

"Will Dr. John E. Walter please take the stand."

In the rear of the courtroom the seventy-six-year-old gray-haired doctor rose and walked slowly forward, a forgotten man whose unexpected appearance took everyone by surprise.

Speaking slowly, Kutner led his witness back more than a quarter of a century, helping him to recall the circumstances of Mamie Snow's visit to the hospital. "Was her clothing disarrayed?" he asked.

"No."

"You examined her for evidence of rape?"

"I did."

"And what did your examination show?"

"It showed that she was a virgin."

More questions followed and Kutner finally fired his parting shot:

"When you found that you were not being called as a witness, why didn't you go the prosecutor and tell him what you knew?"

Dr. Walter wet his lips and shifted nervously in his chair. "He was a man who was very determined," he answered with some hesitation. "He wanted his own way and if he didn't get it there was trouble—and I'm not a fellow who looks for trouble."

Here Kutner rested his case and the court announced that it would be taken under advisement.

The decision came less than two months later—on August 10—and it was front-page news in many cities. In one of the most significant judgments ever handed down in a federal court, Judge Igoe branded Montgomery's trial "a sham" and excoriated the law-enforcement officials and the Klansmen who, he pointed out, had connived to put Montgomery in prison. He declared that Mamie Snow was "a person of ir-

responsible mentality" who had not been raped by Montgomery or by anyone else.

"Society cannot suppress lawlessness by means of lawlessness in prosecution," he went on. "Society cannot inspire
respect for law by withholding the protection of law from
those accused of crime. It was and is the prosecuting attorney's
duty to assist in giving a fair trial to the defendant."

Noting that the prosecution had suppressed material evidence which would have resulted in an acquittal, the court
observed:

"To condone the method of evidence in this case is to
invite grave injustice." He added that such a perversion of
justice must be brought to light "where the public can
scrutinize it and take such steps as are necessary to insure a
true rendition of justice to all, regardless of race, creed, or
color."

At the judge's order Montgomery rose slowly to his feet,
a white-haired man, stooped with the weight of more than
twenty-five years behind prison bars. As his wife, Santoria,
and a sister listened anxiously, the court spoke the words that
opened prison gates with an unconditional pardon.

Tearfully, Montgomery embraced the women and reached
for Kutner's hand. "I'm fifty-six today," he sobbed, "and this
is the greatest birthday present of my life."

While jubilant friends milled about the happy man, a
prison official handed him $10, the state's allowance to very
discharged prisoner—but the matter was not yet closed. Kutner and many newspapers had much to say.

The New York *Times*, reporting the judge's ruling in its
issue of August 11, 1949, stated:

"In freeing Mr. Montgomery, Judge Igoe said that the trial
procedure was dominated by the State's Attorney, that the
State's Attorney threatened retaliation by the Ku Klux Klan
if Mr. Montgomery or his counsel attempted any defense and
that the issue at the trial was not the guilt or innocence of
the accused, but racial subjugation."

In other cities newspapers editorialized on the social implications of the case. Said the Chicago *Sun-Times* on August 16, 1949:

"The case is so shocking, indeed, that it should make Illinois citizens sick at heart. Assuming that the facts are as Judge Igoe found them to be, James Montgomery was the victim of ghastly injustice. What can Illinois do about it? One obvious duty is to compensate Montgomery for the 25 years of useful life which the state took away from him. Beyond this looms the more important question of how Illinois can attain a system of criminal law administration in which such cases won't happen. The fact that there has been one such case brings the question: How many other James Montgomerys are there in our prisons? How many other men are being victimized because their constitutional rights to a fair trial were flagrantly violated?"

Urging adequate compensation for the freed man, the New York *Sun*, on August 12, 1949, said in an editorial:

"Money, although it should be coming, does not fill the bill. It must be accompanied by general determination to stamp out racial prejudices that provoke such outrages."

The St. Paul *Dispatch* asserted:

"The hysteria of racial discrimination is a serious blot on our national records, and its manifestation in any and every form must be compensated with every resource at our command."

Many other newspapers joined in denouncing the injustice suffered by Montgomery and insisted that he must be compensated financially, at least for his loss of earnings if not for false imprisonment. Kutner lost no time in pressing his demands.

First he filed a formal claim with then Governor Adlai E. Stevenson, asking for $150,000. He reached this figure by calculating Montgomery's loss for twenty-five years of the

$3000 annual wage he was earning when arrested. For those years he would have earned $75,000. An equal amount, the lawyer contended, should be paid as "punitive recompense and indemnification."

In reply he received a letter from the governor's administrative assistant expressing regret that the state could not give compensation. There were no available funds, he stated, explaining that such a claim could be met only by legislative action.

Still determined, Kutner filed a new demand in the Illinois Court of Claims and was given a lengthy hearing before Commissioner George M. Tearney on February 1, 1950. Again the lawyer reviewed the entire matter, even citing newspaper editorials to support his claim that Montgomery was entitled to financial compensation.

The Claims Court finally signed a decree granting Montgomery the full amount requested but noted that funds could come only through a special legislative appropriation. Year after year bills have been introduced for payment of the long-overdue sum but in each instance they have died in committee.

As to Kutner, his only rewards for three years of unpaid work and more than $5000 spent out of his own pocket have been his satisfaction and the privilege of serving as best man when Montgomery remarried after his wife's death some time following his liberation.

On the opposite side of the ledger, the lawyer lost three of his best-paying clients because he had defended a Negro and fought the Klan. Yet this was not all. Ironically, the Internal Revenue Service rejected an income tax deduction of $5000 which Kutner had taken on the basis of his personal expenses, and he was obliged to pay the disallowed deduction as well as penalties and interest.

A warm friendship that had developed between client and lawyer continued until July 9, 1962, when Montgomery died at the age of seventy after enjoying slightly less than thirteen years of freedom.

Whether his widow and his sister have a claim against the State of Illinois for his years of imprisonment remains a subject of discussion.

12

HIDDEN EARS

Reno's vigorous, hard-hitting district attorney, William Raggio, was marked for vengeance. He had angered the underworld by daring to arrest one of its most powerful figures, Joe Conforte, who had ignored an order to leave Washoe County and stay out. For his defiance, considering himself well above the law, Conforte now faced the humiliating charge of vagrancy.

In the mind of the resentful racketeer a plot was born—a scheme that could lead Raggio not only to political ruin but even to the penitentiary. Such a downfall for a dedicated public official might have been accomplished but for an intricate little electronic device in the hands of a detective who knew how to use it expertly.

Joe Conforte's maneuver began on a late Friday afternoon —November 13, 1959—with the aid of a young woman as a lure. But with a prosecutor's intuition, the district attorney readily sensed the possibility of a plot. He decided to play out the role of an unsuspecting victim in the hope of trapping those involved. As events developed, however, Raggio acted his part a bit too well.

The scheme had its beginning when District Attorney Raggio's receptionist announced that "a Mrs. Newton" wished to see him. A moment later he looked up from his desk as an attractive, dark-haired young woman, neatly dressed, glided into his office and seated herself in one of his overstuffed leather chairs. He noted that, deliberately or not, she had taken care to cross her legs in a way that amply displayed their shapeliness. Her makeup items—lipstick, rouge, and mascara —were perhaps just a shade overdone.

"What can I do for you?" he inquired formally.

"A divorce," she answered in a subdued voice.

There was nothing unusual about this simple statement— Reno permits its low-paid district attorney to engage in private practice.

"May I have your name and address?" Raggio asked his visitor, reaching for a pad and pencil.

"It's Jacqueline Newton," she answered, "but just call me Jackie."

"Now tell me—Mrs. Newton," the attorney pressed, ignoring the suggestion of informality. "Who recommended me?"

His new client lowered her eyes modestly and then looked up. "Call it luck, maybe," she said. "Coming up from San Diego I asked a woman on the bus who was a good lawyer in Reno and she gave me your name. You're Bill Raggio, of course?"

"William Raggio," he corrected. "You know that six weeks' legal residence here is required."

"Yes, I'm aware of that. Perhaps you could help me find a little apartment somewhere."

Raggio ignored the suggestion and went ahead with routine questions. She said that she was twenty-two years of age; that she had been a "carhop" in San Diego, where she had fallen in love with a sailor named Newton. They had decided suddenly to drive to Tiajuana and be married. Within a week they both had realized that their marriage was a mistake and agreed to go their separate ways.

"I'm not sure I'll have time to handle the case," Raggio commented. "My schedule is rather full right now."

"Oh, please," Jackie Newton pleaded. She leaned forward to open her handbag and take out a cigarette. Her posture accentuated the low neckline of her bodice and Raggio sensed that the move had been calculated. "But you will, won't you?" she went on. "I've got the down payment—the retainer, I guess you call it." Then she placed some currency on his desk.

"All right, then," Raggio asserted. "I'll got in touch with you on Monday. Where will you be staying?"

The girl shook her head. "I don't know—I'm a stranger here. Couldn't you help me find a hotel for the time being?"

Raggio, after making a phone call, escorted Jackie to the reception desk of a nearby hotel. "I'll see you Monday," he repeated, as he left her there and hurried away.

He was deeply engrossed in work the next morning when his desk telephone rang and he readily recognized the voice.

"This is Jackie and I . . ."

"I said I'd get in touch with you on Monday," the lawyer interrupted severely.

"But I have a few questions I want to ask. I've never been through this sort of thing before."

"They can wait—remember I'm calling you Monday," Raggio concluded abruptly and hung up.

By now, Raggio was quite convinced that a plot of some kind was behind his new "client's" case. There was no reason at this time to suspect Conforte's involvement but he concluded that it would be well to proceed with the matter, hoping that before long he might uncover the young woman's real purpose. He did not have long to wait.

The prosecutor had resumed work on a brief when his secretary entered a half hour later to announce that Mrs. Newton was in the reception room and insisted on seeing her attorney. A few moments later Jackie, now clad in a tight, form-fitting dress, stepped into Raggio's private office.

"Didn't I tell you that I'd call you Monday?" the district attorney said coldly.

"Yes, but I'm so troubled and—and you're so sweet."

"Never mind me—just what do you want now? I'm busy."

The girl proceeded with an array of questions obviously intended only to make conversation and to prolong her visit.

Finally she took her handkerchief and dabbed her eyes. "It's awfully lonesome around here," she said tearfully. "Could I possibly persuade you to have a drink with me somewhere?"

It was then that the prosecutor, intent on fathoming the mystery of Mrs. Newton's maneuvers, overacted and made his first misstep. "I'll take you back to your hotel," he told her. "We can have one there."

As they sat down together at the hotel bar, the district attorney looked about for someone he might know and his eye luckily fell upon a friend, the hotel's press agent. Raggio, already realizing his mistake, beckoned to him to join them and the three engaged in a round of drinks. The prosecutor was about to leave when Jackie Newton suddenly swayed on the bar stool. "I'm going to faint," she gasped.

The publicity man quickly obtained a glass of water from the bartender and Jackie soon was revived. "I'll be okay," she said softly. "Just get me to my room so I can lie down."

Raggio again realized that he must protect himself at all costs. He told the girl to wait a moment and hurried to the side of his friend, the press agent. "This thing is more phony than I thought," he whispered. "Take her to her room and I'll stay down here. If everything is on the up and up, ring for a drink. It'll be my signal to come up. I've got to get to the bottom of this business somehow."

The district attorney waited by the bar and after a time heard an order given for a drink to be sent to room 610—the prearranged signal. Still acting out his role of unsuspecting lawyer, he took the elevator and was admitted to the room by the publicist, who nodded in the direction of the bathroom. "She seems okay," he said. "Guess she'll be out in a moment."

It did not take Jackie Newton long to emerge and now she was wearing a skin-tight sweater and Capri pants. "I feel better now," she announced. "Like my outfit, Bill?"

Raggio ignored the question and prepared to leave, but he was held back by his client's questions, all mixed with a by-play of small talk intended to convey the suggestion that he remain with her.

If he had needed further confirmation of his suspicions, the girl's words and actions had provided them but he was still to learn the ramifications of the plot. He took the hotel man by the arm and stepped to the door, promising Jackie Newton that he would still contact her on Monday.

That night he related the episode to his wife and assured her that he would be on his guard.

Monday's developments strongly indicated the nature of the plot and Raggio realized that it was far more dangerous than he had suspected. When a call to the hotel disclosed that his client had checked out without leaving a forwarding address, he started inquiries. A bellboy told him that Mrs. Newton had driven away with Joe Conforte!

It was now more than obvious that Conforte had used the woman in an attempt to compromise the prosecutor in retaliation for the vagrancy charge. The lawyer already knew that Conforte had bragged that he would "even things up" before his trial which was to start before a jury in four days.

There had been open warfare between the two for some time. Conforte, a one-time cab driver, had gained wealth and underworld power from bawdy houses in five counties other than Washoe County of which Reno is the county seat. Once he had owned several such places. Tough and confident, he boasted of his influence and insisted that he was a legitimate night-club operator. He was a lavish spender and liked to drive through crowded Reno streets in his flashy car filled with well-dressed members of the demimonde. He chose to think of himself as a little Al Capone.

To such a man a vagrancy charge naturally was an outright insult. His pride was sorely hurt and he determined to show his contempt for the man responsible. His plot had not succeeded as he had planned but Conforte was not one to be easily thwarted.

His next move came late on the Monday that Raggio was

to have met Mrs. Newton. The district attorney, to his surprise, received a phone call from Conforte's lawyer. "My client, Conforte, would like to talk with you," the attorney said.

"Tell him he knows where I'm located," Raggio answered curtly.

"No, he won't go there—but he'll meet you in my office. He says it's important—very important."

Sensing what Conforte might have in mind, Raggio decided to comply but insisted that for obvious reasons it must be a night meeting. The other readily consented and 8:30 the next night was agreed upon.

The phone call and the events preceding it already had convinced the district attorney that he required professional help of a sort outside his legal field. He put in a call for the man he needed—Harold K. Lipset of San Francisco.

Through more than twelve years of fruitful and often dramatic service to lawyers, businessmen, and many others, Lipset had established a reputation as a skillful private investigator, especially resourceful in the use of electronic listening devices. He had installed them in places and in situations that at first seemed impossible. Lipset had become famed not only as an unusual "private eye" but as an ingenious "private ear" as well.

His career in this field really began when he donned an Army uniform in 1941 and found himself in a basic training school for Military Police. As a commissioned officer, he was later admitted to a criminal investigation school in charge of Melvin Purvis, the celebrated FBI agent, then a colonel. After graduation, Lipset was sent overseas to command an investigation unit of the Army. He returned to civilian life wearing a coveted decoration.

In military service Lipset had learned much about the latest advances in listening devices. They fascinated him and, realizing their potential in civil as well as criminal cases, he

determined to build a career as a private investigator, special-
izing in their use.

Tall and young appearing, with a slender frame and crewcut
brown hair, he does not look the part he plays. His black Ivy
League clothes and heavy horn-rimmed glasses give him the
appearance of a successful business executive. His equipment today is the most modern available and represents an
investment of more than $25,000. He can secrete a recording
device in a room, confident that it will start recording at the
sound of a voice and continue in operation for five full days
without attention. He has metal detectors capable of uncovering hidden microphones. Lest his own operations be thwarted
by similar means, he has found a way to hide a mike deep
enough in a wall to rob the detector of its power. Tiny holes
lead to a plastic tube that carries sound to the microphone.
Should a window intervene in the passage of sound, he can
focus an ultrasonic beam on the glass and convert it into a
sounding board.

Lipset himself wears a small-sized recording machine.
Once, while being questioned by a Senate Committee on
constitutional rights, he was asked about these devices. In reply, he promptly peeled off his coat, displaying a tiny one
strapped under his armpit.

He likes to point out that his equipment can find out in
a day what it would take a month through plodding methods
of the old school, and can establish innocence or guilt against
a burden of contrary evidence. "When a private eye can get
the evidence to upset groundless charges," he says, "there is
real cause for rejoicing."

Once he trailed the plaintiff in a sensational paternity suit
from one part of Europe to the other and returned with twelve
rolls of recording tape that revealed the accuser as joking over
the charges brought against a "sucker." The judge threw the
$125,000 suit out of court, saving the marriage of an in-
fluential Hollywood producer. On another occasion he res-
cued a prominent businessman from a probable prison term

by taping the confession of the government's star witness, who admitted he had deliberately withheld the fact that a large shipment of merchandise was stolen property.

Once, with a tiny recording device concealed under his vest, Lipset visited a young woman who had testified that a professional man's breath "reeked with liquor" shortly before his arrest as a drunken driver. Conversing unsuspectingly with the investigator, she admitted that she had not been close enough to the accused man to smell his breath; in fact she had been a considerable distance from him. When the trial judge heard a recording of her admission, he promptly exonerated the defendant.

In the Reno case, Lipset lost no time in responding to Raggio's call for help. He gathered up his equipment and flew to Nevada with his assistant, Ralph H. Bertsche, whose technical skill has helped to produce many of the devices that Lipset uses.

Raggio told the investigator that to comply with the law he already had secretly obtained the court's permission to "bug" the office of Conforte's lawyer, since he believed that the Newton woman had tried to frame him and that blackmail would be attempted at the night meeting. His only protection, he insisted, lay in secretly recording the conversation.

Lipset accompanied the district attorney to the downtown building where Conforte's lawyer had his office and surveyed the scene with an experienced eye. His delicate task was simplified by two fortunate and unexpected developments. He soon discovered that there was an empty room directly above that of Conforte's counsel. That attorney, some hours earlier, had telephoned his wife saying that he would be detained in another city, that he could not attend the meeting, and that she should give Raggio the office keys.

When Lipset had finished an hour later, a thin wire connecting with a recording machine in the vacant room had been securely hidden deep in the grill work of the air conditioner in the office on the lower floor. A short-wave microphone had been secreted behind a stack of law books and, in case the meeting would not take place there, a similar device was placed under a desk in the reception room. These, too, were connected with the receiving equipment overhead.

Conforte arrived on time and looked suspiciously about. He even inquired whether the place might be "bugged." Several times during the meeting with Raggio which lasted more than an hour, he interrupted to repeat the question, even insisting that the district attorney remove his coat to prove that he had no listening device.

Conforte made it clear that he was not only accusing Raggio of betraying the Newton girl but was proposing a bargain. He would "forget" the entire matter if the district attorney would agree to dismiss the vagrancy charge and publicly apologize for the arrest.

When the recordings were transcribed they filled more than one hundred closely typewritten pages. Typical of the conversation were these excerpts:

CONFORTE: Any bugs around here?

RAGGIO: I haven't got any bugs on me at all. See—I'm emptying my pockets. Now you do the same and take off your coat.

CONFORTE: I'll take your word for it.

(*Both men dig into each other's pockets. Conforte again inspects rooms.*)

RAGGIO: Well, come to the point. Put your cards on the table.

CONFORTE: Okay. This mother of this child—the child's under eighteen—she came to me and she says, "Joe, something happened to my daughter, Joe. Something happened to my daughter. I want advice. What should I do?"

RAGGIO: Go on.

CONFORTE: I told her to let me talk to Raggio first and I can advise her one way or the other. But I'll bet you, Raggio, the attorney general will take this case. I'll make him governor next year.

RAGGIO: Quit talking in riddles.

CONFORTE: If this hits every paper in the country, you might as well pack up and get out. This mother says you did it Saturday . . . at the hotel.

RAGGIO: If you're talking about Jackie Newton, she's a divorce client.

CONFORTE: She's under eighteen. What do you call that? Some kind of rape?

Then followed a long conversation in which Conforte promised that the Newton matter would be forgotten if the vagrancy charge against the racketeer was dismissed and the district attorney made a public apology.

CONFORTE: Dismissal ain't enough. You got to say like this: "Your Honor, we made a thorough research and we realize now that this case is out of our jurisdiction. We ask a dismissal and I want to apologize to Mr. Conforte because he was picked up erroneously—erroneously, do you hear? I want that word said.

At this point Raggio, feigning worry, promised to think it over for a few days and to have the vagrancy trial postponed. With this, the interview ended. Conforte departed and the district attorney, some time later, went upstairs to listen to the taped recording.

On the following day he went into court and swore to a complaint charging Conforte with extortion by intimidation. Hours later the racketeer, protesting vigorously, was arrested and promptly posted bail for his release.

Lipset, however, had finished only half of his work. His next job was to find Jackie Newton and to prove through her that she had been used as a dupe to blackmail a public official. Now he turned to the role of conventional detective.

Who really was Jackie Newton and where was she now? Her name did not appear in any Nevada city directory or telephone book. Inquiries around Reno gambling places brought no results. So Lipset decided to pursue another clue. Jackie had told Raggio the name of the sailor from whom she wanted a divorce. That seemed a possible lead until the investigator found that no such person was on the ship that the woman had mentioned. Neither was there a record of the marriage. Lipset then queried the Navy Department in Washington and was advised that such a sailor lived in Yuba City in northern California.

This man finally was located but he denied that he ever had been married to a Jackie Newton. He did recall, however, that he once had known a girl named Jackie who then lived on a ranch in Yuba City. The detective hastened there only to find that the family had moved. The new occupant gave him a forwarding address—and still more valuable information. He was told that there were two daughters and that Elsie, the elder, a prostitute, had been held in contempt for defying a grand jury investigating vice. Her younger sister was known as Jackie and her description fitted perfectly that of Raggio's mysterious client.

Lipset, starting on a new trail, soon discovered that a relative of the girls once had served in the Navy on the ship named by Mrs. Newton. New pieces were being fitted into a mosaic of facts.

The girls' mother finally was located in San Diego and the mystery began to clear. She told Lipset that Conforte, with whom her daughter Elsie was in love, had fabricated a plot to frighten Raggio into dropping the vagrancy charge. Months before, Elsie had come home and taken Jackie away with her. The mother said she hoped to hear from Jackie in a few days and would get her address.

Lipset's wait was rewarded when the mother called him and gave Jackie's telephone number in San Francisco. A few hours later he was in an apartment, listening to the confession of a frightened, repentant girl. "They wanted me to get in bed with Mr. Raggio in my room," she said, "but, as you know, there wasn't a chance. But Joe told me I'd have to stick to the story he'd made up and tell them we had an affair together."

Since the futile affair in Reno the girl said she had been kept a virtual prisoner of her sister and Conforte, being moved from one place to another. She was pregnant now, having been duped in Seattle and locked in a room with a stranger. Conforte, she said, planned to blame Raggio for her condition.

Indignant now over her betrayal, she promised to tell the whole sordid story in court but Lipset was unwilling to risk another abduction. He kept her in hiding until Conforte's trial on the extortion charge was well under way before Judge Jon Collins, who understood the background of the case and took the precaution of ordering the jury of eight men and four women to remain in the sheriff's custody.

At the proper time Jackie was called as the state's star witness and related the entire story of her experience. Conforte's lawyer subjected her to bitter cross-examination but she could not be shaken. It was a bad day for the defendant and his luck was not to improve.

Elsie took the stand as the main witness for the defense and swore that the plot was solely her own idea, promoted by a desire to even the score with the district attorney, who had asked for her indictment when she defied the grand jury. Conforte, she testified, was only trying to help her. She admitted that she had hid in a closet of her sister's hotel room, hoping to trap the district attorney in compromising conduct with the girl while he was in her room. She was frank in relating her disappointment.

The jury seemed even less impressed when Conforte followed Elsie to the stand to deny that extortion or blackmail was in his mind when he talked to Raggio. He swore that he had merely suggested a friendly way in which one could help the other.

Conforte was found guilty of extortion and sentenced to serve from three to five years in the Nevada State Penitentiary in Carson City. His lawyers appealed to the State Supreme Court which months later rendered a decision sustaining Conforte's conviction, and the one-time racketeer entered the state prison to serve his sentence for a conspiracy that failed.

As for Lipset, he recorded the close of another successful case, grateful that with the help of his hidden microphones he had saved an innocent public official from a plot that might have ended in prison and disgrace.

13

THE TRUTH WILL OUT

Four shots in quick succession and a woman's screams broke the late night stillness of a rural area near the little town of West Shelby, far in the north of New York State.

Awakened by the unusual noise, a farm laborer, Charles F. Stielow, jumped out of bed and raised his window. Seeing nothing, he returned to his covers, suspecting that a troublesome family nearby was quarreling again.

For Stielow, however, those four shots were the beginning of a grim chain of circumstances that sent him to the penitentiary, sentenced to the electric chair.

For George H. Bond, an astute former district attorney and a shrewd criminal lawyer, they were to lead him into the most sensational investigation of murder in his long career, taxing his unusual skill in crime detection. But years passed before the two would meet.

The gunfire occurred on Sunday night, March 21, 1915, at about eleven o'clock. Six hours later Stielow arose and dressed, planning to follow his custom of crossing the road to the farmhouse of his seventy-year-old employer, Charles B. Phelps, where he would perform his early morning chores before turning to the day's work in the fields. His routine, however, was interrupted by unexpected tragedy.

Opening his front door, Stielow was shocked by the sight of a woman's body stretched across the front porch. He

quickly recognized the still form as that of Phelps's housekeeper, Margaret Wolcott. She was dressed only in her nightclothes and Stielow noted a bloodstained bullet hole in her
garment close to the heart.

He ran frantically to the Phelps home and rushed through
the partly open kitchen door. On the bedroom floor lay the
aged man, also in nightclothes, unconscious from bullet
wounds in his head and body. The house was in disarray.

Terrified, the young farm hand returned to his home,
awakened his family, and called on neighbors to notify the
authorities. A short time later Phelps was on his way to a
hospital in nearby Medina but he died before arrival without
regaining consciousness.

It did not take the sheriff's men long to conclude that
robbery had been the motive of the crime. Phelps, a highly
respected bachelor, was known to keep large sums of money
in the house but none could be found. Bureau drawers had
been pulled open and their contents scattered about. The
house and garden were searched in vain for a weapon. However, it was determined later that both had been shot with a
.22-caliber revolver; Phelps three times, the housekeeper
once.

Stielow's story of the late night shooting and a woman's
screams brought a similar account from another neighbor,
Miss Irma Fisher, who reported having heard gunfire at the
same time and a female voice crying out, "Charlie, I'm dying
—let me in." However, Stielow asserted that he had not heard
words—only cries.

Miss Fisher also had attributed the disturbance to a family
quarrel and had dismissed the incident. The noise had not
been heard by anyone else in Stielow's household—his wife,
two children, his brother, Raymond, his mother-in-law, and
a young brother-in-law, Nelson Green.

Officers, surveying the scene, observed a bullet hole through
the glass-paneled door leading to the kitchen and surmised
that the housekeeper had been shot as she fled from the

place. Crimson footprints on the snowy road leading to the Stielow tenant house told the story of her dash for help.

The Stielow family, who had settled in the area only a short time before, and old-time neighbors were questioned for hours. When some of the latter related that Phelps had been in the habit of employing tramp laborers for short periods, officers began moving through the entire region looking for itinerants but they were unsuccessful.

Someone suggested that a farmer, Charles Scobell, living some miles away, had a bloodhound that might be helpful and deputies hurriedly brought them to the scene. Men and women looked on curiously as the dog tugged at its leash and led a party for some distance to a stream where the scent was lost. Hope of picking up the trail elsewhere was soon abandoned.

News of the crime, the first in Orleans County in more than a generation, aroused the entire region and there were demands for swift action, with angry threats against the killer should he be apprehended.

Responding to public clamor, the Board of Supervisors met in special session and voted an appropriation to engage private detectives to cooperate with the authorities. The task fell to a Buffalo agency.

These investigators began by again questioning neighbors, including members of the Stielow household, but they learned nothing that would help in solving the mystery.

The coroner's inquest, a few days later, was little more than a formality. Miss Fisher and Stielow repeated the accounts they had given before. Both Stielow and his brother-in-law Nelson Green were asked if they had weapons in their home on the night of the murder and both replied with an emphatic no. This was a serious mistake as events later revealed.

At the close of the testimony, the jury returned a perfunctory verdict—that Charles B. Phelps and Margaret Wolcott had died at the hands of "a party or parties unknown."

The authorities were urged to spare no effort to bring the guilty to justice.

Though the inquest then was supposed to have served no purpose other than to meet legal requirements, it did give the private detectives something specific to work on. Checking the testimony of every witness, they finally came to the statements by Stielow and Green concerning the absence of weapons in their home on the night of the robbery.

Through an informing neighbor, the investigators learned that the two had sworn falsely, that a rifle and a .22-caliber revolver, the latter belonging to Stielow, actually had been in the dwelling on the fatal night. They were further told that a day after the murders, Stielow had instructed his younger brother, Raymond, to hide the guns in the barn.

Suspicion naturally turned at once to Stielow and Nelson Green, who admitted that they had lied at the inquest. They explained that though they were innocent of any wrongdoing, they were frightened and feared that admitting the presence of the firearms in their home might implicate them. Their story failed to satisfy the detectives who promptly confiscated the rifle and revolver, then turned to a painstaking investigation of the two men—the first possible suspects in the case.

After three weeks of intensive work, the authorities placed the pair under arrest, announcing that substantial evidence had been obtained to justify this action. The nature of that evidence was not divulged but officials pointed to the matter of the firearms and intimated that Stielow's complacency on hearing the shots and screams was a significant point against him.

Immediately after their arrest, both men signed long statements in which they categorically denied their guilt but the officials believed that they were far from innocent and actually could be induced to confess. Undercovermen, dressed as prisoners, were locked in their cells in the hope that the suspects might incriminate themselves.

Days later, on April 23, the community was startled by an announcement from the authorities that both prisoners had confessed to the murders, admitting that they were motivated by a desire to obtain Phelps's money. To many, the news was not surprising, for public statements by the officers had led people to believe that the pair was definitely implicated. However, when a written confession, purported to comprise Stielow's admissions, was given to him to sign, he flatly refused, insisting that he never had made the damaging statements it contained. Green likewise denied having admitted any knowledge of the crime.

The case was turned over to the grand jury and that body, accepting the word of the officials that the accused had admitted their guilt, promptly returned first degree murder indictments against the two. It was decided to try Stielow first and, on July 11, 1915, he faced a jury in the court of Judge Cuthbert W. Pound in the town of Albion, the county seat. Scarcely had the trial begun than Stielow's alleged admission of guilt became a hotly controversial and pivotal issue. While Sheriff Bartlett insisted that Stielow had said to him "I did it," the defense countered with a sharp denial, arguing that even had the accused made damaging admissions, they were obtained by duress and through trickery by the detectives stationed in the cells.

The argument continued for days and it was generally agreed that if this evidence were barred, the case would collapse. Judge Pound finally settled the issue by ruling that the alleged confession was admissible.

The prosecution soon called a ballistics expert who testified that he had carefully studied the four lethal bullets—three from Phelps's body and one from that of Miss Wolcott. A microscopic examination, he said, had disclosed nine abnormal markings on the slugs and these coincided with peculiar "riflings" in the inside of Stielow's revolver barrel.

"What then is your final conclusion?" he was asked.

"There's only one," was the response. "The four bullets

came from the revolver of this defendant, Stielow, and no other." The prosecution had scored heavily.

Defense counsel David White, who earlier had stated that he could easily clear his client, concerned himself with a vigorous attack on the credibility of the alleged confession and a claim that Stielow had remained at home throughout the night of the murders, an alibi supported by his wife and mother-in-law. Since the family had only come to Phelps's farmlands a short time before the tragedy, White had summoned long-time neighbors from a nearby community and all of them attested to the defendant's good reputation.

When final arguments were over, Justice Pound turned to the jury with instructions. Obviously impressed by the state's version of the purported confession, he said:

"I will say very plainly to you at this time that were it not for the introduction of the statement dated Arpil 23 [the unsigned confession] and like statements of the defendant admitting his guilt, it would be the duty of the court to direct you to render a verdict of acquittal."

Obviously, the judge had been impressed by the purported confession rather than by the other evidence of the state, including the testimony of the ballistics expert. However, it was for the jury to decide which of the conflicting claims it believed. As to the spectators in the crowded courtroom, they already had made up their minds. Almost all of them believed that Stielow was the murderer.

The verdict of guilty came after seven hours of deliberation and Stielow was sentenced to be executed in the electric chair at Sing Sing Prison on September 5, 1915.

Nelson Green readily recognized his predicament and was convinced that a trial would doom him to a similar fate. He therefore accepted the advice of his attorney and pleaded guilty to a charge of second-degree murder in the hope of escaping execution. He was sent to Auburn Penitentiary for a term of twenty years to life.

An appeal was taken in Stielow's behalf and his conviction was affirmed. Again he was sentenced to death.

The condemned man, meanwhile, had interested Sing Sing officials in his case and they were impressed by his persistent pleas of innocence together with his claim that even if he had made incriminating admissions, they had resulted from third-degree methods by detectives. On the eve of the second execution date, April 9, 1916, the prison authorities appealed to Governor Charles S. Whitman for a full investigation, and a stay was ordered.

Again the defense lawyer went to court with a motion for a new trial but this was denied and for a third time Stielow was sentenced to be executed.

By this time the case had attracted the attention of the Humanitarian Cult, a dedicated group bitterly opposed to the death penalty. One of its lawyer members, Mrs. Grace Humiston, became active in Stielow's behalf and moved again for a retrial, arguing that the accused, being of an immature mind, obviously had been preyed upon by illegal methods to incriminate himself but at least had sufficient intelligence to refuse to sign the admission of guilt. Her efforts failed—two days before the date set for the execution.

Stielow now abandoned all hope and begged for a chance to bid his family goodby. Warden Thomas M. Osborne of Sing Sing contacted them but was advised that they were without funds to make the trip to the penitentiary. He quickly obtained $45 from a prison welfare fund and rushed it to the heartbroken wife, who arrived at the prison with her children late in the day before the date set for her husband to go to the chair.

A tearful scene followed on what the family believed would be their last meeting, for the doomed man was scheduled to die at 6 o'clock on the following morning.

Before dawn that day, guards completed their grim preparations. They slit Stielow's trouser leg for the adjustment of the electrode and the prison chaplain, who had spent the night in the death cell, prepared to lead him to the chair.

The unexpected came forty minutes before the fateful hour —a telephone call to Warden Osborne. It was a message from New York Supreme Court Judge Charles L. Guy who advised that he had just ordered a stay of execution in response to a plea from a group of prominent lawyers who had informed the judge that they were convinced of Stielow's innocence and wished time to prove their judgment. The jurist later extended the stay and legal procedures were started in behalf of a new trial.

While this move was pending, members of the Humanitarian Cult, working with the little group of sympathetic attorneys, engaged detectives to pursue a new line of inquiry. It was their belief that the murders had been committed by one of the nondescript tramp laborers whom Phelps was in the habit of employing.

Through a clue obtained by Mrs. Humiston, attention suddenly turned to two itinerant peddlers serving sentences in another county. One of them, Erwin King, had been convicted of robbery, and his friend, Clarence O'Connell, had been convicted of perjury in trying to establish an alibi for King. Both were said to have been seen loitering about the Phelps home a short time before the tragedy.

Mrs. Humiston went to the prison accompanied by Surrogate George Larkin and seven well-known lawyers, and the group subjected King to hours of interrogation. Although warned of the consequences of any incriminating statements he might make, King finally broke down and confessed that he and O'Connell had murdered Phelps and Miss Wolcott. He said that he no longer could endure the thought of an innocent man's execution.

King's confession was transcribed and he signed it, after swearing to its truth. A day later he was taken in an automobile for the long ride to Albion where he was to be questioned in court. On the way he repeated his confession, then suddenly repudiated it.

O'Connell, subsequently interrogated, denied that he was in any way involved in the murders.

With King in Albion, a group of the lawyers volunteering their services to Stielow appeared before Judge Adolph J. Rodenback and argued for a new trial. They read King's confession, insisting that in spite of its repudiation, Stielow now more than ever before was entitled to another chance to plead his cause. The court's decision amazed not only defense counsel but those of the Humanitarian Cult interested in the prisoner's fate.

Judge Rodenback, apparently influenced by a strict legal interpretation of the issue, ruled that in his judgment no "new evidence" had been presented in the defendant's behalf and that King's confession and its retraction would not have changed the trial jury's verdict in the Stielow case. The King admissions, the court said, were interesting only as "a psychological study."

Once more Stielow was sentenced to the electric chair—the third time, and by the tenth judge to rule against him.

New appeals were made to Governor Whitman. A public hearing was ordered and the state executive, satisfied at last that all legal steps had been exhausted, commuted Stielow's sentence to life imprisonment, stating that although he considered the man to be guilty, he could not overlook the possibility that he still might be innocent.

The long campaign in Stielow's behalf appeared to be over and the luckless man apparently was resigned to his fate. However, new developments came unexpectedly.

Word reached Governor Whitman that King, back in his jail cell in Buffalo, had been writing letters to friends again admitting his guilt. Some of these began to appear in the New York *World*, which in recent weeks had shown a sudden interest in the case.

The governor sent for King and interrogated him for hours in the capitol. When the meeting was over Governor Whitman announced his conclusion that the prisoner at least had guilty knowledge of the crime and had been evasive on a number of vital points. Admitting that no criminal case brought to his attention had perplexed him as much, the governor made known his intention of launching an independent investigation of his own. A few days later he received from the legislature a special appropriation of $25,000 for this purpose and announced that he had selected a highly qualified man of unquestioned integrity to direct the inquiry.

The man he appointed was George H. Bond of Syracuse, who for six years had served with distinction as district attorney of Onondaga County and was recognized as one of the foremost lawyers in the New York State Bar. He was regarded also as an authority in criminal procedures and was well versed in ballistics and other sciences involved in crime detection.

Bond was sworn in as a deputy attorney general and given a free hand to proceed. He began by studying the trial transcript and, as he admitted long afterward, ended his reading in the belief that Stielow was guilty. He determined, however, to pursue the inquiry with a fair and objective mind.

His appointment by the governor, however, created widespread and bitter indignation in Orleans County where people, with few exceptions, were convinced of Stielow's guilt and saw no reason for reopening the case. King's confession was ridiculed and its retraction was construed as proof of his innocence. Many pointed out resentfully that the Stielow case already had cost the state $50,000 and the additional appropriation for Bond's investigation was regarded as a waste of public funds. Others referred to Stielow's latest supporters as "emotional reformers" who, they said, were interested only in exposing the work of the authorities and establishing a miscarriage of justice.

The governor, himself a stanch Republican, was accused of responding to the pressure of the *World*, a Democratic newspaper.

In the face of such opposition, Bond realized that he

would be obliged to work in a hostile atmosphere in which he could expect little if any cooperation. At the outset he had mapped a number of vital points of inquiry and recognized that ultimately a comparison of Stielow's revolver with the lethal bullets taken from the victims would strongly influence his final judgment. For this reason he soon turned to a ballistics expert whose skill had received national recognition— Charles E. Waite.

For years Waite had participated in the solution of baffling cases involving bullets and firearms. Often he was called to serve the Department of Justice and he already had won acclaim for initiating a nation-wide survey that would finally record and standardize details and measurements of every known pistol and revolver made in the country.

While Waite prepared to make an intensive study of the ballistics elements in the case, Bond went to the penitentiary for his first interview with the prisoner. He began by presenting the situation bluntly and in the simple language that Stielow could understand. In effect he said:

"Nothing more can happen to you. You have everything to gain and nothing to lose by telling the truth. If you are guilty and will confess, you will save the state the expense of this investigation. I will write that into my report with my recommendation that you get time off. If, on the other hand, you are guilty and don't tell me now, I will find it out and write that in my report where it will stand against you always. Do you understand?"

Stielow nodded. "I didn't do it," he replied in his childish way. "If I said I did, it would be a big lie."

They talked about the alleged confession and, as before, Stielow insisted that he had not intended to admit his guilt; that any incriminating statement had been wrung from him either by duress or unfair suggestion. "They badgered me so long I really don't know what I told them toward the end— but, believe me, I didn't do it," he told Bond.

Returning to his office, Bond spent days analyzing the statement which the prisoner had refused to sign. The more he studied it, the more convinced he became that it contained only facts which previously had been common knowledge—and nothing more. He already had scrutinized the Phelps home, inch by inch, with Waite, examining a bullet hole and other physical evidence in a meticulous effort to reconstruct every step in the murders.

As Bond compared the results of this examination with the account claimed to have been related by Stielow, he discovered glaring inconsistencies and details which were not congruous with established facts.

For example, Stielow was quoted as saying that a moment after he had shot Phelps in the bedroom, Miss Wolcott dashed by him after they had met almost face to face, and that she ran out of the kitchen, partly closing the glass-paneled door behind her. "I shot her through the door," Stielow was said to have admitted.

To Bond this statement was wholly illogical. "It just doesn't make sense," he reasoned later with Waite. "Bear in mind that she knew Stielow and must have recognized him. If he had shot her as she fled, why did she run across the road to his house for help? Why did she scream: 'Charlie, let me in'?"

To verify this reasoning, Bond had carefully calculated the position of the bullet hole in the door. It was exactly three feet eight inches from the floor. Considering Miss Wolcott's height and the course of the shot, it would have struck her below the shoulder—not close to her heart.

A drawing of her footprints on the snow-covered path, made by deputies long before, indicated to Bond that she had deliberately taken a zigzag course, dodging bullets as she ran.

When this phase of his work had been completed, Bond was thoroughly convinced that the account of the murders attributed to Stielow in the purported confession constituted a series of physically impossible and unreasonable facts which failed to coincide with evidence and circumstances; that obviously it had been written on the basis of rumor, hearsay and conjecture.

"They've tried to fit a circle over a square—it's that simple," he remarked to one of the defense lawyers.

Probing still further into circumstances surrounding the disputed statement, Bond learned that unknown to the defense, a dictograph had been used secretly to record conversations between Stielow and Green and with their counsel. Bond insisted on hearing the transcriptions and found them to be without a single incriminating statement. He also interrogated one of the detectives who had spent days in Stielow's cell. This man admitted that he had failed to obtain even an approach to a confession; that the prisoner steadfastly denied his guilt.

Use of the bloodhound to track down the murderer had aroused Bond's curiosity. Questioning the dog's owner and others watching its movements around the murder scene, the investigator satisfied himself that the trail followed by scent could not have been Stielow's. In fact, he was told that Stielow had stood close to the bloodhound when it started off; that he had petted the dog which completely ignored the tracks he had made when he first ran to Phelps's home.

The Syracuse lawyer now was ready to turn his attention to what he considered the pivotal issue—Stielow's revolver and the related ballistics problems which the expert, Waite, had been studying for weeks. Together they took the weapon and the lead pellets extracted from the bodies to the New York City Detective Bureau, eager for the help and advice of experts there. They handed the gun to a Captain Jones, the department's revolver expert, and asked him to examine it closely.

"Can you tell us how long ago this revolver was fired last?" Bond inquired.

Jones hesitated, as he scrutinized every part of the weapon. Finally, he pointed significantly at incrustations in the barrel and looked up at his visitors. "Certainly not for three or four years before it was picked up by the police after the murder. It hasn't been fired for a very long time."

Stielow had insisted that he had not discharged the weapon for seven years.

They were now ready for the scientific tests which Bond had said would be the determining factor in his final conclusions. Waite already had spent days in trying to obtain bullets which could be used in the gun, an obsolete model. Failing to find them in New York shops, he had inquired of manufacturers and finally had obtained them from a factory in Connecticut.

In a laboratory of the New York Detective Bureau, Bond and Waite prepared for the tests, assisted by Captain Jones and Dr. Otto Schwartz, the police surgeon. Huge pads of cotton batting were set up and two shots were fired into them from Stielow's revolver. The experts then turned their gaze from the recovered test bullets to the lethal lead.

"You can even tell with your naked eye," Waite exclaimed. "The lethal bullets from the bodies were not fired from this revolver. Look, the mortal bullets are clear and only slightly marked. Those in the test are gouged and gnawed. But we'll confirm this further under the microscope. It really is hardly necessary."

More shots were fired into the cotton bales and the vital specimens finally were gathered together and taken by the experts to Rochester where Waite wished to scrutinize them under powerful lenses with the help of a noted expert in microscopic examinations, Max Poser.

They spent much time with the bits of lead under microscopes, studying and measuring with delicate instruments the telltale "riflings" that are made on bullets by the rough ridges in a gun barrel—the tiny grooves and the ridges between them, known as "lands."

It was Poser who explained their findings. "Note that there are five lands and five grooves on the test bullets," he said. "Note their size, their width. Now look at the lands on the death bullets—see how much wider they are. Such markings speak for themselves."

The group pointed out other differences. Not only were there fewer lands on the lethal slugs but when these scraps of metal were measured with a micrometer and compared with the inside dimensions of the revolver barrel, it was still more obvious that Phelps and the Wolcott woman had not been shot by Stielow's gun.

The experts discussed the earlier report made by the ballistics man engaged by the state and shook their heads. They had no knowledge of his procedures but they considered his conclusions to be incomprehensible.

Bond, who had launched his inquiry believing Stielow to be guilty, now was thoroughly convinced of his innocence beyond the slightest doubt. He set down his reasons in a voluminous, analytical report to Governor Whitman that comprised more than two hundred pages. Step by step he reviewed his procedures, relating his disclosures and their interpretation.

Referring to the disputed confession, Bond declared that the prosecution had found it easy to "work" on their prisoner's simple, immature mind. He remarked that had they been more eager to establish the truth instead of trying to prove Stielow's guilt in which they believed, they would have uncovered glaring faults in their case. He declared that it was nonsense to believe that had Stielow been guilty, Miss Wolcott would have fled to his home for protection.

He even accounted for Stielow's first denial that he had firearms in his home. He had inquired carefully into this matter, he said, and had satisfied himself that Stielow first had refused to hide the weapons in the barn and had done so only on the insistence of the frightened women in the household, who also had compelled him to first deny their possession.

As soon as the report had reached the governor, Bond filed a formal murder charge against King, who in the meantime had made a second confession revealing minor details which supported facts unearthed by Bond in his long investigation. The man even accounted for the money stolen from Phelps —a detail not mentioned in the purported statement by Stielow.

Bond put full credence in King's second confession, for when he had inquired into the retraction of the first, he learned that the prisoner, on his ride from the prison to Albion, had been accompanied by one of the private detectives originally hired by the authorities.

King, after expressing a willingness to plead guilty, was taken into the court of Judge Wesley C. Dudley, who held that since a guilty verdict still stood against Stielow, it would be improper and illegal for King to plead at that time. Instead, he ordered that the entire matter be presented to the grand jury.

Bond and Waite, knowing the temper of the people, were sorely disappointed, but they were not prepared for what was to come.

The inquisitorial body sat for three full days and into the night listening to evidence. First Bond spoke for hours at a time, detailing every move in his arduous inquiry. He admitted the state of mind under which he had started and told the jurors how he had finally become so fully convinced that Stielow could not be guilty. He referred at length to King's confession, pointing out how every detail dovetailed with the reconstruction of the crime. At last came the time for King's appearance.

Seated calmly in the witness chair, King repeated his admission of guilt and insisted that it was the truth. Again he said that in confessing he was motivated only by a desire to save an innocent man. He was frequently interrupted and at one time, near the close of the interrogation, one of the jurors said that he wished to speak frankly with the witness.

"You know that if what you have told us is true, you will have to go to the electric chair," he told King.

"No man wants to die," King replied.

"But what you have told us will send you there. Stielow will go free and you will take his place."

"Yes sir," King said softly, "I know."

The inquiry soon was ended and Bond retired as the jurors began their deliberations. Hours passed before they adjourned after sending a message to the court—a terse note that came as a frustrating blow to Bond. The jurors had voted 14 to 7 that they had "nothing to report." It was a hard slap in the face for Bond.

Stunned and chagrined, he and his colleagues tried to rationalize what had occurred. They became convinced that the jury's action reflected the attitude of a country community that had thoroughly satisfied itself on the guilt of two men and did not wish its conclusions to be changed. They reasoned further that the townsfolk believed they had heard too much of the case for too long and were angered that more than $75,000 of public funds had been expended, even though the money had been used to correct a miscarriage of justice. And there was still another factor—resentment against the employment by the state of an investigator from another county to undo the work of their own elected officials. Against these circumstances, the fate of two of their fellow citizens did not seem to matter.

Bond, however, could not restrain himself from frankly expressing his own opinion and sending it to Governor Whitman. Commenting on the jury's refusal to act, he wrote:

"I am fully of the belief that the grand jury, under ordinary circumstances, would have indicted on evidence less strong, but the circumstances surrounding this case were extraordinary to a degree and the failure of the jury to consider the evidence solely on its merits indicated that the members were actuated by considerations purely personal and local."

Fortunately for the imprisoned men, Governor Whitman held Bond in high regard and was more impressed by his report than by the judgment of the grand jury. A few days later he issued an executive order commuting the sentences of both Stielow and Green and ordered their immediate release with the understanding that they were to be regarded as guiltless. Neither was ever compensated by the state for false imprisonment, and King, after finishing his sentence, left the prison, never to be heard from again.

14

"WE MUST BE CERTAIN"

"We, the jury, find the defendant, Harry Powell, guilty of armed robbery as charged."

As a clerk slowly read this verdict in a crowded San Francisco courtroom, Police Lieutenant Daniel P. McKlem, then head of the Robbery Detail, listened dubiously and shook his head. Visibly worried, he spoke briefly to an inspector sitting at his side, then looked on impatiently while the judge thanked the men and women in the jury box for their services and dismissed them.

Waiting only for the last of the jurors to depart, McKlem stepped briskly to the bench of Judge Herbert Kaufman.

"Verdict or no verdict," he whispered. "I'm still not satisfied that Powell is the guilty man."

"You're not," inquired the judge, obviously puzzled. "You heard three witnesses positively identify him as one of the robbers. They were under oath, and . . ."

"I realize all that," McKlem interrupted impatiently, "but somehow, personally, I have my doubts. We had to book Powell after he had been identified—but I wish I could be certain. Won't you grant a five-day stay before you sentence him? I want to work on this case just a little while longer. I want to be absolutely sure before a man is sent to the penitentiary for a term that could be life."

The delay, with little precedence under the circumstances, was granted and hours before it had expired, the officer ob-

tained still another postponement but many weeks passed
before he could justify his procedure.

Daniel P. McKlem, who became chief of inspectors in
1956, serving until his retirement in November 1962, recalls
the case with pride. He relates the details to prove the soundness of a policy that he followed during his long career and
on which every member of his 188-man bureau was meticulously schooled. "Be absolutely positive before you accuse
any man of crime," he told his inspectors over and over.
"Ask yourself whether the man you are charging would be
justified in accusing you under similar circumstances."

Devoutly religious, he faithfully put the teachings of his
church into everyday practice by admonishing every member of his bureau to "do unto others as you would have them
do unto you." He believes firmly in the overwhelming value
of physical evidence as compared with circumstantial elements in any case, no matter how incriminating they may
appear. "I believe nothing that I hear and only half of what
I see," he has said. "A police officer must be absolutely positive in his accusations and he must always be as eager and
alert in protecting the innocent as he is to convict the guilty.
That determines an officer's worth."

Powell was arrested in San Francisco on May 16, 1945, at
the height of a crime wave in which theaters, bars, and card
clubs were being held up and robbed almost daily by armed
bandits working in groups of three and four. All of the department's resources had been thrown into a search for the
robbers and it was apparent that several different gangs were
operating independently. The press and public were calling on
the police for arrests, yet the most persistent efforts of inspectors and uniformed men were bringing no results. Holdups were continuing despite a steady roundup of suspects
and close attention to every available clue. The situation was
frustrating.

It was during this series of robberies that four men, heavily
armed, walked boldly into the Ace High Club at Sixth and

Natoma Streets, a card parlor in one of the poorer sections of the city where lonely men find recreation in the game of rummy.

Apparently having familiarized themselves with the place in advance, the holdup men divided their attention between a small party of men at a card table and three employees working close by. At gunpoint, they ordered their victims to face a wall and to remove their clothing. After this had been done, the gunmen emptied the cash drawer of close to $1000 and fled.

As soon as police received the alarm, only a short time later, detectives rushed to the place and obtained unusually good descriptions of the bandits from the three employees, who had been careful to note the appearance of the robbers. The patrons, badly frightened, were of little help.

At once new orders went over the police radio and teletype, describing the four bandits and ordering patrolmen everywhere to keep a sharp lookout. Road blocks were set up on highways and inspectors soon spread out over the area on foot and in radio cars as they had many times before. Instructions called for questioning of all suspicious-looking characters.

Two days later a policeman, standing at Ninth and Howard Streets, in the same neighborhood as the Ace High Club, caught sight of a youngish-looking man walking slowly from a tavern. His appearance aroused the officer's suspicions and he eyed the man more closely, recalling the orders that had followed the recent robbery. The stranger seemed to fit the description of one of the wanted men.

Approaching him, the officer asked a few questions and though the man denied all knowledge of the crime, he was taken to headquarters. There he identified himself as Harry Powell, an unemployed steel worker, thirty-six years of age. "You've made a bad mistake," he repeated. "I'm telling you again that I don't know a thing about that holdup."

Although Powell gave the inspectors forthright answers to their questions, they were impressed by the way in which he appeared to fit their description of one of the bandits. Not only was he of the same age and physique, but the police were impressed even more by the fact that he had an unusually prominent Adam's apple, a peculiarity that all of the victims had especially noted.

Men were dispatched to the Ace High Club for the three holdup victims and when they were brought to headquarters a line-up of prisoners was arranged. Powell was instructed to take a place in a group of men and to stand quietly with them when the club employees were brought in.

The trio entered slowly and gazed intently at the men before them. Suddenly they exchanged hurried glances, then looked again, this time more sharply. "That's him," one of them blurted, pointing to Powell. "He's the man—the third one from the left."

"Be careful, gentlemen," McKlem admonished them. "This is a serious charge. Take your time and be absolutely certain."

"We are certain," another of the trio replied. "He's one of them. I'd recognize him anywhere."

"You're badly mistaken," Powell pleaded, disregarding earlier orders to remain quiet. "I'm innocent; you've got the wrong man."

Again the victims assured McKlem that there could be no mistake. "Look at the Adam's apple on that fellow," one of them asserted. "Remember what we told you."

With this positive identification by the three victims of the robbery, Powell, despite his protests, was led to the city prison and formally charged with robbery, a move which the police considered to be justified under the circumstances, although Powell had no previous record.

As days passed, victims of other holdups confronted the prisoner but none were able to identify him, nor could the inspectors find any trace of the other participants in the Ace High Club holdup.

When Powell finally was brought to trial, the three robbery

victims followed one another to the witness chair and testified under oath that the defendant was one of the bandits. Powell took the stand in his own defense, insisting on his innocence, and though his attorney made an impassioned plea of mistaken identity, the jurors chose to believe the prosecution's witnesses.

Pale and trembling, the convicted man was led back to jail, little knowing then, in his despair, of the forces and strange circumstances that were to work in his behalf. Nor was he aware that an indefinable quality in his plea—an unusual note of honesty and sincerity—had so impressed Lieutenant McKlem that he actually doubted the guilt of the convicted man.

McKlem called a number of inspectors into his office and confided his fear that there had been a serious miscarriage of justice. "I'm far from satisfied with the jury's verdict," he told them. "This case requires some hard, old-fashioned plodding. Let's get to work. Let's assume, for the moment, that Powell had not been identified—and start from scratch."

It was while this reopened investigation was under way that Inspector Edward J. Murphy found himself unexpectedly thrust into the case. He had learned to his amazement of a statement made by Powell that "Inspector Murphy framed me."

Murphy, a dedicated officer known for his fairness and accuracy, was shocked, especially since his only part in the Ace High case was to escort victims of other holdups to headquarters to look at Powell, whom they failed to identify.

The inspector met Powell in the jail and the convicted man repeated his accusation. "Do you know who I am?" Murphy inquired.

"Yes, I do," replied Powell. "You're one of the public defenders."

Murphy then introduced himself and the prisoner, visibly embarrassed, admitted that he had made "a dreadful mistake" which he was eager to correct at once. A lengthy conversation followed between the two and when the inspector finally started away he was as doubtful as his superior of Powell's guilt.

He returned to headquarters and quickly reported to Mc-Klem the results of his visit. They discussed the case and agreed that, as McKlem had noted earlier, there was an unusual note of honesty in the prisoner's statements. Then together they called on Judge Kaufman and obtained still another postponement of Powell's sentence until the investigation could be concluded.

Weeks of intensive work followed during which Inspector Murphy, now assigned to the case, pursued one clue after another, as did numbers of other detectives similarly involved. It was a slow, disappointing task. New leads appeared, only to be proved worthless after careful inquiry, and there were times when the officers feared they were doomed to failure.

Then, unexpectedly, one morning there came a new lead that appeared to be better than any of those that had taken the men on fruitless trails. One of the inspectors, following McKlem's orders to check pawnshops constantly for loot taken in the various holdups, located a wrist watch that had been stolen in an earlier tavern robbery. The timepiece had been pawned by a man giving the name of Peter Chavez.

Attention immediately turned to a search for Chavez whose address was unknown and days passed before detectives finally learned that his aunt lived in Stockton, a city eighty-three miles from San Francisco. Stockton police were notified and requested to detain Chavez if he could be located. It was a fortunate move.

On the following morning Murphy received a telephone call from Stockton advising him that the police there were holding one Alfred Tindell and his bride who had just appeared at the home of Chavez's aunt. Tindell had told the officers that he and his wife had just returned from Mexico where he and Chavez had married sisters. Chavez and his bride, Tindell said, were due at the aunt's house at any time.

A police guard was placed there and on the following day, when the couple arrived, Chavez was arrested.

McKlem and Inspector Murphy then drove to Stockton to interrogate the wanted man. On the way, they agreed to move cautiously and to question him first about the various other robberies before mentioning the Ace High Club. To their surprise, Chavez stepped into the trap.

The interview had proceeded only a short time when Chavez, with obvious impatience, interrupted McKlem with an inquiry of his own. "Lieutenant," he asked, "why can't you get to the point?"

"What point?" the officer demanded.

"This point—why don't you ask me about what you came up here to find out?"

"And what's that?" McKlem pressed.

"I know you want to find out about that Ace High job," Chavez went on. "Well, I can simply tell you this—you've got the wrong man in jail. I know that's what brought you here. I was in on that job and I'll tell you just how we pulled it. But the man you nabbed had nothing to do with it. I've never heard of him in all my life."

A stenographer was called and Chavez recounted all of the details of the holdup, some of them so minute and trivial that the officers were convinced that they could come only from an actual participant in the crime. Before he had finished his confession, Chavez had admitted his part in nine recent holdups, including the looting of a post office for which FBI men were hunting him. His crimes extended over the entire length of California.

Tindell then admitted that he had participated in three of these. Together they had netted more than $15,000.

The two were taken to San Francisco and police moved fast to completely verify what now appeared to have been a certain miscarriage of justice. First the three employees of the Ace High Club were brought to headquarters and Powell was placed before them. Again they agreed that he was one of the robbers.

Without a word, Chavez was led into the room and made to stand before the men. The three looked at him in amazement. "There's the robber," they chorused. "We've made a horrible mistake." Then, in turn, they stepped up to Powell and shook his hand, begging for forgiveness. "We're sorry, old man," they said, "but it was an honest mistake."

Powell readily accepted their apologies, and Chavez, looking on, exclaimed, "I wouldn't want to send up an innocent man for a job I'd done." Then he, too, extended his hand to Powell.

As police closely scrutinized the two men, now standing side by side, they were startled to note that while they did resemble each other in some respects, they differed widely in essential details. Each did have an unusually prominent Adam's apple as described by the robbers' victims and both were dark complexioned with dark hair. Otherwise there was no similarity.

Powell was thirty-six years of age, five feet seven inches tall and weighed 143 pounds. Chavez, nine years younger, was four inches taller and weighed an additional twenty-two pounds. Yet Powell had been mistaken for him.

Legal processes soon moved fast to open prison doors for Powell. On September 18 he again faced Judge Kaufman, this time under widely differing circumstances. The court was appraised of Chavez's confession and of the district attorney's request that Powell be fully exonerated. Chavez then took the stand and repeated his confession. The court immediately issued an order that brought freedom to Powell and the happy man announced that he bore no ill will toward those who had wrongly identified him.

A few days later Chavez and Tindell appeared before the same judge and pleaded guilty. "I am sentencing you to a term of from five years to life on each of three robbery charges," the court told Chavez, "but in as much as you saw fit to be honest enough to save an innocent man from going to San Quentin, I feel in my heart that I should do something for you by making these sentences run concurrently."

Chavez bowed his head and Tindell, next called to the bench, received an indeterminate sentence to the penitentiary.

As for McKlem, he left the courtroom content that once more he had lived up to his code of a good officer—and that through his persistent efforts an innocent man had been spared from prison.

In the records of the San Francisco Police Department there are similar episodes—cases like that of young John A. Rexinger, an eccentric, sallow-faced clerk, who was saved from the penitentiary only because McKlem and all of his men were constantly alert to avoid miscarriages of justice.

The crime for which Rexinger was arrested occurred on July 30, 1957, in the darkness of early morning on one of the tree-shaded bridal paths in San Francisco's famous Golden Gate Park. The victims were James Lonerman, a young mathematics teacher, and a pretty nineteen-year-old blonde nurse, whose name the police have withheld because of the revolting nature of her mistreatment.

Lonerman and the girl, returning from a late movie, were talking in his parked car on Lincoln Way in a well-populated section of the city, when they were startled by a sudden knock on the door. Looking up, they saw the dim figure of a young man with a dangerous-looking knife in his hand. He wore heavy shell-rimmed glasses and over his head was a nylon stocking for a hat. "Open the door—quick," he commanded, thrusting his knife against the car window, and the frightened young couple quickly obeyed.

Climbing into the front seat beside the girl, the knife-wielder turned to Lonerman and barked his next command: "Get started—and drive. I'll tell you where to go."

The route he directed took them across Lincoln Way into

the park, then over a dark road that turned and twisted through the wide expanse of trees and shrubs. Now and then Lonerman and his companion looked out anxiously at passing cars, afraid to risk a cry for help but hoping desperately that someone might see the man with the knife in his hands.

"Slow down—get off the road—over on to that bridal path," the bandit suddenly directed. The driver obeyed and was brusquely told to stop his car. Now the man poked his blade at the terrified nurse and directed her to climb over to the back seat and remain quiet. Then, following what appeared to be a carefully prepared plan, he pulled a roll of adhesive tape from his pocket and bound it tightly about Lonerman's mouth and face for a gag. He reached into another pocket for rope and his victim soon was tied hand and foot.

Leaping from the car, the knife wielder then dashed into the back seat, pulled his belt from his trousers, and began brutally beating the helpless nurse. Moaning with pain, she slid to the floor, begging him to stop. His lashes continued for a time; then he took his lighted cigarette and held it against her bare arm while her escort, bound and gagged in the front seat, was forced to look on powerless to interfere.

Suddenly the assailant, without a word, drew a pair of scissors from his jacket and clipped the girl's hair. Then he raped her twice, laughing as she pleaded hysterically with him to stop.

This done, he returned to the young man in the front seat and ripped off his wrist watch. Quickly he moved to the rear seat, pulled a pair of ankle chains from his trousers pocket, and fastened them on the nurse's legs. After making certain that they were secure, he jumped from the car and disappeared in the darkness.

Moments later, the nurse cried loudly for help and soon attracted the attention of a passing motorist who hurried away to notify the police. Before long that section of the park was swarming with officers hunting over paths and bushes for the sex-mad rapist but no trace of him could be found.

At the hospital the girl gave detectives a good description of the man. She said he was about five feet nine inches tall with sharp features and prominent teeth. "I'd recognize him anywhere," she asserted. "There was a lamppost not far away and I took pains to get a close look at him."

The fiendishness of the assault spurred police to swift action and a city-wide hunt soon was under way. Descriptions of the rapist were broadcast over the police radio and a pencil sketch of him, drawn by a deputy sheriff from the girl's description, was sent to newspapers in the hope that it might help in the capture. As a further step inspectors alerted pawnbrokers to keep a sharp lookout for the stolen wrist watch and to detain anyone appearing with it.

Two days of intensive police activity followed, during which officers visited bars and eating places patronized by sex deviates. Suspects were picked up, rushed to the hospital, and shown to the girl who was slowly recovering from her ordeal. Each time she looked up from her bed, eyed the man before her, and shook her head.

It was early evening when Rexinger, on parole from state's prison on a sentence for bad check passing, fell into the police net. He fitted the description of the wanted man only fairly well but when he became evasive about his movements, the officers hustled him into a radio car and took him to the hospital. There the girl raised herself on her elbows, stared at his face, and shrieked: "That's him," she cried. "That's the man who did it. I could pick him out of a crowd."

"Be sure," the officers admonished her.

Again she scanned his features and nodded. "I am certain," she sobbed, and sank back on her pillow.

"But I didn't do it," Rexinger pleaded. "She's made a terrible mistake. What's more, I was home alone on the night this girl was attacked."

Rexinger was taken to headquarters and Lonerman was sent for. He looked at the suspect and said that he could not recognize the man, explaining that he was too frightened to take careful note of the robber's appearance.

Detectives began checking Rexinger's detailed explanation of how he had spent the night of the crime, and the preceding afternoon. It was not long before they learned that he had lied about his lodgings. Actually he had roomed with another parolee, a flagrant violation of the rules.

"If he's lied about one thing, he's lied about others," one of the inspectors commented, "and judging by the evidence, I'm sure we're making no mistake." McKlem alone was still far from satisfied.

"We haven't seen a single piece of physical evidence," he told his men. "Remember, we've searched his clothing and we've gone through his room. What have we found—nothing. Not a single hair of the girl on his clothing; no trace of the tape or even a shred of the rope. No man can devoid himself of every bit of physical evidence. We've got to cinch this case a lot tighter before I'll be satisfied."

"But the girl is positive in her identification," one of the detectives remarked. "In fact, she's identified him twice. Isn't that enough?"

"Not for me," McKlem retorted. "For one thing, I want to find that watch and connect it to Rexinger. And those ankle chains. Let's find out where he bought them."

Plain-clothes men resumed their rounds of pawnshops still looking for the stolen timepiece. Others called at secondhand stores, eager to ascertain where the ankle chains had been purchased.

Two days later they located an Army used-goods store where a clerk told of having sold such chains on the day before the attack. He was escorted to the city prison and a police lineup was arranged. With little hesitation he pointed out Rexinger as the one to whom he had made the sale.

"Now what have you got to say?" they asked their prisoner.

Rexinger shook his head. "I was never in that store, no matter what this man says. He's mistaken, just like that girl at the hospital."

Again the men of the Robbery Detail went into conference and it was still no surprise to them that McKlem, with whose methods they were long familiar, still was dissatisfied. "Like I said before," he commented, "it's the complete lack of physical evidence that worries me. That watch, for example. It should turn up somewhere. Keep on working."

While the inspectors in the ensuing days failed to produce the physical evidence that McKlem demanded, they did uncover a number of vital new facts seriously damaging to Rexinger. His alibi was seriously weakened, if not completely shattered.

At the time of his arrest, he had insisted that he was alone in his apartment from 3:30 in the afternoon preceding the crime until he left for work at 2:30 the following morning—hours after 10:30 P.M., the time of the attack. The officers, however, located a man who was positive that he had seen Rexinger driving his car away from his home at 10 P.M.

The alibi was undermined even further when police learned that two cars with open mufflers had moved under Rexinger's second-story window into a parking lot during the hours that he asserted he was home. Yet in the initial questioning, he had insisted that he had heard no such noises at any time.

There was other circumstantial evidence of an equally incriminating nature. A stocking cap, similar to the one which the nurse had said was worn by her assailant, was found on the front porch of Rexinger's apartment house on the morning after the assault. On the evening of the attack, he had borrowed a pair of scissors from a friend. The rapist had sheared the girl's hair.

Someone else, on the same day, had loaned him darning needles. Both the nurse and her escort said they had been stuck with some sharply pointed object.

Despite these new disclosures and the support which they appeared to give to the case against Rexinger, detectives continued their hunt for physical evidence. A week later they were still visiting pawnshops when the climax came in a way that no one could have foretold. At the corner of Seventh and Stevenson Streets, in an area known as Skid Row, Inspector John Keating recognized a youthful-looking man as a suspected room thief for whom he had been looking. Despite his protests, Marvin N. Bakkerud, an unemployed warehouseman, was taken to headquarters and in his pockets Keating found a number of trinkets reported stolen. "We'll go over to your room," Keating told him. "I want to look around for the rest of the stuff."

Half an hour later the two stepped into a musty-smelling lodging house and walked upstairs to Bakkerud's third-story room. Handcuffed, the prisoner watched nervously as Keating began opening bureau drawers. The detective turned next to a closet crammed with dirty clothes and soiled linen. Keating was rummaging about when his hand fell on something hard and cold. In a moment he pulled out a gold wrist watch and quickly recalled the instructions that had been broadcast. He examined the dial and read the name of a Reno jeweler.

"How'd you get this?" he demanded. Bakkerud shrugged his shoulders.

"Come now," the inspector pressed. "You pulled that job in Golden Gate Park. This is the missing watch. Now let's have the truth."

For a time Bakkerud stared silently at the timepiece. Then he nodded and began to speak. "You've got me cold," he said sullenly. "Yes, I did it. Go look under the bed."

There Keating uncovered what the newspapers had described as the attacker's "torture kit"—scissors, a razor, lengths of rope and tape—even the shell-rimmed glasses and the nylon stocking used as a head cover. The long-bladed knife Bakkerud had thrown away in his flight.

"What in the world made you do a thing like that?" the officer demanded. "What was the big idea in cutting off that girl's hair?"

Bakkerud grinned. "I'd read about a job exactly like that in a magazine and I thought I'd like to try to do the same thing. In fact, I dreamed several times that I had done it. In the magazine, the guy cut off a woman's hair. Look at my crewcut—I wanted her to look just like me."

Keating surveyed the man closely. Only vaguely did he fit the description given by the nurse. He was definitely shorter and he did not have the prominent teeth that she had mentioned.

Later that day, McKlem, who was still anxious for more physical evidence in spite of the confession, sent Bakkerud's clothing to the laboratory of John Davis, chief criminologist of the Oakland Police Department, San Francisco technicians being occupied at the time on another important case. Davis examined the garments under the microscope and reported that he had found fibers of the nurse's dress and a few of her hairs on the prisoner's shoes and socks.

"Now, at last, we've got all of the physical evidence that I've been wanting," McKlem remarked as he scanned the report. "That lab turned up more physical evidence in ten minutes than we got in all our work until that watch turned up."

Bakkerud, with a record of sex perversion and lawlessness since boyhood, was declared insane by Superior Court Judge Walter Carpeneti after an examination by psychiatrists, and committed to a state hospital.

Rexinger, meanwhile, had walked out of the city prison a free man, admitting that he had visioned himself in the gas chamber listening for the drop of the lethal pellets. "Naturally I feel happy," he told newsmen. "I feel as though a steam roller had been lifted off my chest."

15

MISSING RECORDS

When Rabbi Joshua S. Sperka, now of Oak Park, Michigan, wrote to The Court of Last Resort early in 1949 that he believed an innocent man was serving a life sentence in state prison, he opened the door to an investigation that served to deepen rather than to clear a murder mystery which, in many of its complex aspects, remains unsolved to this day.

It brought to light the willingness of individuals to place the burden of guilt on a luckless scapegoat so that a baffling murder would not go unsolved; and it revealed the chicanery of corrupt men determined to keep this innocent man in prison for a motive that never has been fully determined.

In contrast, the inquiry was brightened by the eagerness of two men to delve deeply into a case many years old—one a prosecutor who turned detective for the defense; the other a former police captain whose devotion to justice had brought about his enforced retirement. The prosecutor was the late Gerald K. O'Brien of Wayne County, widely known as a brilliant investigator as well as a clever lawyer. Captain William I. Cross was the retired police officer. But the story should be told from the beginning.

It was midnight on November 17, 1932, when the murdered body of Martado Abrahams, a fifty-eight-year-old Syrian peddler, was found in his bedroom in Highland Park, a suburb of Detroit. A bullet hole in the forehead told its own story but the slayer left behind no weapon or other clue to his identity or motive. Abrahams apparently had been shot in his sleep with a .38-caliber revolver.

Seeking a solution to the mystery, police moved through the Syrian quarter where Abrahams had lived and made his way by peddling notions to his countrymen. From the start there were heavy obstacles. Many of those questioned were taciturn; others could neither speak nor understand English. It was some time before detectives came upon their first lead—they were told of a romance between the murdered man's wife, Zamid Abrahams, from whom he was estranged, and a former acquaintance of theirs. This man, who later assumed a major role in the case, had best be referred to here as Mr. Smith.

Detectives quickly viewed the love affair as a likely motive and theorized that Abrahams probably was killed because he had stood between his wife and Mr. Smith. The latter two were summoned to headquarters and questioned for hours, but vigorously denied that they were involved in the crime. The police, not fully satisfied with the widow's statements, detained her for a time pending further investigation but she was finally allowed to go. The man was not held.

Probing further into Abrahams' background, the officers learned that his married life had been stormy; that he and his wife had been divorced and later remarried. A short time before the murder Abrahams had upbraided her for her friendship with her lodger and she had left him, moving to an apartment a block away.

The police then decided to resume the questioning of Mr. Smith. This time he astonished his interrogators by suddenly recalling an amazing fact that he insisted had escaped his memory during his previous visit to headquarters. He now remembered that a man named Louis Gross had volunteered the information that he had murdered Abrahams.

"Did he tell you why he did it?" the detectives pressed.

Mr. Smith had a ready answer and he seemed anxious to

amplify his accusation. "Gross told me that he had sold Abrahams two rugs and had gotten only a small down payment. When Abrahams refused to pay the balance, suggesting that the rugs were stolen goods, Gross went to see Mrs. Abrahams, he told me, and tried to collect from her. It was during this talk that Gross told Mrs. Abrahams: 'If your old man doesn't pay me, I'll kill him.'"

It was a surprising statement and did provide a suspect, so the police proceeded to Gross's home. He denied emphatically that he ever had made the alleged admission and disclaimed any knowledge of the murder.

Turning the tables on his accuser, he declared that he had met Mr. Smith several times in a neighborhood restaurant but did not learn his name until an afternoon in July 1932 when this man accosted him, introduced himself, and made a startling proposal.

"He offered me a gold necklace which he said was worth a hundred and fifty dollars if I would 'take care' of Martado Abrahams," Gross charged. "Of course I told him that I wasn't interested; I even said that a man could get life for that sort of thing in Michigan—and that ended the conversation."

As expected, Mr. Smith denied that he ever had made such a proposition, so it was now one man's word against that of another and obviously one of them was lying.

The scales tipped in Mr. Smith's favor when a check of police records revealed that Gross had been in previous trouble involving larceny and, though there was no evidence against him now except the unsupported word of his accuser, he was arrested and booked for murder.

The authorities were in no hurry for a trial, preferring to bide their time in the hope that corroborating evidence could be found. It was not until September 1933, ten months after his arrest, that Gross faced a jury in the court of Judge DeWitt H. Merriam, and it was generally understood that the state had succeeded in strengthening its case. Gross was defended by a lawyer whom he had engaged through meager funds contributed by a few relatives and friends.

Mr. Smith was a prosecution witness and repeated every detail of the story he had told originally to the police. He was followed by a man who swore that Gross had asked him for three dollars to buy poison "to kill a man down the street." A woman testified that Gross had offered her three new dresses if she would rent a room near where Abrahams stored his merchandise and entice him there.

The state unwittingly opened the way for a powerful counter-attack by the defense when it called a physician who fixed the time of Abrahams' death as between 10 P.M. and midnight.

This testimony gave Gross's lawyer an opening for which he had been hoping. He called several witnesses who swore that Gross had been playing pinochle with them from 6:20 to 10:20 o'clock on the night of the murder. One told the jury that he and Gross had been together in a coffee parlor until midnight after the game.

The defense believed that this testimony had deeply impressed the jury but its confidence ended soon after the prosecution opened its rebuttal. First the jurors listened to the reading of a statement made to the police by Gross shortly after his arrest, in which he declared that two people, whose names the authorities withheld, had asked him to join in a plot to poison Abrahams. Although Gross insisted that he had rejected the proposal, the prosecutor strongly intimated his belief that the defendant probably had intended participating in the poisoning but that the plotters had decided to shoot their victim instead. Lack of supporting evidence, it was explained later, prevented any move against the two people involved.

The prosecutor then declared he could prove that the defendant, contrary to his statement to the police, definitely had accepted the $150 necklace which he had said earlier was

offered to him by Mr. Smith "to take care of Abrahams."
Gross at that time insisted that he had refused the jewelry.

Gross's alibi next felt the force of the state's barrage. Referring to the defense witness who testified that he had been
with Gross in a coffee parlor up to the hour that the murder
was discovered, the prosecutor produced a sworn statement
made by the same man to the police only a day after the body
had been found. At that time, this man declared that he had
not been with Gross that night but had observed him standing
within a hundred feet of the Abrahams home within the
hours that the murder was supposed to have been committed.

At this disclosure, Judge Merriam angrily interrupted the
trial and ordered the arrest of the witness on a charge of perjury. It was a hard blow to the defense, furnishing the prosecution with new ammunition for its closing argument.

Gross's attorney, pleading for an acquittal, dealt heavily on
the fact that only circumstantial evidence had been presented
against the accused. The jury was told that the state had failed
to prove Gross's guilt beyond a reasonable doubt and it was
admonished not to consider his earlier difficulties with the
law in the present issue.

The jurors finally retired and after several hours of deliberation they returned with a verdict finding Gross guilty of murder in the first degree. Judge Merriam sentenced him to life
imprisonment.

The perjury charge against the defense witness was finally
dropped for reasons that were never fully explained. Apparently, the authorities were satisfied to let the case end with
Gross's conviction.

A few who had followed the trial believed that Gross
should not have been convicted on the evidence presented,
but most people, including the police, were convinced of his
guilt and satisfied that justice had been served.

Protesting that he had been made a scapegoat by the authorities in their determination to convict someone, Gross
went to prison with scant hope of help. With few friends and

no money, he began writing letters to state officials, pleading
for a reopening of his case. Several showed some interest but
the convicted man faced what appeared to be an insurmounta-
ble obstacle. Michigan law then required that a defendant
pay the court reporter for a transcript of trial testimony but
no one was willing to provide the necessary funds. Without
such a transcript, the few who might have helped him were
at a loss to do so.

Despite this difficulty, Gross, who had only a grade-school
education, decided to read what law books he could find in
the prison library and to learn something of criminal procedure. He studied hard, occasionally putting his books aside to
write more letters to those in authority.

Ten years of frustrating appeals had passed with no result
when Judge Merriam agreed to consider a petition for a retrial. The plea, however, was finally denied.

Two years later one of Gross's many letters reached a
deputy in the office of the district attorney who had succeeded
the prosecutor in Gross's trial. With curiosity aroused, that
official decided to inquire into the matter. He looked for the
records in the case but, being unable to find them at first try,
he deferred his quest until a less busy time, the prosecutor
and his staff then being deeply involved in a bitter campaign
for re-election. The district attorney was defeated and before
his deputy could turn again to the Gross case he was out of
office. The new prosecutor was occupied with other matters.

More time passed. His health failing, Gross contracted
tuberculosis and was moved to the prison hospital where his
illness proved to be his good fortune. There it was that he
met Rabbi Sperka, then spiritual leader of Congregation
B'nai David in Detroit, who often visited hospitalized prisoners.

Rabbi Sperka listened to Gross's story and became convinced that the ailing man was entitled to a fair and impartial
investigation of his case. A devout man, the rabbi was deeply
dedicated to the teachings of his faith. One of these precepts,

which he often quoted, was the Biblical command: "Justice, justice shalt thou pursue." So he promised Gross that he would contact The Court of Last Resort, of whose work he had read. It was now early in 1949. Gross had been in prison for sixteen years.

When Erle Stanley Gardner was advised of the basic facts concerning Gross, he decided that he and Dr. LeMoyne Snyder should first meet with Rabbi Sperka and learn all that he could tell them about the case. They took a plane to Detroit and called on the rabbi at his home. The conversation had not gone far before they realized that they were in the presence of an exceptional person.

Rabbi Sperka told them that as a child he had witnessed a pogrom against the Jews in Warsaw, that when he fled with his family he had determined even then to forever be a crusader against injustice. It was this resolve, he said, that had aroused his interest in Gross, although he knew little of the case beyond what the prisoner had told him.

Gardner and Dr. Snyder, deeply impressed by Rabbi Sperka's sincerity, agreed that the facts justified at least preliminary inquiry and that they should start by interviewing Gross himself. In the meantime, the rabbi offered to help by pursuing several new lines of inquiry which The Court men had suggested.

At the prison a week later, Gardner and Dr. Snyder listened to Gross with growing interest yet with a degree of skepticism, knowing that he had a record of earlier offenses. They did agree, however, that his story would be fully investigated by them, progress to be reported regularly in Henry Steeger's *Argosy* magazine—a practice they pursued in most cases in order that the public might follow the course of The Court's activities.

As their inquiry passed beyond the initial stage, they found reason to believe that Gross well might be innocent and that a thorough and far-reaching investigation was warranted. With this in mind, they decided to confer with Gerald K. O'Brien, then the prosecutor of Wayne County, although they doubted whether he could be induced to reopen a case that had been conducted by a predecessor years before and long considered closed.

To their delight, they found O'Brien to be a conscientious official as concerned with vindicating the innocent as he was in sending the guilty to prison. After listening to Gardner and Dr. Snyder, he told them that if they were doubtful of Gross's guilt, it was a prosecutor's duty to investigate and to undo a miscarriage of justice if such had occurred. Promising to personally direct a thorough and impartial inquiry into the entire matter, he assigned three of his best men to work full time on the case. They were Allen De Coursey, George Rose, and Seward Luck. It was agreed that they would carry on in the closest cooperation with the men from The Court. Gardner and his colleague could ask no more, since they already knew of O'Brien's reputation as a fearless and skilled investigator with unusual ability in crime detection.

Their work had not proceeded far before they made a shocking discovery. Almost all of the records in the case had completely disappeared!

Not only had the court reporter's notes been torn from his books, but the prosecutor's files in the courthouse had vanished as had most of the police records!

A document recording the conviction remained intact. Obviously, the papers had been stolen by someone who knew precisely what he wanted and exactly where to look in the courthouse and in police headquarters.

Seeking an answer to this disclosure, the investigators began inquiring into other cases of the same period. All of these records were in their proper places. Only those involving Gross were gone.

De Coursey was instructed to bring the matter officially to the court's attention. The record of that proceeding follows:

THE COURT: Now I understand that you have made a thorough search of the records, the stenographer's records, and you find that the stenographic notes of Mr. Harry Kenworthy, who was the official reporter at the time of the taking of the statements in the Gross case, both in Highland Park and in the prosecutor's office, are also missing.

MR. DE COURSEY: That is right, Your Honor.

THE COURT: And our Mr. Robsen was the official court reporter of this court.

MR. DE COURSEY: That is right. The prosecutor's number of the transcribed record of the Gross examination was A-1758. That file is the only one missing from the package containing the examination of that time, and the book of shorthand notes of Harry Lenworthy, being book No. 196, in which the shorthand notes of the Gross examination were, is also missing from the books in the basement of the Court Building.

THE COURT: I have had Mr. Robson's stenographic notes brought to this courtroom and I examined them myself, and all of the stenographic notes that he took for that particular year, and some months prior thereto and some months subsequent thereto—all the notes that he took are there except the Gross notes, the Gross murder case notes, and they have been systematically taken out, as there has been a systematic rifling of all records in both this courthouse and the prosecutor's office and also the Justice Court in Highland Park. Not only have the notes disappeared, all statements have disappeared, and even the Circuit Court file, together with its cover, has disappeared from the County Clerk's office.

MR. DE COURSEY: That is the jacket containing the complaint and warrant and information.

THE COURT: There is nothing before the court in the way of any official records at all, except the motion for new trial filed by Mr. Gross, which leads me to only one conclusion: that whoever did this knew what he was doing, and had access to the files and records of the County Clerk's office as

well as the basement of the County Building; had access to
the records of the prosecuting attorney's office, which should
be kept under lock and key, as well as here, and had access
to the records, the transcripts and papers in the possession of
the High Park Police Department and the Justice Court in
Highland Park, and the person or persons who took them
certainly knew what they were when they took them. A more
systematic theft could not be perpetrated on the people of
the state or upon Mr. Gross. I am not naming anybody, but
I have my own opinion.

Gardner and Dr. Snyder, together with O'Brien and his
men, now realized that they faced a situation far deeper and
more sinister than they had anticipated. New questions confronted them. Who did the judge have in mind and who
could have been able to loot the courthouse files with impu-
nity? How was it done? And what motive lay behind a plot to
keep Gross behind the bars? They could only wonder. But
first they must learn every fact involved in the police investigation and subsequent trial.

After a long and painstaking search, they uncovered a single
document which the thief had overlooked. It opened the way
to new sources that provided the needed information. The
next step took them to Highland Park where they encountered a strange hostility. It was obvious that some person or
persons did not want the case reopened—that Gross should
remain in prison.

After weeks of futile effort the investigators were told by an
undisclosed informant to look up Captain William I. Cross,
who, before his retirement, had been a highly respected member of the police force. It was rumored that he had incurred
the enmity of a powerful politician because he had undertaken an independent inquiry into the Abrahams murder and
that he had been warned to "lay off the Gross case."

Locating Captain Cross, who was reported to be living
"somewhere in northern Michigan," was not an easy task. The

investigators finally learned his exact whereabouts and drove to his home in a secluded, sparsely settled area. They found a dedicated police officer to whom truth was of paramount importance; a man who believed in justice to the point of sacrificing his career. He told his visitors that he was convinced of Gross's innocence and certain that he had been deliberately framed.

Captain Cross began by giving them a long account of his interest in the case, a concern that began when he returned to the Highland Park force after having been assigned for a time to work with the state police. Gross already had been convicted.

For years Captain Cross had been detailed to cover the Syrian quarter. Gross's friends there, the captain said, approached him on his return and begged him to interest himself in the man's behalf.

Their earnestness induced him to undertake a quiet investigation of his own but he soon found himself the object of mysterious threats.

Captain Cross related that his first moves were to delve into the activities of a certain individual who, he suspected, might be involved. Working in that direction, he was suddenly contacted by a man whom he chose not to name, and emphatically told to "lay off" of the person he was investigating. This order, he learned, had come from an influential political figure with City Hall connections.

Not easily intimidated, Cross decided to ignore the order and continue his course regardless of consequences. He was now certain that Gross was the victim of a conspiracy and that the actual murderer was still at large. Within a few weeks he was to learn the penalty for his dedication and courage.

He was bluntly informed at headquarters that he should retire; that his active service in the department was no longer desired. He had no alternative but accept the edict.

Gardner asked him whether he was fully convinced that his

enforced retirement was the result of his investigation. Cross did not hesitate to answer.

"That order to retire came very shortly after I had refused to 'lay off' my investigation," he declared.

Nevertheless, it did not prevent him from continuing his inquiry and when he finally became convinced that Gross was innocent, he spoke his mind fearlessly. "I told them that I believed Gross to be as innocent as I was," he related, "and that I believed the real murderer, whoever he might be, was alive and walking the streets."

That gave him some satisfaction but what he needed mostly was a job. With difficulty, he found work in an automobile plant, remaining there for a time until he chose to retire and live in the country with his wife.

He now volunteered to contribute his services in any way that would be helpful and at once became a close associate of Gardner and Dr. Snyder, together with O'Brien's aides.

They learned that the murder of Abrahams had taken place at a time when gambling and other forms of vice were flourishing in certain outlying areas of Detroit. Abrahams was losing money at the gambling tables and the investigators theorized that he was probably killed when he refused to pay a gambling debt and had threatened to tell the police what he knew about gambling houses and who was conducting them.

On the basis of their arduous work, they concluded that men involved in these rackets, having influential political connections, deliberately connived to frame the case against Gross and saw to it that the records were destroyed so that with the convicted man in prison, their villainy would be concealed for all time.

Into this pattern, Mr. Smith fitted perfectly, for it was ascertained that he was associated with racketeers and underworld hoodlums. And it was considered reasonable to suppose that Gross, vulnerable because of his past difficulties, had been selected as a scapegoat who would be unable to extricate himself from such a plot.

Certain that perjury had been committed, especially by Mr. Smith in his testimony against Gross, O'Brien directed that he be located and subjected to a lie-detector test.

The man was brought to the prosecutor's office and reluctantly agreed to undergo a scientific examination that would determine whether he had testified truthfully when he swore that Gross had admitted the murder.

A polygraph expert was summoned and after the intricate apparatus had been adjusted, he began by asking the one-time chief witness the usual innocuous questions that enabled the machine to record the subject's normal respiration, heart beats and other reactions before he would be asked anything about the murder itself.

After a time, without warning, came what is known as a "dynamite question"—the climax of the test.

"Did Louis Gross tell you that he had murdered Martado Abrahams?"

"Yes, he did."

As these words were spoken, the delicate needle of the lie detector jumped far and fast. There was no mistaking its significant message.

Before completing their report, the investigators sought to clear two vital points in the strange mystery: Who was the person that Captain Cross was investigating when he was directed to "lay off" and why was the order given? These were questions that they could not answer completely, although they did learn that the order had come from a high official of Highland Park and that the man under investigation was a close relative of Mr. Smith.

O'Brien now fully realized that his main concern involved the future of the unfortunate Gross and that the unsolved reasons for his persecution were a matter of secondary importance and could never be cleared at so late a time. Without further delay he arranged to go with Gardner to confer with Judge Thomas J. Maher and to ask that a new motion for retrial be considered. The jurist listened to their account of the investigation and told O'Brien to proceed through legal channels.

The prosecutor then filed a formal motion for a new trial and while waiting for the court's decision, he sent this letter to Henry Steeger of The Court of Last Resort:

I have filed a motion for a new trial in the Louis Gross case before the Honorable Thomas J. Maher of Wayne County Circuit Court.

As prosecuting attorney of Wayne County, I believe it is my duty to protect the innocent as well as prosecute the guilty. This motion will be heard, in all probability, before the next issue of Argosy Magazine goes to print.

I wish to commend Argosy Magazine, Mr. Erle Stanley Gardner and the whole staff of the magazine for the splendid work they have done in the Gross case.

It is my earnest hope that the Circuit Court will grant the motion that has been filed.

Sincerely yours,
Gerald K. O'Brien
Prosecuting Attorney.

The hearing was set for October 28, 1949, before Judge Maher. Sixteen years had passed since penitentiary doors had closed behind Louis Gross.

With new hope, the prisoner, heavily manacled, was taken to Detroit and led into the courtroom where O'Brien sat ready to report all that the prolonged investigation had disclosed. Before presenting his case, he announced with perfect frankness that he intended first to argue for a new trial and that if this were granted he would move for a dismissal of the murder charge, since he would have no intention of subjecting Gross to another trial. Granting of his motion, he said, in effect would clear the slate for Gross.

The hearing lasted for hours as O'Brien forcefully emphasized what he regarded as the five major points produced by his investigation. First he dealt with the stolen records and stressed their implications. The work of the authorities leading to Gross's arrest he termed as "suspicious." He told the court that witnesses who had been expected to testify in Gross's behalf had suddenly changed their stories and appeared against him.

To the judge's amazement, O'Brien declared that one witness on whom the defense had leaned heavily to support its case, had been arrested on a pretext and held mysteriously in a suburban jail until the trial had ended.

Lastly, he placed great emphasis on the results of the lie-detector test of Mr. Smith and to the "lay off" orders given to Captain Cross before his enforced retirement.

While it had been expected that the court would take the matter under advisement, Judge Maher acted with surprising haste.

First he reviewed, slowly and methodically, all of the points that O'Brien had made, explaining that his decision would be based on their soundness and relevance. "It appears to me," the judge finally said, "that this man, Louis Gross, has been framed."

He then granted the motion for a new trial and complimented the men involved in the investigation, paying special tribute to what he termed "the diligent work of Mr. O'Brien, who believes his job is not only to prosecute the guilty but to protect the innocent."

O'Brien, elated, promptly moved for a dismissal of the murder charge against Gross and the court granted his request without further comment. Louis Gross, now fully vindicated, was restored to freedom after sixteen years in prison. He left at once for New York to visit relatives and was last heard from in 1950 living comfortably in Paterson, New Jersey.

The murderer of Martado Abrahams was never apprehended. O'Brien and his colleagues were convinced that suspicion pointed strongly at Mr. Smith but with the passing of years since the crime, the disappearance of records and other complicating factors, it was agreed that it would be useless to bring him to trial.

16

MEDICINE—THE LAW'S ALLY

Medical science often plays a major role in solving murder mysteries. One of its many necessary functions is to determine the exact time of death when this becomes a vital factor in a perplexing investigation.

A victim's lips are sealed. There may be physical evidence at the scene of tragedy but the precise time when life has ceased may be the pivotal issue in solving the crime. It can prove or shatter a suspect's alibi.

Medical men may differ in their judgments as they sometimes do, but law enforcement officers and juries are influenced by the findings of highly qualified physicians whose work in this field has established their reliability beyond doubt.

That is why Dr. LeMoyne Snyder, nationally recognized as a medico-legal consultant, occupied so important and valuable a place in The Court of Last Resort. A member of both the American Medical Association and the American Bar Association, he has often demonstrated his rare ability to bring medicine and law into interplay to decide highly technical, involved questions of paramount concern in enigmas of crime.

The case of Gerald C. Wentzel of Pottstown, Pennsylvania, challenged all of Dr. Snyder's varied talents, though his major task was to determine within a matter of minutes the time that an attractive divorcée met death at the hands of a strangler. On that vital point his work was of a highly technical rather than spectacular nature, but it was all-important since his decision would establish or disprove a convicted man's claim of an alibi. However, before the long investigation had ended, he was to demonstrate not only his knowledge of medicine in relation to legal procedures, but his skill with the lie detector and his readiness to assume the role of a plodding detective in pursuit of facts.

Throughout the inquiry, he operated in close association with Bob Rhay and Tom Smith, the ace investigators of The Court of Last Resort, who carried on much of the tedious leg work requiring fast traveling from place to place. Most of the time they worked under Dr. Snyder's direction, especially when it became necessary for them to find important medical details buried in masses of court records and to delve into facts vitally essential to his scientific studies.

The victim in this case, twenty-seven-year-old Mrs. Miriam Greene, was found garroted to death at 2 o'clock in the afternoon of Monday, December 9, 1946, when the manager of an apartment building in Pottstown, alarmed by a call that her tenant had not reported for work, entered the small suite with a passkey. A blue scarf was tightly knotted around the woman's neck.

Although it appeared certain that Mrs. Greene was dead, the apartment manager summoned a nearby physician who said at once that undoubtedly the woman had succumbed some time before. However, he was persuaded by the first police officer on the scene to have her rushed to a hospital should there be any chance of resuscitation. On arrival she was immediately pronounced dead and the coroner was summoned.

Police, after examining the apartment, were convinced that robbery had not been the killer's motive since expensive jewelry lay on the bureau and neither drawers nor closets had been ransacked or even opened. There were no signs of a struggle and a close-by neighbor had heard no unusual noise from the rooms during the past few days. The officers believed that Mrs. Greene had been dead for some time—just how long they were unable to hazard. That would be a decision for the coroner.

The victim's former husband, George Greene, was summoned but he was unable to throw any light on the mystery. He explained that he and his former wife had been separated for more than a year. In fact, their divorce had become final that day. He said that he had not even seen her for months.

When more thorough investigation failed to reveal any clues to the murderer, detectives sought to locate the woman's relatives and friends, hoping to learn something of her background. They were told of a close friendship between her and George C. Wentzel, who was employed as a master die caster by the Doehler Die Casting Company of Pottstown.

Wentzel appeared at headquarters where he insisted that his friendship with Mrs. Greene had been only casual and that he knew little of her affairs. However, after further questioning a day later, he admitted that there had been a romance, explaining that his earlier statement had been prompted by a desire to keep the affair from his wife.

Suspecting that he still knew more than he was willing to divulge, detectives continued their grilling and were finally told by Wentzel that he had called at the woman's apartment at eleven o'clock on the Sunday night preceding the discovery of her body and had found her dead. Overcome by fear that he might become involved in a murder case, he had hurriedly left the place without notifying the police or telling anyone that Mrs. Greene had been killed. "I felt confident that her body would be found sooner or later," he stated, "and the police, I knew, would find the murderer. What I wanted was to keep out of the whole business altogether."

Though not completely satisfied with this explanation, the police permitted him to leave and they moved about in an effort to uncover at least some tangible clue that would lead to the capture of the killer.

The physician who had first seen the body told detectives that he had not examined it closely enough to determine the exact time of death but on the basis of his meager observation the officers proceeded on the theory that Mrs. Greene probably had been murdered some time during the previous Saturday. This was at variance with the findings of the autopsy surgeon who estimated the day of death as Sunday.

When continued investigation left the police as mystified as ever, they turned again to Wentzel as a possible suspect and ordered him to detail his movements for several days up to the Sunday night when he said he had discovered the murder. With no hesitation, he proceeded to account for every hour from three o'clock on the preceding Thursday afternoon until his arrival at Mrs. Greene's apartment. "I was two hundred miles away from Pottstown on a deer hunting trip with about fifteen members of the East End Rod and Gun Club," he related, "and when we got back to town I left them and went directly to see Mrs. Greene. Why don't you talk to the boys I was with—I'll tell you who all of them are."

The officers jotted down the names and busied themselves rounding up every person who Wentzel said had been with him during the entire outing period. To a man they corroborated his statements in every detail.

The police now faced a serious dilemma. Despite what appeared to be Wentzel's airtight alibi, they chose to proceed with his prosecution as the murderer. Obviously, they had no other suspect and were ready to gamble on their chances of obtaining a conviction regardless of medical testimony.

In such a situation, the precise time of Mrs. Greene's death assumed paramount importance to both the prosecution and the defense. The authorities thus were obliged to radically alter their theory and proceed on an entirely new premise—that the murder had been committed at eleven o'clock Sunday night by Wentzel when, by his own admission, he had entered the dead woman's apartment. By no other supposition could he logically be accused in the face of his well-corroborated alibi.

Although Wentzel insisted that he was not responsible for

the woman's death and knew nothing of the circumstances, he was formally charged with murder and the state pushed for an early trial. Defense counsel, leaning heavily on the alibi, was confident that it would be an easy matter to convince any jury of the defendant's innocence.

The trial has been described by some as a fiasco. The state's medical testimony was weak and confusing. The physician who was the first to see the body was uncertain as to the time of death, admitting that he had observed the remains carefully for no more than five minutes.

He was followed to the stand by the coroner's autopsy surgeon who had seen the body at seven o'clock Monday evening —five hours after the murder was discovered. It was his opinion that death could have occurred between twelve and twenty-four hours before—a time that coincided with the prosecution's new theory. However, under cross-examination, he was forced to admit that Mrs. Greene might have been dead for seventy-two hours.

Disregarding this, the prosecutor hammered hard in support of his contention that Mrs. Greene had been killed at eleven o'clock Sunday night by Wentzel and made much of the defendant's contradictory statements to the police as strongly indicating guilt. The jury appeared to be impressed.

The defense, eager for medical testimony that would coincide with the defendant's alibi, called a well-known mortician as one of its principal witnesses. Testifying that he had cared for several thousand bodies during his long career, he said he was convinced by the condition of the remains that Mrs. Greene had been dead for at least eighty hours when she was found.

Wentzel's hopes for a fast acquittal rose high as he listened to the judge's instructions to the jury. "If you find that Miriam Greene did not die at eleven o'clock on December 8 [Sunday night]," said the court, "then Gerald Wentzel did not kill her."

The jury retired and the accused man kept his eyes on the

clock, expecting a quick verdict that would set him free. Spectators told him that he would not have long to wait.

Some hours passed before the jurors returned to the courtroom and the foreman handed a slip of paper to the clerk.

Wentzel could scarcely believe the words he heard:

"We, the jury, find the defendant, Gerald C. Wentzel, guilty of murder in the second degree."

There were gasps in the crowded courtroom. Wentzel paled and drooped in his chair, unable to comprehend it all. A few days later he stood before the judge and heard himself sentenced to serve from ten to twenty years in Eastern State Penitentiary in Philadelphia.

An appeal was taken to the Supreme Court of Pennsylvania which sustained the conviction by a vote of four to three. It was some comfort to Wentzel that Chief Justice George W. Maxey rendered a dissenting opinion 10,000 words in length in which he assailed the conviction as a gross travesty of justice. The force of his opposing views is evidenced by these two paragraphs:

"A careful study of this record convinces me that the Commonwealth produced no evidence which justifies a verdict of guilty of murder against this appellant and the trial judge should have given binding instructions for acquittal. He could well have said as other judges have said under the circumstances, 'No man can be guessed guilty in this court.'

"If the evidence in this case does not prove the defendant's innocence beyond a reasonable doubt, it certainly preponderates in his favor. Wentzel found himself enmeshed in a set of circumstances which raised a suspicion of his guilt, but each of these circumstances is consistent with his innocence. There is no rule at law or at logic that several suspicious circumstances, each one of which is consistent with the innocence of the accused, becomes proof of guilt when they are considered together. Four or five times nothing is still nothing. In this case it is impossible to find a single fact cited against the accused which is not consistent with his innocence."

In spite of the significance of this dissenting view, Wentzel appeared doomed to remain in prison—but he could not have anticipated strange and wholly unexpected developments. To his amazement two women came forward in his behalf—the mother and a sister of the murdered Mrs. Greene! Publicly stating their belief in Wentzel's innocence, Mrs. Katy O'Mara, the mother, and her daughter, a Mrs. Eckenroth, offered a reward of several thousand dollars for the capture of the real murderer! And they did still more. They brought the case to the attention of The Court of Last Resort.

Erle Stanley Gardner and Henry Steeger were moved by the plea for help that reached them from the closest relatives of the murder victim. Realizing at once that the conflict in medical opinions would call for the services of their colleague, Dr. Snyder, they sent for him and outlined the situation. It was finally agreed that their first step would be to send Rhay and Smith to Pottstown to learn everything that they could about the puzzling case.

Undertaking this assignment, the two interviewed every man and woman who possibly might have a shred of information. After this had been done they were convinced by facts and circumstances that the murder had taken place Friday evening or Saturday morning—not at eleven o'clock Sunday night as the state had contended.

They reached this conclusion after spending hours at the Firestone plant where Mrs. Greene had been employed. After questioning scores of workers, they finally located two women who had accompanied the victim to her apartment on Friday evening. As far as the detectives could learn, Mrs. Greene was never seen alive again by anyone.

An examination of the company's records showed that she had not reported for work on the following day, Saturday, nor had she called to say that she would be absent, as was her unfailing custom when illness kept her away from her job.

Rhay and Smith pressed still further. They ascertained the names of several previous employers and when these were interrogated, they all affirmed, after a careful checking of their records, that Mrs. Greene invariably had telephoned whenever she was obliged to remain away.

The men from The Court next looked to the victim's mother, Mrs. O'Mara, for assistance. They went to her home in Reading and learned from her that Mrs. Greene had made plans to visit her mother after work on Saturday as she did on every weekend. She did not go, nor did she telephone her mother to advise that she would not be there. Mrs. O'Mara stated that this was the first time that this had ever occurred. "Miriam was very dependable," she said, "and she never failed to let me know when she could not come to spend a weekend."

Since Mrs. Greene had failed to pay her customary Saturday visit to her mother and had not been seen after her return home Friday night, Rhay and Smith now were satisfied that she had not left her apartment after that time. To further corroborate this belief, they interrogated the officers who had first seen the body and were told that at this time the victim's clothing, which she had worn to work on Friday, had been found neatly folded on a chair beside her bed.

When Dr. Snyder was advised of these facts, he decided that the time had come to utilize the lie detector on two people. The first was to be Wentzel himself. Before doing this, however, he expressed a desire to accompany the two detectives to Pottstown where he personally interviewed officials as well as Mrs. Wentzel. The latter assured him that she could throw no light on the tragedy, having been completely unaware of her husband's affair with the murder victim—a statement which Rhay and Smith had corroborated some time before. He also interrogated George Greene, the former husband of the murdered woman, but he was equally at a loss to account for what had occurred.

Dr. Snyder then took a lie detector to the penitentiary. He had talked to Wentzel before and was impressed by the prisoner's straightforward answers to all questions and his vigorous denial of guilt. When a test with the polygraph was proposed, the convicted man not only consented but said he was heartened by this opportunity to establish his innocence. The test proceeded and when it was completed, Dr. Snyder announced that all of the recordings indicated beyond doubt that Wentzel had told the truth.

The apparatus was taken back to Pottstown where a test was given to a man whose earlier statements the physician wished to verify. This person, too, proved to have truthfully denied any knowledge of the case.

Dr. Snyder purposely had deferred to the last a decision on what was regarded as the pivotal point in the case—the exact time of Mrs. Greene's death. At the start of the investigation he had expressed a desire to first clarify the many other elements involved so that a background based on fact might be established. Now he turned to the final issue which would support or destroy Wentzel's alibi. On his instructions, Rhay and Smith already had assembled all of the testimony and medical records as well as official photographs of the body. This, however, was only a small part of their assignment in preparation for the scientist's major task. They had been directed to ascertain the temperature of Mrs. Greene's apartment when her body was found, the size and number of her windows, outside temperature and atmospheric conditions, and a myriad of other details pertinent to changes in the body of the murdered woman after she had been strangled.

Utilizing all of this material, Dr. Snyder finally went to work, spending days and nights in a meticulous study of everything that lay before him. His report, which ultimately reached the Board of Pardons and Paroles of Pennsylvania, resembled a lecture that a professor in a medical college might give to his students on the changes that a human body undergoes after life has ceased. In minute detail, he reviewed the testimony given by the physician, the autopsy surgeon, and others who had testified at the trial concerning the condition of the remains, challenging their conclusions and giving his reasons for doing so. It was a document of six full pages, single-spaced, technical in some respects but written so that laymen could follow his clear, deductive reasoning. In a word, he sought to prove that the physical condition of the body, as described by witnesses, did not coincide in any way with the time that they had fixed for her death. To establish this, he probed with scientific depth into accepted medical rules and facts relating to body changes after death.

"The problem" his report began, "is to try to determine whether or not it is likely that Mrs. Greene came to her death at about eleven o'clock on Sunday, December 8, or at some time in advance of that hour. In order to intelligently appraise this problem, one must have some understanding of the mechanism of death due to strangulation and also the changes which take place in a body following death."

After first explaining the effects of strangulation, he launched into a long explanation of rigor mortis before turning to the specific questions involved. Defining rigor mortis as "a stiffening of all muscle tissue due to chemical changes which take place [after death] in the muscle itself," he noted that this change does not come over the entire body until from eight to twelve hours after death. It then remains, he stated, from twelve to twenty-four hours when it begins to disappear and is gone after between eight to ten hours. Decomposition follows.

Then he posed a key question:

"If Mrs. Greene had met her death at eleven o'clock Sunday, December 8 [the state's contention], by strangulation, what would have been the expected findings when the body was discovered at two P.M. the following day and autopsied five hours later?

"Fifteen hours after death the entire body would have been extremely rigid due to rigor mortis while the face, neck and possibly the shoulders might be somewhat dusky in color. . . ."

With this as a premise, he turned to reports and testimony

of the medical men, which he insisted did not support their conclusions as to the time of death. For example, he noted the autopsy surgeon's report on the temperature of the body five hours after it had been found. Reckoning the usual "loss of one degree per hour after death in relation to room temperature" (which he had ascertained earlier), he rejected the official's final judgment as to when the victim had succumbed.

Using other information which Rhay and Smith had gathered at his direction, the expert had calculated meticulously the effect of a partly open window, the physical condition of the apartment, the degree of steam heat and other details. There were many other arguments, equally technical, but all of them supported this final conclusion:

"Considering all of the factors involved, and based on the time the body was autopsied—7 P.M. December 9, 1946—it is highly improbable that death had occurred less than 48 hours previously and it is my belief that Mrs. Greene expired during a period from sixty to eighty hours before she was observed by the autopsy surgeon."

His report now completed, he sent it to Gardner and Steeger, who viewed it as a dramatic and conclusive climax to the long investigation. To them, Dr. Snyder's findings were nothing less than a complete refutation of the prosecution's theory and a full vindication of Wentzel on the basis of his alibi, for if Mrs. Greene had died before the ill-fated Sunday night, the man convicted as her murderer could not have committed the crime.

They hastened to prepare their detailed report of the entire inquiry but while this was under way sensational news reached Gardner and his associates most unexpectedly from Mannheim, Germany.

In the United States Army's Eugon Prison in that city, a twenty-four-year-old soldier from Pottstown, serving a sentence for armed robbery of a German taxicab driver, walked into the office of the commandant and bluntly stated that he was the murderer of Miriam Greene. He said that he had worked with

Wentzel in the die casting plant in their home town and that jealousy had developed between the two over their attentions to the murder victim.

Relating his visit to Mrs. Greene's apartment "a couple of days before Thanksgiving in 1947 . . . shortly after midnight," the soldier told the commandant:

"Miriam and I became involved in an argument about her association with Wentzel and I told Miriam it had to be him or me, that she had to make up her mind. She just said she would see him as much as she liked . . . Miriam laughed and just said I was crazy. I told her to stop laughing or I would kill her. She continued to laugh. At that time I picked up a blue bath towel from the bed and wrapped it around Miriam's neck, tightening it from behind. I tightened the bath towel and she continued laughing. After tightening the towel for about five minutes (sic) she fell off the bed on to the floor. I then picked her up and laid her on the bed. I thought she was dead, so I felt her pulse but there was no beat. I think I remained in the apartment for ten minutes or more but I don't know what I did. I left the apartment about 0130 or 0200 hours [1:30 or 2 A.M.]. I was unable to sleep the rest of the night so around 0700 hours (7 A.M.) I got up and started drinking. I stayed drunk for four days. This incident has been on my mind all the time. Every time I hear the word kill, I think of it. I could just hold it no longer."

He signed this statement and was ordered transferred to the Federal Penitentiary at Lewisburg, Pennsylvania. There, on the advice of friends, he completely retracted his confession and insisted that actually he knew nothing of the murder.

An investigation was undertaken by the prosecuting attorney who concluded, on the basis of two serious discrepancies, that the confession was a hoax. He pointed out that while the soldier had said that he killed the woman "a few days before Thanksgiving in 1947," the murder had occurred in December, 1946; and that while he had told of using a blue bath towel, Mrs. Greene had been strangled with a blue head scarf.

In spite of the prosecutor's rejection of this man as the killer, members of The Court of Last Resort were puzzled for a time as to whether his statement should be seriously considered. They had noted with some suspicion that the color of the ligature, described by him as blue, had not been mentioned either in newspaper accounts of the murder or at the trial.

They finally decided to ignore the episode, reasoning that The Court, not being a police agency, should concern itself only in proving Wentzel innocent.

The Court's full report was then presented to the State Board of Pardons. After prolonged study of the findings, that body, by unanimous vote, recommended to Governor John S. Fine of Pennsylvania that Wentzel should be pardoned. One member of the Board stated publicly that of the 15,000 cases he had reviewed since taking office, this was the first in which he was absolutely positive that the petitioning prisoner was entirely innocent.

On May 21, 1951, Governor Fine signed an order that opened the prison doors for Wentzel and he soon returned to his former position as master die caster at the plant in Pottstown.

The strangler was never apprehended.

"COULD THIS HAPPEN TO ME?"

Could this happen to *me*—now?

The question is often asked today by men and women familiar with one or more of the cases related here or of similar ones in which innocent people, through no fault of their own, have been caught in the web of circumstance, prejudice, or police bungling.

The answer is that it still could, but that it is far less likely than ever before because of the many safeguards—scientific, legal, and moral—that have been set up in recent years to prevent such miscarriages of justice. A strong public conscience supports such advances.

As has been noted before, probably the most significant progress has been made in the attitude and philosophy of law enforcement officers themselves who have come to realize, more and more, that truth and justice are their main objectives, whether their work results in conviction or in vindication.

Not only is this new concept being accepted at top levels, but it has been passed down to those of lower ranks—from the district captain to the foot patrolman on the beat. It has become both a matter of principle and of education. What once was known as the "police business" is now a science, a profession. In our modern metropolitan police departments there are large numbers of alert young men, college trained in procedures involving law enforcement and crime detection.

Guess work of a few generations ago is being replaced by exact scientific techniques. The officer who first reaches the scene of a crime knows precisely what to do to preserve vital physical evidence.

Police criminologists are equipped with the latest facilities for making silent evidence talk and mobile crime laboratories are maintained by departments in large cities, ready to move immediately upon discovery of a crime so that skilled men accompanying them may make permanent records of evidence before it is tampered with or obliterated.

In schools and colleges, men are taught how to reconstruct a crime, to ascertain with scientific accuracy the "what, when, and how" of a murder or other major offense. No longer do they rely, in most departments, on their own haphazard, unproven theories of how it *might* have happened or what *could* have been the motive.

Throughout the country police officers and other law enforcement agents follow the scientific pattern set down soon after the turn of the century by such pioneers in scientific crime detection as Edward Oscar Heinrich of California, who often said that "the criminal virtually labels every crime he commits"; that the skilled investigator need only to apply the natural sciences to interpret the debris left at the scene of the crime—evidence that inevitably can be made to betray the offender's method.

Such progress, in itself, has been a powerful factor in protecting the public against miscarriages of justice. But, in the police field alone, there have been other important advances of a different nature working in the same direction.

A new and improved relationship has been developed between the public and the police, and a better image of the man with the star has emerged. No longer is he viewed by many as a symbol of abusive authority, but rather as a dedicated public servant concerned primarily with the peace and safety of his fellow citizens. It is the policeman who has

changed the image—through his own efforts and his perform-
ance.

Brutality and abused power, as we have seen it in some
cases reviewed here, is relatively rare and when it does occur,
it is condemned and severely punished by those in command.

As public concern has turned to the need for bettering race
relations and solving the problems of minorities in our communities, peace officers have recognized their responsibility
in this phase of human relations. Police academies and officer training schools, once interested only in procedural subjects, now focus major attention on the proper attitudes and
policies toward racial groups and the need for intelligently
understanding their problems in a heterogeneous community.

In some large cities, like San Francisco, departments have
created special bureaus, manned by trained staffs, to deal
specifically with interracial problems. Such a program is aug-
mented by neighborhood councils under police sponsorship
to deal with tensions within the area. The policeman thus
becomes a partner with community leaders in working toward
a healthier, happier, and better integrated people.

Racial and religious bigotry, responsible in measure for
prejudiced juries and hate pressures, is being fought throughout the country by civic-minded men and women, working
through unity councils, fair play commissions, church groups,
business organizations, and the like. That, too, is making a
significant impact.

The machinery of the law is moving toward a guarantee of
equal justice for all; toward eliminating the unfair disadvan-
tages of the poor and ignorant. We have seen how innocent
people, wrongly accused, have suffered conviction and imprisonment through their inability to engage competent counsel
and eminent medical witnesses. Mostly, it has been the poor,
the uneducated, and the friendless who have suffered through
miscarriages of justice. Only the defendant of at least some
means has been able to finance really adequate defense in
competition with the resources of the prosecution.

Such inequalities are being overcome not only by the creation of public defenders departments in many states but by basing staff appointments in such divisions on ability rather than on political influence. Thus the state, using public funds, accepts as its obligation the defense as well as the prosecution of those accused. Certainly, the services of a public defender should be available in every community.

As still a further protection of the poor and underprivileged, some states, like California, now require an automatic appeal to the highest court in all cases involving the death penalty. In this way no man, because of poverty, is put to death without an opportunity of having his case reviewed.

The status of the court-appointed defense lawyer also has undergone a change. In many jurisdictions, courts impose this obligation on skilled, experienced lawyers rather than only on recent law school graduates interested merely in an opportunity for experience.

Those who have studied the problem of equal justice report a turning point in public conscience. The cry for vengeance after a heinous crime has changed to a call for justice, and the forces that once goaded law enforcement officers to make *any* quick arrest to satisfy public demands, gradually have come to more temperate attitudes, to an urge for the capture of the *right* man; not *any* man. Prejudging of defendants, in advance of trials, is diminishing, in the press and in the community generally.

Such are the changes under way in our American society today. And there are ways in which John Citizen can cooperate in guaranteeing justice for himself as well as for his neighbor. One of the first rules is to speak the truth in every situation. We have seen how Charles Stielow in New York involved himself in a serious miscarriage of justice by a "little lie" at a coroner's inquest. Had he told the truth at the outset instead of resorting to perjury, he might have been spared from years of imprisonment. His case is a grim illustration of the proverbial "tangled web we weave" when we resort to deception.

As witnesses in any case, and especially where liberty and life are at stake, we must be cautious and objective, endeavoring to relate only what we actually have seen and heard, rather than what we think might have occurred or what we believe we should have observed. By so doing, we can eliminate in great measure the bugbear of mistaken identity which has been responsible in many instances for convicting the innocent.

We can cooperate more closely with the police and accord them the respect to which they are entitled. And when major crimes occur, we can accept it as our duty to impart such *reliable* information as we may have, being always cautious not to permit unverified hearsay, conjecture, or personal bitterness or vengeance to become a motivating factor.

Such help to our authorities from the citizenry will be of material assistance in crime detection, in protecting the innocent and convicting the guilty. Miscarriages of justice can and will be reduced to the lowest minimum. The trend is strongly in that direction but because human error is always possible, despite the most stringent and earnest precautions, opponents of the death penalty continue to press their cause so that no innocent person ever will be put to death through a weakness in our legal procedures that cannot be corrected once a life has been taken.

The progress of recent years for better, more honest, and more efficient administration of justice continues to be the concern of those who hold the lives and liberty of men and women in their hands. Their outlook is well expressed by a highly respected expert in the field, Dr. David H. Wilson, a member of the Criminology Department of the University of California and a special consultant to the widely known "scientific police department" of Berkeley, California.

"The function of the law," Dr. Wilson says, "is to adjust differences peacefully in our society. Punishment of offenders is but a means to this end and effective only in this context. Vindication and assistance to innocent citizens are equally important functions of law enforcement agencies and this philosophy is replacing the outmoded punitive orientation of the latter.

"Great progress has been made in this direction and more is anticipated as the standards of law enforcement continue to be raised in the future."